ALPHA GIRLS

"... it remains only for women to continue their ascent, and the successes they are obtaining are an encouragement for them to do so. It seems almost certain that sooner or later they will arrive at complete economic and social equality, which will bring about an inner metamorphosis."

—Simone de Beauvoir, *The Second Sex*, 1949

"Women of my generation survived the conflict and became stronger from it. We did not want our daughters to experience either the repression or the mandatory rebellion . . . They don't have to live by our narrow strict rules, the rules of rebellion and resistance. Their lives are rich with porous boundaries, combinations of possibilities that we could not imagine. They can be wildly sexy, soft and smiling, and still be welders and journalists and CEOs."

—Judy Upjohn, 50-year-old feminist mother

"My generation takes it for a *fact* that girls are equal to boys."

—Dora, 16-year-old alpha girl

ALPHA GIRLS

Understanding the
NEW AMERICAN GIRL
and How She Is
Changing the World

DAN KINDLON, PhD

RODALE

Rodale books may be purchased for business or promotional use or for special sales.
For information, please write to:
Special Markets Department, Rodale, Inc., 733 Third Avenue, New York, NY 10017

Printed in the United States of America
Rodale Inc. makes every effort to use acid-free ♾, recycled paper ♻.

Illustrations by Sandy Freeman

Book design by Tara Long

Library of Congress Cataloging-in-Publication Data

Kindlon, Daniel J. (Daniel James), date
    Alpha girls : understanding the new American girl and how she is changing the
world / by Dan Kindlon.
        p.   cm.
    Includes bibliographical references and index.
    ISBN-13 978–1–59486–255–7   hardcover
    ISBN-10 1–59486–255–9   hardcover
    ISBN 978-13: 1–59486–732–3   paperback
    ISBN 978-10: 1–59486–732–1   paperback
    1. Girls—United States—Psychology.   2. Emotions in children.   3. Emotions in
adolescence—United States.   4. Sex role in children—United States.   5. Femininity—
United States.   I. Title.
HQ777.K56 2006
305.23082'0973—dc22   2006018444

Distributed to the book trade by Holtzbrinck Publishers

2   4   6   8   10   9   7   5   3   1   hardcover
2   4   6   8   10   9   7   5   3   1   paperback

LIVE YOUR WHOLE LIFE™

We inspire and enable people to improve their lives and the world around them
For more of our products visit **rodalestore.com** or call 800-848-4735

CONTENTS

ACKNOWLEDGMENTS

Much like a non-narcissistic movie star when she or he prepares to speak after receiving an Academy Award, I find myself remembering how many people I have to thank for the position I now find myself in. With apologies in advance for those I omit, let me begin with Suzanne Gluck, my super-agent, who believed in the project, provided the momentum that got it off the ground, and has been an inspiration throughout. Leigh Haber, my editor at Rodale, helped give the book its structure at the beginning, fine-tuned it at the end and was a delightful collaborator in between.

Special thanks go to my in-the-trenches compatriots: Kenneth Wapner and Amy Sapp. Ken is my longtime personal editor and was involved in every dotted I and crossed T. I can't conceive of writing a book without him. Amy, a brilliant Harvard graduate student, played a major role in every data point, chart, and statistical analysis. The background research she did was stellar and her perspective as the only woman on Team Alpha Girl was invaluable.

I owe a huge debt of gratitude to the administrators, teachers, and parents who not only graciously gave us access to their schools and homes but patiently answered our questions about the girls for whom they cared so deeply.

I also owe immeasurable thanks to Dr. Catalina Arboleda. Several years ago, at her suggestion, we began writing a proposal for a book on the importance of the father-daughter relationship. Although the proposal was never completed, her ideas were part of the germinal matrix from which this book grew. Moreover, she was an extremely understanding partner and co-parent throughout a very difficult period in our lives.

Finally, I deeply thank all the girls and women, alpha or otherwise, who told us the stories that form the backbone of this book. I hope I have faithfully represented you.

INTRODUCTION

Not long ago, I was talking with a group of girls at Greenfield High, a suburban high school in northern New Jersey, about Mary Pipher's bestselling book, *Reviving Ophelia*, which was assigned reading in their English class. The girls' reaction to *Ophelia* was one of confusion. They disagreed with the book's premise—that girls are robbed of vitality and self-esteem as they enter adolescence. According to Pipher, our sexist society causes girls "to stifle their creative spirit and natural impulses, which ultimately destroys their self esteem."

"Who are the girls in this book?" asked Sarah, a Greenfield sophomore. "I mean, I feel sorry for them, but they're pretty much losers. We're not at all like *them*."

From what I could see, she was right. The girls I met were vital. They appeared *more* confident than many of the boys. They had not "lost their voice," something that psychologists typically say happens to girls as they enter adolescence. They feared neither competition from boys nor the consequences of outperforming them.

Were these girls for real? Isn't the average American girl[i] supposed to be a psychological mess? Recent books on teenage girls have painted a grim picture. Peggy Orenstein, the author of *Schoolgirls*, has eloquently expressed the prevailing wisdom. Orenstein says that a girl's passage into adolescence is "marked by a loss of confidence in herself and her abilities, especially in math and science. It is marked by a scathingly critical attitude towards her body and a blossoming sense of personal inadequacy."

If the prevailing psychological thinking was correct, why were Greenfield's girls so mentally healthy? Had I wandered into an exceptional classroom with exceptional students? Or was it time to start thinking about girls in a different way? As the father of twelve- and fifteen-year-old daughters, I had a vital personal as well as professional interest in these questions.

When I lectured at American and Canadian high schools, I began to gauge whether the girls I met were more like the self-hating portraits in popular books on adolescent psychology or the self-confident girls at Greenfield High. I immersed myself in cutting-edge scientific literature about gender and sex differences to see what there was to teach me about the girls of my daughters' generation. This twenty-first century scholarship—most of it written by women—provided me with the latest data on girls' mental health, academic achievements, and attitudes.

I gradually became convinced that the new American girl was fundamentally different from her sisters of previous generations. I began to think of her as an "alpha girl"—a young woman who is

[i] The term "girl" is used instead of "woman" or "young woman" because the emphasis of the book is on female development during the period covered by *pediatric* medicine, that is, up to age 21.

destined to be a leader. She is talented, highly motivated, and self-confident. The alpha girl doesn't feel limited by her sex; she is a *person* first and then a woman. Issues of sex and gender, dependence and independence, and dominance and subordination are largely irrelevant to how she sees herself in the world.

It became clear to me that the generally accepted view of girl's psychology was missing the mark in many important respects and that a new psychology of contemporary American girls was needed. Exploring that psychology—giving it shape and substance—and describing the effect that this new wave of women is having on our society is what I have set out to do in *Alpha Girls*. At its core, this book is an attempt to understand this new generation of women of which my daughters are a part.

The psychology that I describe in *Alpha Girls* reflects the radical changes our society has experienced over the last generation as new laws and social policies have guaranteed women equal rights and equal opportunities with men. It is a psychology shaped by the ever-increasing number of strong female role models for young women, often including alpha girls' own mothers. It is a psychology that owes much to the way a new generation of involved fathers has affected how their daughters think and feel. It is a psychology unencumbered by assumptions of low self-esteem and warped body image. It stands in stark contrast to the largely negative, anxious, and defensive portraits of American girls that have dominated academic and popular psychology for the past twenty-five years.[1]

Clearly not all girls are alphas. Some lack self-confidence and are anxious, depressed, anorexic, or bulimic. Sexual harassment and date rape are real problems that affect too many women and girls. What I want to show in this book, however, is that the psychology of

American girls is changing and that a substantial number of our girls are thriving.

The first chapters of *Alpha Girls* describe the distance women have traveled in the last four decades and the new role of fathers in their daughters' lives. I then look at traditional and feminist views of women's psychology and contrast them to the psychology of over 150 girls from all socioeconomic backgrounds and regions of the United States and Canada who I interviewed for the book.[2]

I conducted interviews in charter schools with largely black and Hispanic populations, urban and suburban public schools, and private schools. I told the schools that I wanted to meet with talented, high-achieving girls who were leaders, or at least appeared destined to be, and they chose the interview subjects. They picked girls who were class presidents, captains of their basketball teams, and social leaders. Many had stellar grades and a wide range of extracurricular interests. I supplemented the girls chosen by schools with girls who came to me by word of mouth. It seemed that everyone knew at least one alpha girl. "Oh, you've got to talk to so and so," people would say. "She's perfect for your book."[3]

There were 113 girls in the interview sample, 32 in grades 6 through 8, 81 in grades 9 through 12. They came from 15 different schools in eight states and one Canadian province. These schools are not a representative slice of the North American educational pie. There are more private than public schools and, given the demographic realities of independent schools, the affluent and white are overrepresented; approximately 15 percent of the interview sample was non-white, the majority of these African American. Appendix A contains the details of the sample's characteristics.

Because our society is not a true meritocracy—educational achievement, occupational attainment, and mental health are all enhanced by economic advantage—the alpha girl interview sample will be more representative of the group of students who will someday move into societal positions of power and influence than girls drawn from a random sample of schools. Alpha girl psychology, on the other hand, appears to transcend barriers of race and class. In the voices of alpha girls from both advantaged and disadvantaged backgrounds, one hears the same emancipated confidence. Even though an alpha girl chosen by a principal of an urban public school might be less accomplished "on paper" than an affluent alpha girl at a high-powered prep school, she is no less an alpha. In fact, her alpha status is in some ways more deserved given the greater obstacles she has had to overcome.

The quotes in the book are mostly verbatim. I have tried to keep as close to the interviewees' words as possible, but, in order to protect their privacy, details have been changed, and, in a few cases, I have constructed composites. My overriding concern, however, was to stick as close as possible to what the girls actually said. The names of students and schools used in this book are fictional.

In addition to the interviews, I administered the Adolescent Life Survey, a questionnaire assembled for *Alpha Girls*, to a sample of over 900 girls and boys across the United States and Canada.[4] I wanted to see how *all* girls in this particular generation had been affected by the changes in family and society that we describe, not just the subset of high-achieving alpha girls. I wanted to measure girls' self-esteem, their expanded sense of who they can become, and their academic achievements, even in areas formerly reserved for boys. The survey helped elucidate what makes the alpha girl tick—what she values, how she feels about her parents, her religious and political leanings, and how she understands herself in relation to others.

The survey also helped identify other alpha girls from this wider pool. A girl had alpha status conferred on her by satisfying four of these five criteria based on her responses to the ALS:

1. A GPA of 3.8 or higher.
2. At least one leadership position from the following areas: band; drama; dance, cheerleading, or step; individual or team sports; hobby clubs, such as French club; community service; newspaper or yearbook participation; membership in the National Honor Society or student government, or serving as an officer of a school academic organization.
3. Participation in extra curricular activities, in or out of school, for a minimum of ten hours a week.
4. High achievement motivation score based on eight items, with an average response of "very important" to questions about the importance of: a) getting a college education; b) owning one's own home; c) making a great deal of money; d) having a well-paid job; e) having a good reputation in the community; f) studying hard to get good grades; g) working hard to get ahead; h) saving money for the future.
5. High self-rating for dependability with a minimum score of 11 out of 12 on three items: a) I usually get things done on time; b) I'm the kind of person others can depend on; c) I always do what I say I'll do. (4=strongly agree).

By these fairly strict criteria, around 20 percent of girls were alphas.

The ALS results are described in some detail in the final chapters of the book, which examine the seismic cultural shifts that will occur as alpha girls exert their influence. Like the interview sample, affluent white girls and boys are overrepresented. To correct for potential biases created by our unbalanced school sample, all analyses included statistical corrections for socioeconomic status, sex, and race/ethnicity. The details of these analytical methods are presented in Appendix A.

Our forecasts about the future place of women in society are informed by state-of-the-art statistical projections generated for *Alpha Girls.*

What was fascinating to watch unfold as our survey results came in was the ways in which these prototypic alpha girls shared many similarities with their non–alpha girl peers. We came to feel that, in many respects, when we talked about alpha girls we were talking about a whole generation. The alpha is a leader in a generation of girls on the rise. She is deployed in large numbers at the borders of adulthood—ready to make her mark on our world.

ALPHA GIRLS

CHAPTER ONE

DAUGHTERS OF THE REVOLUTION

6:00 p.m. The January evening in Atlanta, Georgia, is unseasonably cold as four upperclasswomen from St. Ann's, an all-girls prep school, drive to the municipal courthouse. They are on their way to a fourth-round match of the National High School Mock Trial Championship.[1] The Mock Trial was founded in 1984 to give high school students a taste of America's judicial system, and, perhaps, kindle their ambition to become lawyers and judges.

The Mock Trial case this year, *The State v. Terry Woodward*, is based on an actual lawsuit that went to trial and was posted on the Georgia Bar Association's Web site in November as a pdf file. Trial teams across the state downloaded it and began studying intently, preparing to do battle in court.

The case involved the leader of a country music band who allegedly murdered the group's former manager in a dispute over royalties.

Before sending it out to students, volunteer attorneys doctored the case, planting loopholes in both sides. Teams alternate in each round as the defense and prosecution. The Mock Trial isn't about who wins or loses, but which team argues most effectively. The students need to understand rules of evidence, prepare opening and closing statements, and present cogent objections. Teams are awarded points by a panel of three volunteer jurors, attorneys chosen by the Young Lawyers Association, which runs the program. The court is presided over by a volunteer attorney.

Tonight the St. Ann's girls will face their number-one rival, St. Luke's, an all-boy's school, for the city championship. If they win city, they advance to state. They are St. Ann's A Team, and they know they're in for a fight. The boys have already beaten St. Ann's B Team, who are younger and less experienced.

"We know the boys will be cocky," says Nora, one of the team's attorneys, who is hoping to attend Dartmouth next fall. "We eat lightly before the trial—we're keyed up and nervous and we don't want throw up in court. To get in the mood for the case, we put good country music on the car stereo. We play the Dixie Chicks really loud, sing along, and get pumped up. We like the Dixie Chicks because they're adversarial."

Tonight, Nora and her colleagues will argue for the defense. That suits her co-consul, Walker, whose nickname is Winky. "I like defending," Winky says. "It's more intense and interesting than arguing for the prosecution. You're breaking down something instead of trying to build it up. The prosecution's job is simple, ABC, construct a logical argument. I'd rather raise doubts, demolish arguments, hound witnesses. I like to swirl all the evidence around and turn it into a messy puzzle. But in real life I don't think that I'd be objective enough to be a defense attorney. I don't think I could do my best to help someone get off who I thought was guilty. I wouldn't want to wonder what he would do next."

The girls, dressed in suits, enter the building, go to the law library, and refine their opening and closing statements before heading down to the courtroom itself. The St. Luke's team is also in suits, two of the boys with their long hair pulled back in ponytails. The judges enter, the court is called to order, and the trial begins.

"The strongest point for the defense is reasonable doubt," says Nora, who handled the opening statement for St. Ann's. "So we hammered away at that. We go through the prosecution's case and show that it is a house of cards. We tell the jurors that if even *one* of those cards is in doubt, the whole house collapses, and they can't convict."

One of St. Luke's attorneys, a talented actor, tries to control the proceedings with theatrics, a ploy that worked against the girl's B Team. But that strategy doesn't work against St. Ann's A Team.

"The St. Luke boys were drama queens when we competed against them for city," says Winky. "They tried too hard to rely on style and charm. The fact is that we know the rules better than they do. We *know* what we're talking about."

St. Ann's captured the Atlanta title and went on to win second place in the state championships, losing in the finals to a magnet school in Savannah.

"We were pleased with second place," says Nora. "But we would have liked to have won."

"I didn't sense too much disappointment on the way back," said Susan Croy, a history teacher and the girls' Mock Trial coach, in her Georgia drawl. "I mean, second in the state isn't bad. What these girls really like is running *over* the guys in the city rounds. They consistently display tremendous confidence—and this confidence can be intimidating."

Croy described a witness on the St. Ann's team named Lindsay, who spoke fluidly even when she was on shaky ground. This often caused opposing attorneys to drop damaging lines of questioning: They simply assumed Lindsay knew more than they did.

"These displays of confidence rattle the boys," said Croy. "Boys, of course, often display confidence, too. But it's easy for it to slide into arrogance and bravado. Girls tend to maintain a fine line more effectively."

I met Croy in the faculty room of St. Ann's newly expanded campus of three-story brick buildings with white shuttered windows and an Episcopal church at its center. Each day the school's 600 girls fill the long wooden pews in a light-filled chapel, where they sing hymns, pray, deliver announcements on events and school policies to the student body, and giggle as senior girls hone their public speaking skills by delivering humorous homilies on the trials and tribulations of growing up.

I asked Croy about her students. "You know, I've been here fifteen years," she said. "And in the last ten I've noticed a definite change in who these girls are. Many of them fit your alpha girl profile. I give them a questionnaire each year about their career goals. The last five or six years I've been getting more and more responses like 'Senator' and 'Astronaut.' Winky is a good example. She has AP [advanced placement] physics down cold. But *that* isn't even her subject. What she's really interested in is *history*. These girls are locked and loaded. They don't even blink. These girls say, *bring it on*. They feel like they can do anything. And they can."

The *bring it on* confidence of alpha girls, the feeling that they can do anything, is part of what characterizes them. The alpha genera-

Dan Kindlon, PhD

tion is *full* of girls who feel empowered. This is at least partially due to the fact that they are entering a culture in which many women are already high achievers. Teenage girls today are entering an environment of achievement and possibility that is unlike anything that existed for women in the past.

When I asked Winky about her career plans, she said she was interested in law, politics, or intelligence work with the CIA. At St. Ann's, I also met Minnie, who wants to be a senator or president; Becky, who wants to produce films; and Gertie, who has been accepted at West Point.

"Why do you want to attend West Point?" I asked her.

"I want to be challenged," she says. "I know that I could be intellectually challenged at many colleges. But West Point has physical challenges, mental challenges, leadership-type challenges. I really wanted to push myself. That's why I chose the Point."

Bring it on, indeed.[i]

∼

American girls today are the daughters of the revolution—the first generation that is reaping the full benefits of the women's movement.

[i] Recent research by Colonel Karl Friedl published in the *Journal of Women's Health* determined, based on the results of over 130 studies, that assumptions about women's inability to handle the rigors of military training were "astoundingly wrong." These studies were produced courtesy of a 1994 $40 million Congressional mandate. Among the findings that exploded long-held beliefs were that intense military training has no adverse effect on women's reproductive systems or their bones. The report concluded that "women are just as good as men—and in some cases, perhaps even better—at handling intense exercise and decompression sickness."

Their mothers and grandmothers fought and won the battles that produced the 19th Amendment to the U.S. Constitution, giving women the right to vote. They spearheaded the efforts that resulted in the 1973 Supreme Court decision of *Roe v. Wade*, which legalized abortion. They pressed for Title IX, giving girls equal access to sports participation in school. Thanks in part to the courage and perseverance of these foot soldiers, women today play a wide range of professional sports, have easy access to effective contraception, and attend Ivy League colleges and West Point (Harvard and the U.S. military academies didn't admit women until the mid 1970s).

From a *psychological* point of view, the move toward economic and social equality for women has made our daughters see themselves in ways that are unfamiliar to those of us who are older. Girls today are growing up in an environment where the status of women is at an all-time high. The oldest members of the cohort of alpha girls we studied were born in the late 1980s—a tipping point of sorts—just as women began to outnumber men in college. They have grown with women's ascendance. Consider the following:

➤ The newest data from the National Center on Educational Statistics show widening gaps between men and women at the undergraduate and master's degree levels. For the first time, women earned more first professional degrees than men.[ii] In the 2004–2005 academic year, 59 percent of all degrees were granted to women (see Figure 1-1). Women earned 62 percent of all associate's degrees, 59 percent of all bachelor's degrees, 60 per-

[ii] First professional degrees are degrees that require at least six years of college work for completion (including at least two years of pre-professional training), such as MD, DDS, and law degrees.

Dan Kindlon, PhD

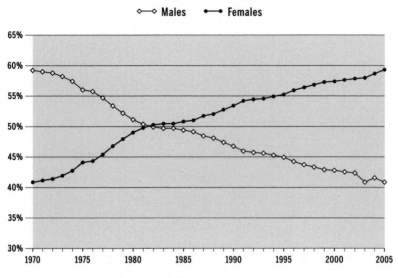

Figure 1-1

PERCENT OF DEGREES (ALL LEVELS*) AWARDED TO MALES & FEMALES, 1970–2005

◇—◇ Males   ●—● Females

*Includes Bachelor's, Associate's, Master's, Doctorate, and First Professional Degrees

cent of all master's degrees, 48 percent of doctorates, and 51 percent of professional degrees.[2]

➤ The professions of law, medicine, and business administration are increasingly gender-balanced. In 1970, fewer than 10 percent of students earning graduate degrees in these fields were women. In each decade since, that number has increased. Today women earn approximately 40 percent of these professional degrees[3] (see Figure 1-2 on page 10).

➤ The 109th U.S. Congress (2005–2007) contained a total of 84 female members—the highest number in its history, with 14 women in the Senate and 70 in the House, including the Minority Whip. In 2006, there were three states where both senators were women—California, Maine, and Washington.[4] As a point of comparison, in 1991 there were only four female senators and 28 congresswomen in total[5] (See Figure 1-3 on page 11).

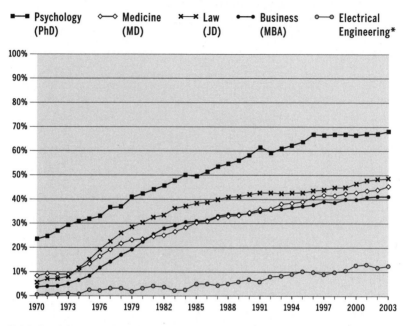

Figure 1-2

PERCENT OF DEGREES AWARDED TO FEMALES–SELECTED FIELDS: 1970–2003

■—■ Psychology (PhD)   ◇—◇ Medicine (MD)   ✕—✕ Law (JD)   ●—● Business (MBA)   ○—○ Electrical Engineering*

*Includes Master's, Doctorate, and First Professional Degrees

➤ Since 1971, the number of women serving in state legislatures had increased more than four-fold. In 2006, 22.8 percent of the 7,382 state legislators in the U.S. were women. Women held 20.8 percent of the state senate seats and 23.6 percent of the state house or assembly seats. Three women served as presidents of state senates (CO, ME, WA), and two women were speakers of state houses (OR, VT). Additionally, women had been elected to statewide executive offices in 49 of the nation's 50 states and held 25.7 percent of these positions across the country[6] (see Figure 1-4 on page 12).

In *The Second Sex,* an enormously influential book published in 1949, Simone de Beauvoir argued that there is a direct link between

Dan Kindlon, PhD

the *status* of women in a society and the attitudes and expectations of that society's girls.

De Beauvoir wrote: "If a caste is kept in a state of inferiority, no doubt it remains inferior; but liberty can break the circle. Let the Negroes vote and they become worthy of having the vote; let woman be given responsibilities and she is able to assume them. The fact is that oppressors cannot be expected to make a move of gratuitous generosity; but at one time the revolt of the oppressed, at another time even the very evolution of the privileged caste itself, creates new situations; thus men have been led, in their own interest, to give partial emancipation to women: it remains only for women to continue their ascent, and the successes they are obtaining are an

Figure 1-3
NUMBER OF WOMEN IN THE U.S. CONGRESS, 1979–2005

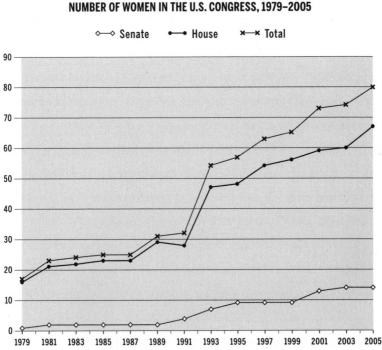

Source: Center for American Women and Politics, 2005

Figure 1-4

PERCENT OF WOMEN IN U.S. STATE ELECTIVE OFFICES, 1979–2005

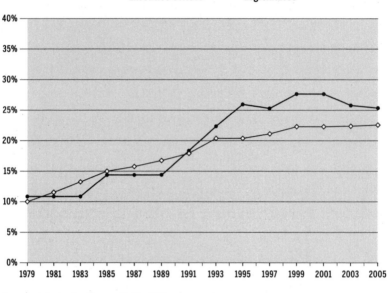

Source: Center for American Women and Politics, 2005

encouragement for them to do so. It seems almost certain that sooner or later they will arrive at complete economic and social equality, which will bring about an inner metamorphosis."

The alpha girls we interviewed showed us that de Beauvoir's inner metamorphosis has occurred. Large numbers of girls are feeling the effects of the feminist revolution and no longer carry the conscious or unconscious assumption that they are a second sex.

It makes sense that there is a time lag between cultural and personal change. For psychological transformation to occur, a girl needs to be *born* into a society in which women's status is already high.[7] The way we parents treat our daughters from a very young age—the kinds of assumptions that we make about their potential and role in the world—shapes their psychology. If the status of women is high,

Dan Kindlon, PhD

parents will instill the expectation of accomplishment and attainment in their daughters.

Children are also shaped by what they perceive society values as well as by how they themselves are treated. They are adept at picking up subtle social cues that point to what is and is not acceptable, and they adapt to their environment. Although we like to think of ourselves as autonomous, self-created beings, most of us carry the imprint of the world we were born into.

Our daughters' inner assumptions about themselves reflect the ascendant status of women. But how profound, really, is this change? Has social and economic equality for men and women been achieved? In the United States, women earn only 77 cents on the dollar compared with men and the boardrooms of the Fortune 500 companies remain over 90 percent male.[8] We've yet to have a woman run as the presidential candidate for either major political party, and the boardrooms of the Fortune 500 hundred companies remain over 90 percent male.[9]

Nevertheless, what the trends show is that there is a powerfully accelerating movement *toward* equality. Although some of the girls we interviewed recognized that there were clear inequities still in place, they were sanguine about their futures. They felt opportunities were now tilted in their favor in what had been male-dominated professions: Employers would tend to hire them *because* they were female. If they bumped up against glass ceilings, their attitude was that they would deal with that when it happened; and even the girls at the younger end of our spectrum, in their early teens, were aware that they would have legal recourse if they were sexually harassed or discriminated against on the basis of sex.

Many of the girls we interviewed felt that their mothers and grandmothers had paved the way for them, that they owed them for their sense of empowerment and opportunity (the only thing that any of the girls we interviewed thought they *couldn't* do was play pro football). They recognized the struggles and sacrifices women in earlier generations had made. Some (to the extent that this is possible for adolescent girls) were even grateful. But their attitude was that things had changed and now it was their turn.

Despite all the benefits they had gained from feminism, *few* of the girls we interviewed considered themselves to be feminists. They associated feminism with an overly aggressive, antimale attitude.

"I'm not the old type of stereotypical feminist," said Terry, a junior at a private school in San Francisco suburb who plans to study political science at Berkeley. "I'm not the militant type who hates men or thinks that women are better than men. I think women deserve all the same opportunities as men. All *people* deserve the same opportunities."

Seventeen-year-old Molly, along with many of her alpha peers, unequivocally resisted the feminist label. "I'm not a feminist. I'm an *equalist*," she said. Molly is a senior at a New York City school that draws kids from all over the world. "I see feminism as not only about equality for women, but about being antiman. It's about fighting men."

Susan—a straight-A student from a large public high school in Portland, Oregon, and the star of both her varsity swim and volleyball teams—smiled as she told us the following story. Her mother, a scientist, and her aunt, a professor in the gender studies program of a large university, sat her down one day to talk to her about where she was applying to college. Susan, whose areas of interests are biology and political science, had a list that included Oberlin, Kenyon, and St. Olaf's in Minnesota. Her applications had been directed at schools that offered merit scholarships because her parents had told her that she needed to contribute to her education. She planned to work while she was in college.

"My mother and aunt sat me down for tea at the kitchen table," said Susan. "It took them a little while to spit out what they wanted to say. They felt that the schools to which I wanted to apply weren't 'feminist enough.' They wanted me to apply to Smith, their alma mater. 'But I'm not a feminist,' I told them. That stopped them in their tracks. My mom said that later, after I had left the room, my aunt began to cry because I didn't consider myself a feminist. My mother confessed that she, too, had been upset. I guess they felt that they had been unable to pass along much of what they had spent their lives fighting for. But they got over it."

More than 75 percent of alpha girls we surveyed had mothers who had worked outside the home, a percentage roughly equal to the national average.[10] Terry's mother was a stockbroker; Nora's, an attorney; Susan's, a biochemist; Molly's, a photographer (see the tables on page 16). Many girls need look no further than their own family for examples of self-assertive, independent women with dynamic, fulfilling careers. Many of the girls we interviewed said their mothers were an inspiration to them, even when they felt that some of their mothers' attitudes, toward feminism, for example, were outmoded.

"My mother is a top-notch commercial photographer," said Molly. "She does still life, magazine work. Her career has been enormously fulfilling for her. She *loves* what she does. She's freelance, her own boss. Without feminism, she would have had a much more difficult time in her career. My mom encountered sexist attitudes early on. She was a pretty blonde trying to get jobs. It was all about assisting guys. In fact, my mom worked for my dad as his assistant—that's how they met! Guys would ask her: 'What's a pretty blonde like you doing in this business?' But she came out of it on top. Look where she is now—more successful than the people who dissed her."

Molly's admiration for her mother was common among the alphas we interviewed. Many cited their mothers as a role model. Survey results show that alphas had a close relationship with their mothers. They often said their mothers could tell when they are upset about something. They could tell their mothers about their problems. Their mothers helped them talk about their difficulties, trusted their judgment, cared about their point of view, and understood them. A close relationship between mothers and daughters is not something new. But in our alphas we saw the mother's role expanded. Not only can girls cry on their mothers' shoulders, they can come to them for advice about their work since many of their mothers have had careers. Alphas are actually more likely than non-alpha girls to talk frequently with their mothers about future career plans, and they are more likely to value their mothers' opinions.

Girls' responses to:

"I value my mother's opinions about my future occupational plans."

	Non-Alphas	Alphas
Strongly disagree/Disagree	14.0%	10.5%
Neutral	65.5%	62.1%
Strongly agree/Agree	20.5%	27.4%

"I often discuss my future occupational plans with my mother."

	Non-Alphas	Alphas
Strongly disagree/Disagree	5.2%	2.4%
Neutral	20.2%	17.6%
Strongly agree/Agree	74.7%	80.0%

Dan Kindlon, PhD

Molly's parents divorced and her mother never remarried, although her father has. I called Molly's mother, Mara, to get her perspective on the difference between her generation and her daughter's. She laughed to hear herself described by her daughter as a "pretty blonde" who was "dissed" way back when.

"It's true," she said, "that men didn't take me seriously back then because I was a 'pretty blonde.' But they have to now. The kind of photography I do, studio work and still life, is highly technical. It was, and it still is a male-dominated field. I think it's been important for Molly to see that I've always had my *own* studio."

Mara said that she has always tried to give Molly as much information and as many choices as possible. "My mother tried to shield me from life," Mara says. "But I raised Molly to be empowered, to be in control. My daughter and her friends are coming of age in a time where they have every option. That's created in them a sense of openness and confidence and energy."

Judy Upjohn, a mother in her early fifties, is a staunch feminist who works as a writer and has started an alternative secondary school. We asked her what she feels her generation has passed along to girls today. Judy e-mailed us this moving, eloquent response:

> In a real sense the mothers of young women today [are] not free; we were tearing ourselves away and demanding freedom: our choices were more exhilarating, perhaps, than our mothers', but still proscribed and limited.
>
> We could reap some benefits, but we were saddled with unconscious conclusions from our childhoods (about how ladies should be) and astonished by what a phenomenal job our mothers had done—cooking, cleaning, sewing, ironing,

raising families, and looking flawless when our fathers brought the bosses home—when we could barely sew on a button. We were still caught. Who were we, really? Thus arose the tough women in men's garb; rejection of men and rejection of femininity; rejection of family; and then the supermom. You had to fit in one of a few hard-defined categories.

Not so, today. We women who fought through the initial slapdown waves of protest and refusal have given rise to a generation of girls with real choices. They don't have to merely comply or rebel. They don't have to tear themselves away from the models of their mothers, and as a result, they don't have to start searching for themselves anew in their twenties and thirties and forties. Women of my generation survived the conflict and became stronger from it. We did not want our daughters to experience either the repression or the mandatory rebellion. . . . . They don't have to live by our narrow strict rules, the rules of rebellion and resistance. Their lives are rich with porous boundaries, combinations of possibilities that we could not imagine. They can be wildly sexy, soft and smiling, and still be welders and journalists and CEOs.

Compliance or rebellion; repression or resistance. These were the choices open to alpha mothers. The alphas embody, as Judy notes, a much wider range of choices on how to be a woman. Their mothers' legacy to them is the *assumption* of equality that characterizes their generation. Dora, a 16-year-old alpha girl interested in rock climbing and riflery, expressed the view that we heard over and over in our interviews. "My generation takes it for a *fact* that girls are equal to boys."

Some alpha girls have already bumped up against what they consider the atavistic vestiges of the patriarchy. In the 2004 Mock Trial competition in western Massachusetts, a high-powered team of student attorneys from an all-girls school competed for the county championships. Beverly, a senior who is on her way to Yale next year to study economics, said that the judges of their cases were mostly men.

"I found that odd," said Beverly. "And in the county championships, I found it particularly so. The judge in that case, I would guess, was about your age. We were clearly winning. But at the end of the trial, the judge spent at least twice as long praising the other team's lawyers—who were all boys. He used fishing analogies to demonstrate his points. Critiquing one of our lawyers, he said: 'When you're addressing someone at the bench you should use the urinal stance.' And he proceeded to demonstrate that posture."

"What did you think of this guy?" I asked.

She looked me straight in the eye. "Dinosaur," she replied.

The "equalist" attitude expressed by alpha girls comports with "Third Wave" feminism that gender studies authors and activists have written about in recent years. Rather than a movement, the Third Wave is a generation, of which alpha girls are a part—girls born to Beverly's generation of women, who have grown up with the fruits of feminism as part of their culture and politics. They feel entitled to equality—gender and otherwise—as they increasingly reap the benefits not only of feminism but also of other social justice movements such as the gay-lesbian rights movement, antiracism movements, and labor movements. Consequently, many young women have carved out identities that reflect their understanding of the interconnection of social justice issues—identities that stand in stark contrast to the exclusionary, militant image of feminists constructed by the media during the 1980s and 1990s.

The media is important, and not just because it contributed to the way the current generation of girls perceives feminism. Although the alpha generation was not the first to grow up with television, it has witnessed its expansion, first by cable, then by satellite and mobile technology; children now tune into their favorite shows on their laptops, iPods, and cell phones. The average child over six years of age in America watches close to four hours of television a day.[11] Most children spend another hour or two per day playing videos games or tooling around on a computer.[12]

Boys and girls in our survey sample didn't spend quite as much time glued to the tube as the average American teenager. On average, they watched two hours of television per day and spent another two hours on the Internet for non-school-related purposes. Consistent with their seriousness of purpose, alpha girls, on average, spent slightly less time playing on the Internet than the rest of the sample.[13]

What we see on television can affect how we behave. Watching sexist images doesn't *necessarily* lead to sexist behavior, but it increases its likelihood. We are a species of imitators.[iii] Within the first days

[iii] Much of what psychologists know about how the media affects behavior comes from a huge body of research on the effect on children of viewing violent TV and movies. Research shows that the statistical relationship between watching media violence and aggression is nearly as strong as the relationship between cigarette smoking and lung cancer. It is stronger than the relation between calcium intake and bone mass, condom use and sexually transmitted HIV, and much stronger than the statistical relationship between homework and academic achievement. See for example, Huesmann, L.R.; Moise-Titus, J.; Podolski, C.; and Eron, L.D. (2003), "Longitudinal relations between children's exposure to TV violence and their aggressive and violent behavior in young adulthood 1977-1992." *Developmental Psychology, 39*, pp. 201–221.

Dan Kindlon, PhD

of life, sometimes even within the first hours, children can imitate behavior. Imitative ability quickly advances, and by the time a child is three, she can mimic the complex behavior that she sees on television.[14] Scientists have recently discovered a specialized set of amazing "mirror neurons" in the brain that appear to explain why humans learn complex behavior and attitudes so easily. These neurons essentially "copy" observed actions. When you watch a tennis match, for example, your mirror neurons that are involved in running and swinging activate. Other animals, such as monkeys and dolphins, have rudimentary mirror neurons, but only human brains are capable of copying complex behavior. Researchers believe that mirror neurons are the key to understanding feelings of empathy—why televised violence may predispose us to act violently and pornography can sexually excite us. Patricia Greenfield, a psychologist at UCLA, believes that mirror neurons provide a biological explanation for the power of culture to affect human behavior: ". . . we see that mirror neurons absorb culture directly, with each generation teaching the next by social sharing, imitation and observation."[15] Humans, it appears, are hardwired for imitation.

Since the 1960s, feminists have recognized the power of media to shape attitude and beliefs and have pressed for changes in the way women are portrayed on television. Although television today isn't a land of equal opportunity, there have been significant changes in the sexism that was rife just a generation ago. Until recently, women were typically portrayed as ancillary to men; men far outnumbered women in leading roles; and there was a dearth of women characters who were intelligent, competent, or self-sufficient. The oldest alpha girls in our study were born at a time when television, advertising, and film began to present girls with a wide variety of strong, independent female characters, and their generation consciously and unconsciously imitated these characters and internalized their stories.

The mass media, especially children's television, provides more positive role models for girls than ever before. There are roughly the same numbers of boy and girl characters on television. There are no significant differences in the way they are portrayed; although girls are more likely to show affection and boys are more likely to be aggressive.[16] Many kids' shows feature strong female characters who interact with their male counterparts on an equal footing. There are strong role models on television for teens as well.

Despite the trend toward parity,[17] gender role stereotyping in prime time still exists. A study of the 2004 television season showed that male characters more often held positions of power than female characters. Even when men and women had the same job title, such as "attorney," men were more likely to be a senior lawyer and women a junior. Also, while men and women were equally likely to be portrayed in a number of high-status roles, women still outnumbered males in several lower-status roles including domestic workers (67 percent), clerical workers or secretaries (76 percent), nurses (81 percent), and homemakers (an amazing 100 percent).

There has been an explosion of "action chicks" in film, physically imposing women who routinely overpower their male foes.[18] Given what we are learning about the power of observational learning, it isn't surprising that our culture is experiencing a rise in physical violence among girls.[19]

Female stars like Angelina Jolie as Lara Croft or Lucy Lawless as Xena have qualities that feminists wanted to see in female characters. They are powerful, independent, and decisive. They redress stereotypic images of women as yielding, subordinate, and submissive. But they are powerful in a way that is sexualized. They wear skintight body suits, reveal cleavage, and masterfully wield a gleaming array of weapons. They are a Hollywood version of the male sexual fantasy of the dominatrix—infinitely desirable but dangerous. A large part of their audience is teenage boys. They embody an impossibly stylized version of feminine beauty—a version whose genesis is in male adolescent sexual fantasy. Their physicality is an unattainable ideal that the vast majority of girls can never hope to emulate. They are female equivalents of the sculpted male physiques that have dominated action films in the last decades, the Schwarzenegger spin-offs who are all brawn but no brain and leave legions of bodies in their wake before becoming governor of California.

Across all forms of media, women's bodies are more likely than men's to be portrayed in glamorized and unrealistic ways, although men, too, are subject to this kind of sexual objectification.[20] Body image problems still affect far too many girls and there is little doubt that the media is a prime culprit, inducing our daughters to starve themselves and plunging them into depression when the girl they see in the mirror doesn't resemble the emaciated waif in the huge fashion poster adorning Times Square. If this sounds simplistic, look at cases where television is introduced in new areas, such as Fiji in 1995, where hitherto unknown eating disorders then emerge in large numbers.[21]

There is some indication that there is a new kind of advertising that is bucking this trend. In 2004, Dove first launched their Campaign for Real Beauty, an advertising campaign that has since gained national attention for its rejection of the wafer-thin models that have dominated advertising since the 1980s, which have in part been blamed for eating disorders and low self-esteem in girls. Glorifying curves and wrinkles rather than bony limbs, the Dove advertisements and commercials encourage women everywhere to appreciate the bodies that they have been given rather than to yearn for unhealthy ideals. Furthering this message, Dove released a short film called *Evolution* that was posted on YouTube. An instant hit, the film shows how a normal-looking model is transformed by makeup and extensive photoshop editing into a billboard beauty. It reveals the falseness of the media's version of beauty.

Similarly, Nike started an ad campaign in 2005 that celebrated women's "big butts, thunder thighs, and tomboy knees." One ad shows a well-rounded posterior. The copy reads: "My butt is big and round like the letter C, and 10,000 lunges have made it rounder but not smaller. And that's just fine. It's a space heater for my side of the bed. It's my ambassador. To those who walk behind me, it's a border collie that herds skinny women away from the best deals at clothing sales. My butt is big and that's just fine. And those who might scorn it are invited to kiss it."

Feminist Gloria Steinem, the founder of *Ms.* magazine, responding to these ads, commented: "It is a change that women—and some men, too—have been agitating for 35 years. I spent 15 years of my life pleading for ads that reflected our readers by age, race and ethnicity. We could demonstrate that women responded better to ads that were more inclusive of them, but they just weren't coming."

Nike's U.S. ad director said that Nike was consciously trying to target a new generation of girls who, she said, are "more personally independent about who they can and should be" than girls were ten or twenty years ago. "One of the things we've noticed is if you go to an exercise class, if you go to a marathon, women come in a lot of shapes and sizes."

Dan Kindlon, PhD

A blogger, Christine, on the Web site for *Ms.* magazine, however, isn't convinced. She writes: "One [Nike] ad features a close-up of a woman's thigh in a pair of running shorts. The copy has the owner of that leg proclaiming, 'I have thunder thighs. And that is a compliment because they are strong and toned and muscular.' Let's be clear. These are not thunder thighs. These are runner's thighs. Biker's legs. They are not 'real.' And there is nothing average about them. They are spectacular and inspiring. They make one want to rush out and buy a new pair of Nike sneakers, strap on an iPod and start training for next year's Marine Corps Marathon. Nike is selling a fantasy just as surely as Victoria's Secret is."[22]

Christine's position has been receiving a growing amount of support from the public—especially advocates for girls—who argue that companies should be accountable for the images they produce, which should include a greater number of realistic, diverse images of girls and women. There is evidence that these voices have begun to be heard. The Canadian public, for instance, prompted their government to implement Gender Portrayal guidelines, which help prevent offensive portrayals of women in advertisements.[23]

In the U.S., Kellogg answered the public's requests by releasing an ad campaign for Special K cereal in the late 1990s, which used pictures of older and larger women and text such as "the Ashantis of Ghana think a woman's body gets more attractive as she ages. Please contact your travel agent for the next available flight." The ads were so well received that they were followed up by a television campaign in 1999.

Special K is the exception, not the rule. Girls are being aggressively targeted by manipulative images of femininity that have nothing to do with helping them live richer, more rewarding lives and have everything to do with selling product.

Many alphas were aware that they were being manipulated. "Women can be sucked into what the media tells them they should look like," said Lynn, a 17-year-old alpha at a prep school in Toronto, Canada. "Girls get the message that they can be lawyers, but only if they're anorexic. Or that they can run a company, but only if they have plastic surgery."

Lynn said that some of the girls at her school are already planning to customize themselves. "You could ask almost any girl what plastic surgeries she wants," said Lynn, "and she'll give you a list. Most girls have really spent a lot of time thinking about this. They lose sleep over it." Looking over the list of girls her school had chosen as interviewees, she said that alphas "were more focused."

Alphas as a whole don't define themselves solely by their appearance. They are resisting the pernicious need that advertising tries to engender in girls by giving them the message that they need to buy products in order to be attractive and successful.

Perhaps one of the most important ways in which assertive, independent female characters in media are breaking with traditional stereotypes is that they present alternatives to what has been called the "myth of inevitable domesticity."[24]

Narratives of inevitable domesticity were particularly popular in nineteenth-century literature. They often began with a talented tomboyish girl who morphs into an adolescent filled with dreams of a career and a life independent of men and then is irresistibly drawn into marriage and motherhood.

Dan Kindlon, PhD

A case of a prototypical alpha girl who succumbs to inevitable domesticity is Jo March from *Little Women,* which was published in 1868 and has been read by millions of girls. When the book opens, Jo is 15 and wants to join her father, who is a soldier in the Union Army. "It's bad enough to be a girl anyway when I like boys' games, work, and manners! I can't get over my disappointment in not being a boy; and it's worse than ever now for I'm dying to go fight with papa . . ."

By age 19, Jo wants to be a famous writer: ". . . great plans fermented in [Jo's] busy brain and ambitious mind, and the old tin kitchen in the garret held a slowly increasing pile of blotted manuscript, which was one day to place the name of March upon the roll of fame . . ."

Jo hones her craft and eventually earns the handsome sum of $100 for a manuscript. "[Jo took] great comfort in the knowledge that she could supply her own wants, and need ask no one for a penny."

Jo becomes a successful writer, but after the death of her younger sister, Beth, to whom she was quite close, she begins to feel lonely and notices "how happy" her married sister Meg is with a "husband and children." Jo decides that "Marriage is an excellent thing after all. I wonder if I should blossom out half as well as you [Meg] have if I tried it."

Meg replies: "It's just what you need to bring out the tender, womanly half of your nature Jo."

As her 25th birthday approaches, Jo is despondent: "Almost 25," she thinks, "and nothing to show for it."

When an older man takes an interest in her, Jo is swept away. They become engaged and after her aunt dies and leaves Jo her farm, Jo decides that she wants to start a school for boys, which she imagines as "a good, happy, home-like school . . . I should *so* like to be a mother to them."

In place of her writing, she tells stories to her students. Thinking back over her previous dreams of an independent life, Jo says, ". . . the life I wanted then seems selfish, lonely and cold to me now. I haven't given up hope that I may write a good book yet, but I can wait . . ."

Little Women's author, Louisa May Alcott, was a suffragette—the first woman in Concord, Massachusetts, registered to vote in local elections. She went to Washington, D.C., and became a nurse during the Civil War. She never married herself, so her characterization of Jo may have been dictated by the conventions of the nineteenth-century novel, rather than by Alcott's personal feelings about the inevitability of marriage and motherhood. A percentage of women have always lived outside the perimeter of marriage and motherhood; but for most, the pressures pushing them toward inevitable domesticity have been overwhelmingly strong.

Jo March speaks to the fear that many girls had as they looked at a future that didn't involve marriage. Inevitable domesticity was a catechism drilled into them to ward off the loneliness that only a man can appease, rescuing women from the unenviable fate of a cold heart and barren health and empty womb. When Jo says she wants to "blossom" in marriage, she speaks to the perennial fear that without marriage and motherhood a woman won't flower and is doomed to become, instead, a shriveled old spinster.

I am not implying that Jo March is necessarily a bad model for girls. As we shall see, the trend today is to want a family, to embrace domesticity. The point is that characters who portray girls and women as happily independent and self-sufficient give girls a wider array of models to imitate than they have had in the past. That, I think, is what is ultimately most important in the new Nike ads. Girls today have more choices about how to act, who to be, and what is considered "normal," culturally sanctioned behavior. This is precisely what their mothers and grandmothers fought for—the ability and freedom to *choose* how to live one's life.

Karen, a senior with 3.8 grade point average at a midsized rural high school in upstate New York who planned on going to Georgetown University to study politics, articulated what many alphas felt about the future that their mothers and grandmothers had bequeathed to them.

"I know that if I work hard I can do whatever I want," Karen said. "I'm interested in government, and I have a lot of female friends who are interested in government, too. I was part of the National Youth Leadership Conference in D.C. and the Harvard Model Congress. I impersonated a senator from Illinois. We debated a bill on racial profiling. My mother is very politically active. Always has been. She's into labor organizing. Women's rights. She runs an organic coffee roasting business. They only buy from socially conscious growers. I grew up in a very politically engaged household. My mother raised me on her own, and I got a lot my values from her.

"Aside from politics, I'm into theater. Who was it that said that politics is showbiz for ugly people? Politics is like theater. They're both group activities. Politics is all about showmanship, song and dance. I like the energy of politics. The intensity. The drama. I know discrimination against women is still out there. But I feel totally free to choose how I want to live my life."

Nowhere is the freedom to choose more important for women than whether or not to conceive or have a child. Thanks to the pioneering work of Margaret Sanger, today nearly three million teenage girls in the United States use contraceptives.[25]

Sanger coined the term "birth control" and founded the American Birth Control League, which in 1942 became the Planned Parenthood Federation of America. For many girls, owning and controlling their own bodies is largely a reality. It was an impossible dream for many twentieth-century women, including Sanger's own mother, who died as a result of weathering 18 pregnancies and 11 live births.

The battles their mothers fought to broaden access to birth control and legalize abortion have made possible the kinds of lives many girls today envision for themselves. They can postpone marriage and motherhood without denying or compromising their sexuality. They can choose to live independently or balance a relationship and a career. Or they can become traditional stay-at-home moms.

The alpha girls we interviewed see themselves as unconstrained. Unfettered. They feel that they have limitless choices. They are savvy enough to realize that their sex may be an advantage rather than a disadvantage as they move into occupations that have been formally dominated by men. They think of themselves as a post-feminist generation. They are the living, breathing embodiments of the inner revolution that women in the last generations so ardently desired and fought for.

CHAPTER TWO

MALE WAYS OF BEING

She's as competitive as I am . . . In her teens, I think sports
will be a big way that she relates to boys—
the way she makes that connection.
She speaks the language.

−Tony Green, 50, on Anna, his eldest daughter

The women's movement and new female role models have deeply affected the psychology of alpha girls. But there has been another decisive influence on their psychology. Closer relationships exist today between fathers and daughters than have existed in the past, and this has had a profound impact on the way many girls think and feel, how they interact with the world, and what they want and expect from life.

The trend toward this new type of relationship is startling. The May 2004 issue of the journal *Pediatrics* summarizes:

→ The average amount of time fathers in two-parent families spend with their children, directly engaged or accessible, has increased in the last decade to 2.5 hours per weekday and 6.3 hours per weekend.

→ The number of father-only households increased almost 25 percent from 1995 to 1998, to 2.1 million. The 2000 U.S. Census revealed father-only households increased to 4.3 million, or 4.2 percent of U.S. households. In Illinois alone, the number of children living in father-only households increased by 109 percent, from 47,000 in 1985 to 98,000 in 1995. Additionally, father-only households seem to be headed by men who are highly involved in their children's lives at home and school.

Our society increasingly supports fathering. Courts rule for shared-custody arrangements; men have more work flexibility than they have had in the past (largely because of telecommuting and flex time); and the media portrays the positive effects of highly involved fathers on their children.

One of the most striking differences between our sample of alpha girls and their non-alpha peers was how much more involved their dads were in their lives.[1] Three out of four alpha girls said that the quality of her relationship with their father was either very good or excellent; only a handful rated it as fair or poor. The alphas felt accepted by their fathers and trusted by them; many even described being able to discuss their emotional problems with their fathers.[2]

By cultivating closeness to their daughters, fathers are both deliberately and unconsciously passing along to their girls what I call male ways of being—and these traditionally male attitudes have become an intrinsic part of the psychology of many alpha girls.

Nowhere is this more apparent than in sports. Many fathers take an active interest in their daughters' athletic abilities.[3] Historically, important concepts about how to act in the world were taught to boys—and boys only—through sports, along with metaphors that structure male ways of thinking. Boys learned that it was "Time to step up to the plate," "You can't win them all," and my favorite,

"There is no 'I' in team." When they were hurt, they were told to "Suck it up" or "Walk it off."

Title IX passed in 1972 and gave girls access in schools to a wide range of sports from which they had been excluded in the past. Girls with fathers like me, who coach them or take an interest in their athletic abilities, are now exposed to these lessons—and I think it is having a profound impact on the way girls think and feel.

One of the first things that I noticed when I began coaching the Tigers, my younger daughter Julia's fifth-grade girls' softball team, was that many of the girls shrieked hysterically when a ball was hit toward them. "From now on," I decreed, "anyone who screams has to run laps." The screaming stopped.

"You may wonder why there is no screaming in softball," I explained. "Your first reaction shouldn't be to run away from the ball when it comes at you. I don't want you to be *afraid* of the ball. If you're afraid of it, you're not going to be able to catch it or hit it."

Boys will flinch when they have to field a hard grounder or a line drive, but they've been socialized not to scream. They put up a façade, because fear is considered girly. "You're screaming like a little girl" is a phrase that boys use to taunt each other.

The screaming response smacks of hysteria. In sports as in life, I tell my team, hysterical screaming can often be counterproductive. It's important to learn not to succumb to it. Screaming takes you out of your body. You lose focus. Concentration.

Some Tigers are amazed the first time they catch a ball. They look proud—as all of us are when we overcome fear and succeed. I coach them with high expectations and lots of praise.

"Play the ball; don't let the ball play you," I say. I stress that they should be in control. In command.

Last year the Tigers went undefeated, and we have a perfect record so far this season. I don't think that's because we're more athletically gifted than the teams we play, but because I follow the example of soccer star Mia Hamm and her U.S. Olympic teammates. They asked their coach to treat them like women but coach them like men. The Tigers rise to the challenge, and they are thrilled when they play well.

When I first started coaching them, many of the girls didn't know how to throw. To put it bluntly, they threw like girls.

"Get your elbow out first," I told them. "Snap your wrist. Put your body into it."

Boys can generally throw better than girls because they have practiced throwing from a young age, emulating male role models in professional sports and elsewhere. They also have a genetic advantage. But if you don't think there are girls who can put mustard on the ball, you have never taken a hard throw from any decent high school softball player.

Mandy, a Tiger who had trouble throwing in her first year on the team, now has a solid arm. I sometimes play her at third, a position called the "hot corner," since many balls that come down the third base line have been pulled hard and are traveling fast. She needs that arm after she fields the ball for the long throw to first.

Mandy relishes the challenge from which she used to shrink. "Put me over there, Coach," she says. "Let me play the hot corner."

In the batter's box, similar cultural stereotypes come into play. Girls tend to swing only with their arms and shy away from the ball. I teach them to root themselves in the ground, rotate their hips, and draw power from their core.

"Swing like you mean it!" I tell them. "Don't bail and wail."

I have recently been teaching them how to slide. I told Julia about Ty Cobb, one of the game's most ferocious players and accomplished base-stealers.

"Baseball was war for Cobb," I said. "He sharpened his spikes. When he slid, he kept his spikes in the air. He sent infielders out of games with stitches."

Julia gave me an odd look. I *was* getting a little carried away. Still, I don't regret letting her absorb the traditionally male lesson that says "Keep your spikes sharp." I know that Julia and the other Tigers will absorb and adapt it to their own personalities and feminine selves.

The Tigers wore gym shorts the day we practiced slides. I sent them barreling in from third base and sliding home. Although they slid on grass, their legs were taking a beating, getting ripped up and bruised. They would not, however, stop. They wanted to learn and wore what they considered their battle scars with pride. Almost without exception, they seemed completely unaware of the notion that girls are supposed to be fragile and fearful and that to be otherwise isn't feminine.

Finally, my Tigers are living proof, week after week, that girls are competitive. They want to win. Their appetite for victory is keen—as sharp as the spikes on Ty Cobb's shoes.

I was much gratified in an exhibition game at the start of this year's season that they chose to play the Meadowlarks, a team of 12- to 14-year-olds that were mostly bigger, stronger, and faster than my team of 11- and 12-year-olds. *Bring them on*, they told me. Win or lose, they were up for the challenge.

Late in the game, I waved a girl home from the coach's box at third when I shouldn't have. I was too aggressive. She was out by a mile.

We lost by one run.

I don't know if all my Tigers are alpha girls, but the lessons they're learning at softball will instill them with confidence, help them assert themselves, and show them that they can succeed.

I'm not the only father out there who coaches his daughter in athletics or shuttles her to sports practice and is in the stands when she competes. This kind of involvement is a clear way for us fathers to show our daughters that we care about what's important to them. In our post–Title IX environment, the world of women's athletics is taking off,[4] and as Figure 2-1 shows, alpha girls are no exception. They are as involved in sports and say that sports play is just as important to them as it to boys[5,6] (see Figures 2-1 and 2-2).

Sports are not the only way fathers and daughters connect. Alpha

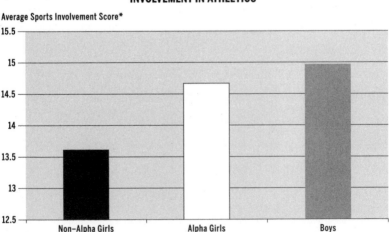

Figure 2-1
INVOLVEMENT IN ATHLETICS

Average Sports Involvement Score*

*Sports involvement score combines responses to questions that asked respondents about their involvement in 21 different sports, for which they rated their level involvement on a four-point scale, ranging from "not involved" to "very involved."

Dan Kindlon, PhD

Figure 2-2

PERCENT OF SURVEY RESPONDENTS WHO SAID THAT PLAYING SPORTS OR BEING ON AN ATHLETIC TEAM IS A "VERY IMPORTANT" PART OF THEIR LIFE

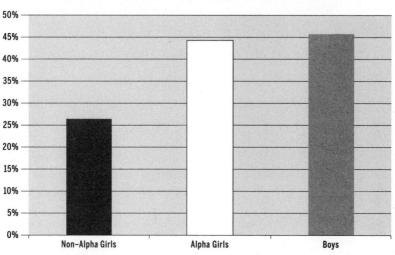

girls and their dads also bond around academics. They'll discuss homework, college choices, and career. In our sample, 75 percent of alphas said that they discussed their occupational plans with their fathers and said that they valued their father's opinion about their future careers.[7] (If you're feeling left out, rest assured that even these amazing alphas don't take their parents too seriously. Fewer than half of the alpha girls who said that they often talked with their fathers about their careers said they valued that advice.)

For the most part, all girls, including the alphas, felt closer to their mothers than their fathers and were more likely to discuss emotional problems with mom, but this trend was much less lopsided among alpha girls. Close to a third said they were equally close to both parents[8] and more than a third said that they could count on their fathers to listen when "they needed to get something off their chest."

Male Ways of Being

37

The more balanced relationship alpha girls have with their parents is an important part of their psychology. Many alphas are hybrids, incorporating aspects of each parent into their personalities.

Fathers today are often more involved in their daughters' lives, in part, because women have pushed men to shoulder more childcare responsibilities. Women have done this because they work, because they wanted to be unshackled from what can sometimes be the unremitting drudgery of parenting, and because they have wanted their children to have close relationships with their fathers.

It does fathers a disservice, however, to think that it is only women's prodding or their careers which have spurred them to become more emotionally connected and spend more time with their children. Many men of my generation feel that they would have liked more time and a closer emotional rapport with their own fathers. Many of us grew up in families whose fathers worked outside the home and whose mothers were responsible for the lion's share of the childcare.

This has changed. The closeness that fathers are engendering with their daughters often comes from the kind of day-to-day nurturing that has, in the past, been a mother's purview.

"There's nothing now that girls can't do," said Tony Green, a Washington, D.C., book packager and writer who is the father of three girls, aged 5 through 12. "My oldest, Anna, is totally into sports. It's what she lives for. Soccer, basketball, baseball. She plays third base, and she's got a great arm."

"Hardball?" I ask.

"You bet. And she's a monster at the plate."

It's Saturday at noon, and we're sitting in Tony's sunny kitchen.

Dan Kindlon, PhD

He's serving his girls lunch: he does all the cooking in the house. His wife, an executive in educational publishing, often travels for work, and Tony is frequently left alone with the kids. Even when his wife is at home, Tony has a more flexible work schedule, so it often falls to him to shuttle his girls to and from their relentless round-robin of sports practices and playdates.

Tony has the lunchtime routine down pat: tuna salad sandwiches work for the older two; the little one, nicknamed Vixen, will eat only peanut butter and jelly. "Breakfast, lunch, and dinner, if I let her," Tony says. "Oh, and she likes Peking Duck." He stops for a moment and considers. "It's perverse."

"Do you want to play H-O-R-S-E?" Anna asks me.

"A challenge!" Tony cries. "Eat your tuna first."

"She's as competitive as I am," he says. "She loves to win. But she's very polite—she always tells you that she's sorry after she beats you."

After scarfing down her tuna, Anna stands me fifteen feet from the basketball hoop. "You can shoot first," she says.

Two minutes later Anna has shot around, while I have made shots for just two letters—H-O.

"I'm sorry you lost," she says.

"What did I tell you!" says Tony. "She has the killer instinct, but she's also empathetic. In her teens, I think sports will be a big way that she relates to boys—the way she makes that connection. She speaks the language."

"You said before that there's nothing that girls can't do. What did you mean?"

"They have it all. Nothing limits them. Girls today can be sports stars. They can class presidents. They can beat you in H-O-R-S-E. But they can also gossip, play with dolls, and bare their souls."

"What do you think is different about having three girls rather than a mix of boys and girls, or just boys?"

"Perish the thought," Tony says. "But living with three daughters and a wife can have a downside. I'm in an estrogen mosh pit. It's a tough emotional climate. My primary emotional expression is anger—and they think their variety of emotional expression makes them superior beings."

Tony cooks and takes care of the kids, traditionally a mother's purview, while his wife works, yet he is still able to pass on his male ways of being to his daughter. Anna is a typical alpha generation hybrid, combining what has traditionally been thought of as the male competitive urge to win with empathy, a trait generally associated with women.

Until quite recently, psychological studies routinely found that fathers of girls tended to be distant parents. Surveys of expectant dads around the world indicated that they were much more likely to express a preference for having a boy.[9] If the new arrival turned out to be a girl, fathers tended to become increasingly detached, and by adolescence, psychologists characterized the father-daughter relationships as the one that was most emotionally distant, with the lowest level of interaction of the four parent-child dyads.[10]

Some research suggests that even emotionally distant fathers have an impact on their daughters. Studies conducted in the 1980s and early 1990s concluded that fathers have a greater influence than mothers on gender role development because, if they were involved with their daughters at all, they tended to reinforce stereotypes. Dads observed playing with their 4-to-6-year-old children paid more attention to daughters when they expressed what the study's authors termed "submissive emotions" (fear and sadness, for example) and

Dan Kindlon, PhD

more attention to sons when they displayed "disharmonious emotions," such as anger.[11] Another study found that dads were much more likely to give approval and attention to their daughters when they were playing with "feminine" toys, such as dolls, than when they were playing with "boy toys," such as trucks.[12]

Although in the past fathers have tended to enforce traditional models of femininity, our interviews with alphas suggested that many fathers today are encouraging their daughters in what in the past have been typically male activities, and that this can sometimes influence the direction of their daughters' lives.

Audrey's father, Bill, is an inspirational example of how a father passed along parts of himself to his daughter, teaching Audrey about what interested him and, in the process, showing her the high priority he placed on spending time with her and how much she meant to him.

Despite Bill's 60-hour workweek as an emergency room doctor, on evenings and weekends he found the time and energy to do building projects with Audrey in the living room of their suburban Lexington, Kentucky, home. When I interviewed her, Audrey was a freshman at the Massachusetts Institute of Technology (MIT), majoring in computer science.

I met Audrey on the MIT campus. She was still excited from her choir concert the previous evening. "We did my favorite piece," she said. "Mozart's *Requiem*. We got a standing ovation. It was awesome."

As Audrey and I walked to a nearby Marriot, she pointed out MIT's new Stata Center.

"That's CSAIL. I'm working there this summer," she said.

"What does CSAIL stand for?"

"Computer Science and Artificial Intelligence Laboratory."

Audrey is one of only two undergraduates to be hired by this prestigious lab.

At the Marriott, we found a quiet corner, and I asked Audrey about her father. "I learned construction from him," she said. "My dad is eclectic. When he feels like doing something, he gets a book, reads it, and gets it done. He built our barn and did most of the carpentry, plumbing, and electrical work on our home."

"Did you learn those skills from him?"

"You bet. But my own construction plans are modest. I'm installing new lights in my dorm room. You're not supposed to do anything to the rooms but everyone does. I've also been thinking about putting in a hardwood floor over the summer."

Audrey studied Ancient Greek in high school and plans to take Modern Greek at Harvard next fall. She sings alto in choir, plays the flute, is an accomplished cook, and has a black belt in tae kwon do. But her real passion—and the reason she chose MIT over the many other colleges that would have loved to have her—is the study of artificial intelligence, which she describes as "trying to get computers to do more of the things people can do."

Because of her interest in AI, Audrey has become fluent in several computer languages—Python, C, LISP, SCHEME—and she is conversant in C++ and JAVA. Her father helped launch her into cyberspace.

"When I was four, I was in a car accident," Audrey said. "Out of school for half a year. My parents bought me a computer to help me keep up with schoolwork and keep me occupied. I played around with DOS. Explored the program. Learned the language."

"How did your parents respond to your interest in computers?"

"My dad encouraged it. When I was a little older, we would build circuit boards together in our living room. We'd spend hours and hours, working closely together, taking computers apart and rebuilding them."

"What else did you build?"

"One of our coolest projects was a radio. We installed it in our basement. It was *really* cool. We had wires running everywhere." Audrey paused to make sure that I was still on the same page. "The main thing with a radio is the length of wire."

"You mean the antenna?"

"Yeah. We got the best reception in the basement. *What fun!* I thought. Somebody else might have a normal radio. But I *built* mine! Another real cool thing I did with my dad was model rocketry. We spread our stuff all over the living room. My brother was more into building *models*. But I liked things that went places or had moving parts."

Audrey and Bill are a clear example of how an involved father can shape his daughter's interests and give her a firm foundation on which to build her life. It doesn't always work out this way, of course. But Bill is following a long line of illustrious examples.

Former dean of Fine Arts at Ohio University Henry Huan Lin's daughter, Maya, designed the Vietnam Veterans Memorial in Washington, D.C. In a 2002 interview with the *New York Times*, Lin said that her closeness with her father was "the single biggest thing that contributed to me getting to do what I wanted to do. My brother formed a unit with my mother, and my father and I formed our own. I got the same attention from him that would in those days have been given to a boy. I was completely aware that it was unusual. And that made all the difference to me."[13]

Ms. Lin's account of her relationship with her father is similar to the connection between Sigmund and Anna Freud, Alfred Roberts and Margaret (Roberts) Thatcher, and Jawaharlal Nehru and Indira Gandhi. These examples show an intriguing similarity. Each woman, as a girl, gravitated towards her father because of her mother's death or lack of interest. In each case, the close father-daughter bond inclined the girls to look to their fathers as role models for their careers. Anna Freud eventually replaced Sigmund as the leader of the psychoanalytic movement. Margaret Thatcher's father was mayor of Grantham, the small English town where Margaret spent her childhood. She went on to become Britain's first female prime minister. Indira Gandhi, India's first female prime minister, occupied the post her father had held.[14] But the relationships of these women to their fathers were not atypical of past generations.

Audrey felt that her relationship with her father and the time they spent together was the reason that she was at MIT and had become interested in engineering. Many of the alpha girls we interviewed told us a similar story. They recognized that they had had close relationships with their fathers—relationships in which their fathers took them seriously and taught them skills that in prior generations would have been considered "too masculine." Freud, Thatcher, and Gandhi are fast becoming the norm instead of anomalies and exceptions.

Sports and career paths are not the only areas in which girls are being influenced by their fathers. Her classmates regarded Katie, a seventh grader in Lexington Country Day School (LCD), as the smartest kid in her class. (A+ is Katie's *lowest* grade.)

Katie's father, a neurologist, tried to interest her in his work. "It just didn't take," Katie said. "I feel kinda bad. When I was about six, my dad bought me a model brain, and every night at bedtime he'd talk to me about the different parts of it. But it wasn't meant to be. Now that brain has a Cleveland Indians baseball cap on it. I'm really more of an English person."

"Are you more like your mom?" I asked.

"I look more like my mom," Katie replied. "But I'd say that I'm more like my dad. We're both easygoing. My mom was rebellious. He was more of a good kid. I'm a pretty good kid, too."

Lynda, an eleventh grader who attends a prep school in a San Francisco suburb, also said that she felt her personality was similar to her father's. When I interviewed Lynda, the school day had just ended. Students lounged on the grass. One girl used her prone friend as a pillow while they read their history assignment.

I commented that Lynda didn't seem at all self-conscious about being seen with me—clearly an outsider in the small school community.

"I'm one of those 'high-profile' students on campus," she said. "I'm used to being stared at because I'm so tall—for a girl, that is."

"How tall are you?"

"Six-one in my stocking feet."

Height was not the only reason Lynda stood out. Her accomplishments would give Audrey a run for her money in an alpha girl poster child competition. Lynda is da Vinci–like in her interests—a straight-A student who speaks four languages and an accomplished painter, she whizzed through her advanced placement (AP) physics and calculus classes.

"Are you more like your mom or your dad?" I asked her.

"My dad."

"How are you two alike?"

Her response was typically alpha.

"My dad and I have the same interests," Lynda said. "We remember things the same way. We're the same politically. We have the same sense of humor. And the same things that get me really get him."

The relationships with their dads described by Audrey and her fellow alpha girls contain important information about the unique ways in which fathers interact with their children. Fathers and mothers even tend to play differently with their babies. The father jazzes the baby up—throwing her in the air and making her scream with delight (and a dose of fear) until she can barely breathe. Typically, Mom sits close by during these exhibitions, tense as a tautly tuned guitar string, begging him to be careful.

A similar scene was enacted almost every night at bath time in my house when our children were young. If my wife did the bathing, she would sit close to the tub and coo softly to the girls as they played games with our little family of yellow rubber ducks. But if I was in charge, I would transform into "Bath Man," don my superhero towel cape, grab my magic scrub brush, and burst into whichever room the hapless child cowered. "It's BATH MAN!" I would bellow. Swooping the squealing child into my arms, I would "fly" her to the bathroom for a raucous splashfest.

Research on sex differences in parenting shows that our family's bath time rituals were typical. Fathers tend to spend more of their parenting time playing with their young children than mothers, who spend more time care-taking. Father play tends to be more vigorous, louder, and physically rougher than mother play.

It's odd that these differences and their implications are not more studied. The vast majority of psychological research on parent-child relationships—including books written for parents—has focused on

Dan Kindlon, PhD

mothers.[15] Much of the research on fathers has centered on the negative aspects of his role. Reams of books have been written about absent fathers and "deadbeat dads."

When the contribution of fathers who are engaged with their children is studied, however, the results are clear: children of involved fathers are at lower risk for delinquency, substance abuse, low self-esteem, academic underachievement, and behavior problems. Involved fathers contribute to a child's social competence and self-control.[16] The quality of any child's relationship with his or her father is important for his or her mental health. For all the boys and girls in our sample, those with better relationships had higher self-esteem (see Figure 2-3).[i] In addition, girls who had better relationships with

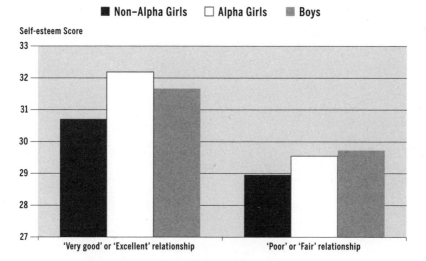

Figure 2-3

SELF-ESTEEM SCORE BY QUALITY OF RELATIONSHIP WITH FATHER

■ Non–Alpha Girls   □ Alpha Girls   ▥ Boys

[i] In addition, boys who had higher quality relationships with their dads were less likely to drink alcohol and got better grades in school. The latter relationship also held for alpha girls.

their dads also had more internal locus of control—that is, they were less passive and felt that they had more control over their lives.

Despite the paucity of books on the subject, the body of work on fathers who are involved with their children shows that both fathers and mothers make a unique contribution to their child's well being and that the father's rougher more playful parenting style especially benefits girls. There is evidence (from rat studies anyway) that vigorous play in and of itself contributes to brain development. Baby rats that are vigorously handled are smarter than those that aren't.[17] Father play can help girls develop a sense of humor, and that can help girls alleviate anxiety. In general, the alpha girls in our sample were less tense than non-alphas. They were also more open to experience—less shy and more eager to "try new things" (see Figures 2-4 and 2-5).

Play by its nature is fun. Fathers can help their daughters learn to

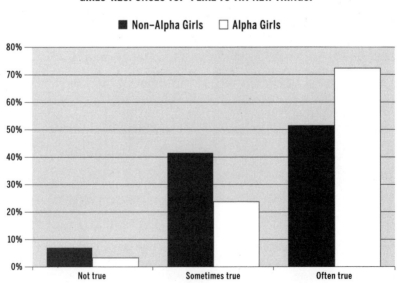

Figure 2-4

GIRLS' RESPONSES TO: "I LIKE TO TRY NEW THINGS."

■ **Non–Alpha Girls**   □ **Alpha Girls**

Dan Kindlon, PhD

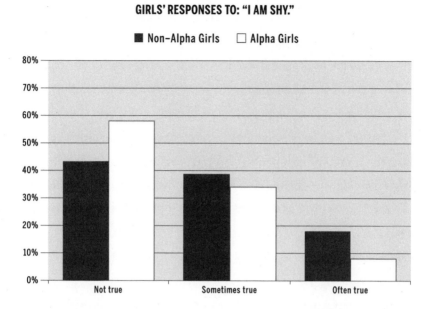

Figure 2-5

GIRLS' RESPONSES TO: "I AM SHY."

■ **Non–Alpha Girls** □ **Alpha Girls**

have fun and relax. Many girls we interviewed said, "My dad and I have the same sense of humor." I can relate. There are many nights at the dinner table when my daughters and I are in near-hysterics, laughing about something we saw on television. We read the funnies in the newspaper each morning before school, and I goad them about the misadventures of their latest celebrity heartthrobs. I genuinely enjoy these activities, just as I genuinely enjoy playing board games with my kids.

This deliberate silliness, getting down to their level, is something in which, I confess, I take pleasure, and it's a big part of the connective tissue of my relationship with my daughters. These activities are uniquely ours. My wife consciously ceded my daughters and me this space in which to connect and be close; and she is circumspect—she doesn't want to intrude. By removing herself, she has helped foster the intimacy I like to think that my daughters and I share.

I know that I'm not the only dad who relishes getting down to his kids' level. Audrey's father bedded down in the living room with his children to watch James Bond movies. "We'd all get our sleeping bags," Audrey reminisced, "and lay them out in the living room in front of the TV. And my mom would say, 'You all are crazy. I am not sleeping on the floor.'"

Another way father play helps daughters is by teaching them to take risks. According to Margaret Henning, author of *The Managerial Woman*,[18] one the biggest benefits to businesswomen of having involved fathers is that they teach their daughters not to be afraid of risk taking. Men can see both the upside and the downside to risks, while most women, according to Henning, see only the downside because they are afraid to lose.

One girl we interviewed, Rebecca, a 16-year-old public high school sophomore in Portland, Oregon, with a 3.9 average who is already a starter on the school's volleyball team, said that she routinely plays Texas Hold 'Em poker with her father. "When I was just starting to learn the game, he accused me of wussiness. He taught me to raise with nothing and call him when I thought he was bluffing."

Father play can help daughters learn how to relate to men, especially in competitive situations. Given that in the past, and to a large extent today, many professions are male dominated, women who are comfortable around men will be more successful.

As I talked to girls during our interviews, I could not detect anything psychologically unhealthy about their attachment to their parents. I didn't see evidence of some variant of an Oedipal triangle, in which the girls had effectively defeated their mothers in the competition for their father's attention[19] (see Figure 2-6).

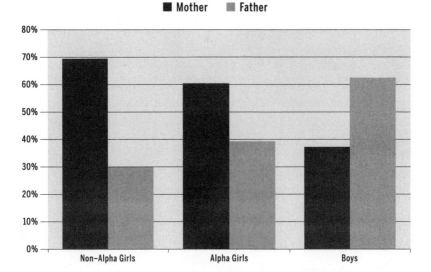

Figure 2-6

RESPONSE TO: "ARE YOU MORE LIKE YOUR MOTHER OR FATHER?"

■ Mother   ■ Father

A father's influence on his daughters goes beyond the psychological. A remarkable 1999 study led by Bruce Ellis at Vanderbilt University found that the age at which a girl begins puberty—her first menarche—can be predicted by *the quality of her relationship with her father.* This finding of the later onset of puberty in girls with involved fathers was replicated in a more recent study of Finnish twins.[20]

The amount of time the father spent doing childcare and the greater the affection between father and daughter (measured before the girl entered kindergarten) were predictors of later pubertal timing in daughters by the time they entered seventh grade.[21] In other words, girls who are close to their fathers tend to start menstruating as a later age than girls who aren't as close to their dads.

We found a similar effect among the girls in our sample. Although we could not assess the quality of relationship girls had with their dads when they were toddlers, we did find that the better a girl rated the quality of her relationship with her dad, the older she was when she got her period[22] (see Figure 2-7).

Figure 2-7

RELATIONSHIP QUALITY WITH FATHER AND AGE OF FIRST PERIOD

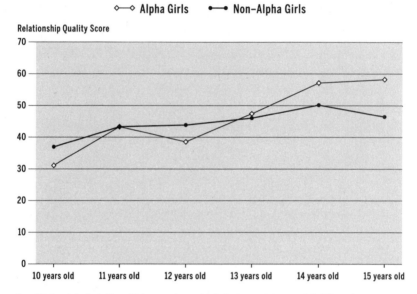

Age of first period adjusted in multiple regression models for body mass index, race/ethnicity, and socioeconomic status. Association between relationship quality and age of first period significant for alpha girls (β= 3.02, SE= 1.30, p=0.03) but not for non–alpha girls (β = 1.19, SE= 0.65, p=0.07).

Ellis explains this phenomenon in the following way: Very young girls notice at a biochemical level whether men are important assets in child rearing. If a girl's father is present and involved, her body will delay the onset of puberty until she is older and thus more able to have an involved father for her offspring. If her father is not involved, her biochemistry, shaped by eons of evolution, pushes her to start bearing children as soon as possible.

Most research indicates that a later rather than earlier menarche

Dan Kindlon, PhD

is healthier for girls. In the article that documented his findings, Ellis writes: " . . . early maturing girls are at greater risk later in life for breast cancer and unhealthy weight gain . . . [They] have higher rates of teenage pregnancy, are more likely to have low-birth-weight babies and tend to show more disturbances in body image, to report more emotional problems such as depression and anxiety, and to engage in more problem behaviors such as alcohol consumption and sexual promiscuity." Indices of pubertal timing in both boys and girls suggest that most dimensions of pubertal maturation are sensitive, in unknown ways, to structural variation across families. These initial studies generate a host of important unanswered questions that remain for future research, and they underscore the certainty that pubertal maturation is a complex and dynamic process, one for which simple metaphors, such as the steady and synchronous advancement of a biological clock, are woefully inadequate.

The contingent of girls today who identify with their dads do so not because they have been neglected or pushed aside by their mothers, but because they are *choosing* to broaden their repertoire and learn a range of skills that have been traditionally associated with *both* masculinity and femininity. They are "whole," in the sense that their conception of womanhood encompasses a wider range of attributes—including some that in the past were exclusively male—than at any other point in human history. Gender, the psychological meaning attached to each sex, is not fixed—social forces shape it. Today, a girl's conception of what it means to be female—her gender identity—is likely to be different from her mother's, and, perhaps, even her older sister's.

It is, of course, also vitally important to girls' expanded sense of themselves that so many of their mothers and other formative female role models have also adopted traditionally male roles in the world, working out of the house and forging careers. But I think many mothers would agree that fathers are helping form their daughter's psychology in ways that would have been inconceivable 50 years ago.

Many alpha girls gravitate toward their fathers because they identify with them. They feel they are like their fathers in fundamental ways. Other alphas gravitate toward their dads because they are aware of some of the compromises their mothers have made, and they don't plan on making the kinds of sacrifices that have been common among women in the past.

Violet, a ninth grader at St. Ann's who is the vice president of her class and wants to be an attorney, recognizes the sacrifices her mother made for her husband and family. Both her parents are lawyers, but her father's job prosecuting white-collar criminals was far more interesting to Violet than her mother's less demanding position. "She's done the same thing all these years," Violet said. "She works shorter hours than my dad and takes days off to be with the kids. But that's not what I want."

"Perhaps you'll feel differently when you're older," I suggested. "When you, too, want kids and a family."

"I don't know," said Violet skeptically.

"Do you think one day you might have a family?" I asked.

"Yes. Definitely. I want kids. But I would never do what my mother did."

"Go into real estate law?"

"No. Not just that. Not just being slowed down in her career. My mother comes from the Northeast, but she moved down to Atlanta, to the south, which she hates, to be with my dad. I'd never move to

Dan Kindlon, PhD

my husband's hometown the way my mom did. I'm more ambitious than she is. I know that I have a lot of potential, and I'd like to fulfill that potential. It's the right thing to do."

Rabbi Daniel Goldstein, the father of Rachel, another straight-A St. Ann's student, was among the most moving fathers we interviewed on the subject of the way he and his daughter were connected.

"My father was a rabbi," Goldstein told me. "When I studied at the Harvard Kennedy School, I was undecided on my career. I thought that I might go into law or public service or teach. But one of my professors told me not to spend my life climbing the ladder. 'Do something meaningful,' he said. So I became a rabbi. My daughter also has a rabbinic personality. She's open and loving. Perhaps, like me, she's too much of perfectionist. We're working on that. Every child comes into the world with a blessing. His or her own soul or nature. Our job as parents is not to shatter or ruin that soul— to love our children for who they are, but, ultimately, to get out of the way. You know, Rachel is my oldest. My second child was a boy. When he was born, a congregant said to me, 'Well, Rabbi, now you've finally got your son.' I couldn't believe he said that! Do people still think that way?"

"Less and less," I replied. "Less and less."

CHAPTER THREE

SEPARATION AND CONNECTION

"My best friend was on third, and I didn't want to get her out."
—Michelle, age 10

The "new psychology of women" developed by feminists that emerged in the 1980s and 1990s told us that men and women have fundamentally different identities. Men live their lives as separate individuals, independent of others, egocentric and competitive, while women experience themselves as part of the "web of human relationships" and relate to others in ways that are interdependent and cooperative rather than competitive.[1]

Feminist psychologists insisted that female connectedness had value, that it was, indeed, psychologically healthier than male autonomy. Carol Gilligan wrote in 1982 that the male psyche is "out of balance, favoring the separateness of the individual self over connection to others, and leaning more towards an autonomous life of work than towards the interdependence of love and care."[2]

Feminists felt they needed to defend the psychology of connectedness because, beginning with Freud, it had been systemically denigrated in psychology through much of the twentieth century.

Freud had argued that during early childhood, boys, but not girls, go through a process that inclines them towards separateness. He said that women never achieve the same degree of autonomy as men do, and, as a result, are at a psychological disadvantage. They have less ego strength.[i] They are more likely to be hysterical (a word taken from the Greek word for *uterus* because it was a disorder peculiar to women). He characterized women as overly emotional and hypochondriacal. Freud's views on women developed, in part, because many of his early patients were women who he diagnosed as suffering from hysterical neurosis—a condition that he thought resulted when sexual desire was repressed or frustrated.[3]

After Freud, male psychologists took up his mantle, treating women as though they were emotionally fragile. They took the position that the male path toward autonomy and independence was the healthy norm, while the female failure to separate was synonymous with a failure to develop into a strong, independent, fully individuated person.

As if that wasn't enough, in the 1970s and 1980s, Lawrence Kohlberg, a Harvard child psychologist (like me, but with a much nicer office), established his career by developing a theory of moral development in which women were *morally* inferior to men. Kohlberg dominated the field of moral development, and his theories about how children's moral reasoning evolved were taught in virtually every introductory psychology class in America.

---

[i] **Ego Strength**: Each person's ego has the ability to deal with reality and stress differently. Ego strength is the extent to which one is able to deal effectively with stress and continue to maintain emotional stability.

In the 1960s when Kohlberg's star was rising, Jean Piaget's stage theory of cognitive development had become very influential. Piaget had demonstrated that children pass through stages, from the completely egocentric preverbal "thinking" of the infant to objective, abstract adult reasoning.

Kohlberg applied Piagetian concepts to his stage theory of moral development. A child's moral reasoning, Kohlberg argued, progressed through six stages of development based, in part, on how egocentric his thinking was. At the first stage, a child makes moral decisions based on which choice brings *him* the most pleasure and least amount of pain. As a child gets older and is able to think about the needs of others, he may move to a stage where he recognizes that laws are necessary and must be obeyed. At the next stage, he moves beyond a simple "it's the law!" or "that's the rule" moral standard and applies the principles of the "social contract" as his basis for moral action.

Kohlberg developed a way to assess a child's stage of moral reasoning. He presented moral dilemmas to children; the most well known was a story asking whether a man should steal a rare drug in order to save his wife's life. Kohlberg was less interested in what decision the child made, but rather the type of moral reasoning he used. Thus, a child at the earliest stage of moral development might say the man should steal the drug because "he would be sad if his wife died," while a child at a higher stage of development might say the man shouldn't take the drug "because it's against the law to steal."

Boys, on average, scored higher on the moral development scale than girls. Boys were more likely use moral imperatives, *rules* that could be applied to reach a solution in any moral dilemma, just as the rules of baseball or golf that could be used to solve disputes during a game gave boys a scoring edge. Girls gave diffuse "well, it depends" answers; they were not as systematic; their moral reasoning was more diffuse and as a result didn't fit as neatly into Kohlberg's system.

In the early 1970s, Carol Gilligan, who had been Kohlberg's research assistant, set out to rethink moral development. She used the separation-connection dichotomy to analyze sex differences in moral reasoning, publishing her results in her highly influential book *In a Different Voice*.[4]

Gilligan theorized that because women and girls feel connected they use a "care orientation" when faced with a moral dilemma. Their moral decisions will be based on how they affect other people's feelings and whether the outcome of these decisions will harm their relationships. Men and boys, on the other hand, consistent with their individualistic self-concepts, have a "justice orientation." They base their moral reasoning on how established rules or laws should be applied, rather than on the feelings of those affected by their decisions.[ii]

In a competitive game, Gilligan said, a girl's primary goal is not *win* but to maintain relationships. Gilligan observed that girls do compete, but in a way that makes sure feelings don't get hurt, sometimes even at the expense of the game itself.

Soccer moms and dads I know make the same observation. They note clear differences between their sons' and daughters' games. In a boy's game, when an opponent falls down, the boys on the opposing

[ii] As an example of this separate-connected orientation, in her research interviews, Gilligan contrasts the moral reasoning of two 11-year-olds, Jake and Amy. Gilligan interprets Jake's moral reasoning as akin to doing "a math problem with humans," while Amy's involves "a narrative of relationships that extends over time." (p. 28).

team see it as an opportunity to score. Girls, on the other hand, will often stop to check if the felled opponent is injured before resuming play.

Gilligan's observations are acute, and they were driven home to me a couple of years ago when I was coaching the Pheasants, a softball team of third, fourth, and fifth graders. In one early-season game, we held a slim lead, but the opposing team had loaded the bases with only one out.

Given the dire importance of the situation, I called time-out and strolled to the mound to discuss strategy with Michelle, my pitcher.

"If the batter hits the ball, she will probably hit it right back at you," I told Michelle. "Will you be ready for it?"

"Yes, Coach," Michelle replied.

"You will then have two options. You can run to home plate or toss the ball to Meredith [the catcher] for the force-out. Are we clear on this?"

"Yes, Coach, Dr. Kindlon." Michelle vigorously nodded her head.

"It's late in the game. They're threatening, and we don't want to blow our lead."

"Threatening. Right, Coach."

Just as I predicted, on the next pitch the batter dribbled a grounder back to the mound.

"Home! Home!" I yelled at Michelle to reinforce my previous instruction.

She cleanly fielded the ball, looked home, then turned and threw the ball over the first baseman's head. A run scored.

I called another time-out and made my way back to the mound, trying to calm myself sufficiently for the talk that I was about to have.

Dan Kindlon, PhD

"Michelle," I said in the most even-tempered voice I could muster "We just discussed this situation. Why didn't you throw home?"

She scuffed her feet. "My best friend was on third," she replied, "and I didn't want to get her out."

I had to laugh. "I understand," I said. "But remember—you have some loyalty to your teammates as well as your friends."[iii]

This exchange helped me understand Gilligan's point about how girls respond to moral dilemmas[iv] by asserting the value of connection and care—a moral perspective that was at least as valid as boys' focus on the abstraction of rules.

Freud and Kohlberg, among others, had sown the seeds of dissatisfaction with male-dominated psychology. Now it was up to women to create a psychology that applied to them and, especially, to their daughters.

As feminist psychologists began to develop their own theories of women's psychology, they were in a bind. On one hand, they wanted to dispute the Freudian model. On the other hand, even as they insisted that the psychology of connectedness had value, indeed, was superior in many ways to the male *disconnected* self, they had to use

[iii] For those competitive readers who are on pins and needles, the Pheasants—despite our pitcher's care orientation—went on to win the game, which is, of course, the whole point to playing. Isn't it?

[iv] I should note that I tend *not* to see this kind of care orientation in the older girls I coach. For the large majority, the competitive aspect of sports predominates. This may be true, at least in part, because as children get older, their sports competitions tend to be against strangers rather than friends.

the Freudian model of how children develop to make their case if they wanted to be taken seriously by the psychological mainstream.

It is hard to imagine today how Freudian theory, or more broadly the psychoanalytic movement, completely dominated psychology well into the 1970s. Senior psychoanalysts always had the last say in any interpretation of a patient's case, and their assertions could be neither disproved nor verified. (A major problem with Freud's theories is that they are almost impossible to test scientifically.) Those with differing views had very little leverage to use to make their arguments. In short, if women psychologists, feminist writers, or women intellectuals of any stripe wanted to be taken seriously, they had to be fluent in Freud, especially his ideas about how boys and girls develop.

In 1908, Freud published "On the Sexual Theories of Children," in which he discussed the case of "Little Hans," who at the age of 3 had developed several phobias after concluding that his newborn sister had lost her penis. Freud used Little Hans to develop his ideas about the "castration complex." Around 3 or 4, Freud said, children begin to notice and think about the anatomical differences between men and women; moreover, they have a strong incestuous desire to possess the opposite-sexed parent and eliminate the same-sex rival. These desires come with a price: anxiety. Children notice that their parents are more powerful than they are—especially the father, who is bigger, scarier, and, according to Freud, far more influential than their mother. Boys are anxious that they will be castrated and lose their penises, which is what they assume has already happened to their mothers and sisters.

Freud postulated that castration anxiety was at the core of the Oedipal conflict, the primary shaper of personality.[5] In the Oedipal

Dan Kindlon, PhD

conflict, a boy tries to reconcile his strong sexual desire for his mother with the fear that accompanies it. The boy takes a cold, hard look at the reality of the situation. Like a hostage with Stockholm Syndrome, he eventually solves his dilemma by adopting a kind of "if you can't beat him, join him" attitude and tries to be like his former rival, his father. For a young boy, then, his identity development is simple: separate from mom, be like dad. Like what dad likes. Do what he does. When the boy *identifies* with his father, he "internalizes" him. It is almost as if a boy acquires a little internal father, a kind of a conscience that tells him when he is being bad (not like dad) or good (like dad).

It's not so simple for girls. According to Freud, little girls assume that they have already been castrated and recognize that their fathers have something *important* that they have "lost," a condition that goes by the unfortunate term "penis envy." The young girl blames her mother for the loss. (And why not—girls seem to blame their mothers for everything else, don't they?) The girl also feels contempt for her mother and all like her who do not possess the important male appendage. These feelings weaken her connection to her mother.

Although the little girl knows she can't have her lost penis back, she draws closer to her father, hoping to have his baby as a kind of consolation prize. Thus, the young girl is highly motivated to get as much affectionate attention from her father as she can. Her self-worth depends on it. For the most part, she does this in socially acceptable ways—by being cute and flirtatious. As she gets older, the girl continues to base much of her self-worth on how much attention she can get from men.

The little girl's conflict is sometimes referred to as the Electra Complex, after the character in Greek tragedy of Electra, the daughter of Agamemnon and Clytemnestra, who plotted to have her mother killed.

It is clear from the Freudian perspective that a girl's identity development isn't as straightforward as a boy's. She doesn't have as much to fear from her mom-rival as a boy does from his rival dad. She has, after all, already been castrated. She doesn't internalize and emulate either her father or mother. She doesn't identify as strongly with her mother as a boy does with his father. As a result, her conscience is not as strong[v] and her identity is more diffuse.

One of the most influential books to first shake the foundation of the Freudian view of the way male and female personalities developed was *The Reproduction of Mothering: Psychoanalysis and the Sociology of Gender,* by Nancy Chodorow, a California psychoanalyst, which was published in 1978.[6]

Its jacket copy proclaimed that the book was a "Copernican revolution" in child psychology. Just as Copernicus had scientifically demonstrated that the sun rather than the earth was the center of the solar system, Chodorow set out to demonstrate that a girl's psyche did not revolve around her relationship with her father: instead, Chodorow said, it centered on her mother.

Chodorow opened her argument with the observation that much had changed since Freud's time. Fathers were no longer the absolute

[v] This theory about girls having a weaker super ego, of which the conscience is a part, is at the root of the thinking behind the lower level of moral development for girls seen in Kohlberg's work.

Dan Kindlon, PhD

monarchs they had been in Freud's turn-of-the-century Vienna. Chodorow wrote: "Freud assumed a strong patriarchal family with authority vested in the father, and the theory of the Oedipus complex relies on a family of this description. But even since Freud's time, this authority has declined . . ." Furthermore, she observed, "In Western industrial society, biological or adoptive mothers have tended to have nearly exclusive care for infants."[7]

If men are largely absent from child rearing, Chodorow argued, it followed that castration anxiety and the Oedipal conflict cannot be the major forces in personality development that Freud had claimed they were. Still, Chodorow wanted to "remain firmly psychoanalytic," and she drew on the same Freudian theory that she wanted to critique.[8] She looked at the influences that predate the Oedipal phase and theorized that psychological differences between the sexes don't emerge from a struggle to come to terms with a powerful castrating father but because, as very young children, boys and girls are *mothered* differently.

Freud hadn't completely ignored a mother's influence on her children. He had written that newborns merge with their mothers—a blissful symbiotic state that is experienced by *both* mother and child. Chodorow provided a new emphasis and perspective to the Freudian model. She said that when the developing girl confronts the reality that she isn't "one" with her mother, she figures out ways to retain as much of that original bonded state as she can. Contrary to Freud, Chodorow argued that girls don't run off to try to get attention from their dads but instead stay connected to their moms.

On the other hand, mothers encourage boys to separate from them and be like their fathers. Chodorow said that mothers work harder to maintain the primary bond with daughters than they do with sons, in part because they want to return to the bliss of their own infantile bonded state. A mother's bond with her infant daughter is a way of reproducing her close connection with her own mother.

Chodorow and then other psychologists said these differences in rearing resulted in the distinct personality styles of the two sexes. The symbiotic mother-daughter bond tended to incline a girl's identity development toward a self-definition that consists not so much of her separateness from other people but of her connection to them. In contrast, a boy's experiences with his mother leads him to perceive himself as a distinct, separate individual.[vi]

One can also see that the ways in which children do or do not separate from parents, particularly their mothers, is at the core of Chodorow's thinking about the development of a sense of self. Her basic model of child development—her adaptation of Freudian theory—became the foundation on which the new psychology of women was built.

An important book that emerged from the seeds Chodorow had planted about women's connectedness was Jean Baker Miller's *Toward a New Psychology of Women*.[9] Miller added a political dimension to the discussion of separation and connection. In her view, subjugation of women by men was also part of the process that had produced women's connected identity. Men had forced women to adopt helping roles. Miller argued that connectedness, which had often been interpreted as "unhealthy dependency" in male-dominated psychology, was the result of "the influence of patriarchy on women's minds and women's specific psychological reaction against it . . . [f]or women, as we have seen, the very structuring of the relationship to

---

[vi] Chodorow does not take issue with the basic Freudian dynamics of the Oedipal conflict as it applies to boys.

Dan Kindlon, PhD

other people is basically different than it is for men. Serving others is one way of describing the fundamental form in which women's ties to others are structured."[10]

Miller, much like Gilligan, defended this way of relating to the world. She said that a truly evolved society would value affiliation, cooperation, and connection instead of conflict, competition, and bare-knuckled self-interest. Miller wrote: "Another important aspect of women's psychology is their greater recognition of the essential cooperative nature of human existence. Despite the competitive aspects of any society, there must be a bedrock modicum of cooperativeness for society to exist at all."[11] The premise of feminist psychology was that the dominant patriarchal structures tend toward violence and alienation and the connectedness of women points in the direction of a more compassionate and peaceful world.

Both Chodorow and Miller argued that the separate and connected personality styles resulted from early relationships with parents and society's expectations. Others, especially evolutionary psychologists, think that these differences are genetic, the result of thousands and thousands of years of different selection pressures on men and women in hunter-gatherer groups. Men hunted. Women gathered.[12] What makes humans a unique species, however, is that we are able to adapt to changing environments. We can *learn* new behavior even if it is at odds with our biological inclinations.

Whichever force, genetics or environment, singly or in tandem, produces these different male and female personality styles, it's clear that they show up even in very young children. Some distinctly male and female characteristics are universal: they are present in every culture on earth[13]—in the ways boys and girls play, for example. I noticed that difference the first time I was the designated as a "parent aide" in my younger daughter Julia's class at the Sudbury Co-op, a parent cooperative preschool.

Julia was thrilled when it was my turn to monitor her group. She chattered in the car on the way to the Co-op about her little pals. Always a responsible child, she reminded me of my duties: "You have to help wipe off the tables when we're finished with snack," she said. "You have to vacuum the playroom before we leave, and you have say 'use your words' if kids are fighting over a toy."

"Thank you for that advice. I'll do my best."

"Don't worry. If you forget, *I'll* remind you."

When we arrived, Julia grabbed my hand, bounced up and down, and pulled me toward the building. As soon as she entered the playroom, she raced to her friends and completely ignored me. I might have been a piece of furniture; and I had the ridiculous feeling we occasionally have as parents of being snubbed by our own children.

That feeling was dispelled by the raucous commotion of a room full of 4-year-olds, who were quickly and without any effort on my part coalescing into organized groups. The playroom was stocked with toys, including a jungle gym, a large sand table, and a dress-up area, from which the kids could choose costumes and props.

Boys played exclusively with boys; girls with girls.

The boys donned plastic fire helmets and began a rescue mission on the jungle gym, which they pretended was a burning building. They quickly formed a hierarchy. A wiry, dark-haired boy was dominant, while another boy, the largest in the group, was his lieutenant.

Dan Kindlon, PhD

A brigade of workers carried out their animated gestures and shouted commands, running here and there, squirting toy hoses at the imaginary inferno.

The girls were more subdued. They clustered around the sand table and made imaginary cookies and cakes. There was no clear leader or hierarchy in their group. They exchanged toys, shared tasks, and enunciated in what sounded to my ear like an unintentional parody of civilized, grown-up talk.

It was hard to believe how completely these 4-year-olds were acting out traditional gender stereotypes. The boys were saving the world, organizing themselves into what amounted to a military unit that was engaged in a do-or-die act of rescue or conquest. The fire could have been a wicked dragon or the armies of Troy. The girls were imagining themselves as nurturing domestics, and the mood of their interaction was based on sharing and cooperation rather than hierarchy and commands.

No one is quite sure why boys and girls start, at about age 4, to play in groups almost exclusively with members of the same sex, but it is a universal phenomenon, true the world over. Both sexes, however, play the same *kinds* of games: acting out fantasies or playing "pretend" are the most popular. The *themes* of their play are, however, usually quite different. Little girls generally play some variant of "house," acting out domestic and family roles; little boys prefer to pretend they are superheroes or other powerful characters.[14]

If these play patterns are universal,[vii] isn't that irrefutable evidence

[vii] The boys-with-boys and girls-with-girls play pattern was not quite universal at the Sudbury Co-op that day. There was one boy, Larry, who played alone on a rocking horse in the middle of the room. He was wearing a dress.

that the separate and connected personality styles in men and women are biologically determined? And if this is true, shouldn't we just accept this and help our children adapt to their "natural" roles in life? The most straightforward answer to that question is "No," and to understand why, we need to take a closer look at how children learn gender roles—the kinds of behavior that our culture deems appropriate for each sex.

What is the process in early identity formation through which kids come to construct their notions of gender? By age 2, most children can accurately state whether they are boys or girls. Shortly thereafter, children acquire a working knowledge of gender and quickly begin to form gender stereotypes. Children often say things like "Girls can't be firemen," or "Boys don't play with dolls, girls do." They sort attributes and behavior into male and female as if they are assigning endings to nouns in romance languages. Toddlers aren't comfortable with complexity. Their worlds are colored in sharp blacks and whites. When they assign occupations, toys, activities, and clothes "for boys" or "for girls," it is not because they're sexist: They simply don't have the cognitive maturity to see gray areas.

Still, it's amazing how easily children pick up these stereotypes. The reason that they assign these gender roles with such conviction is, to some extent, because they want predictability and a sense of control—a way to orient themselves, understand new experiences, and master their environment. The unpredictable produces anxiety.

Children's preference for same-sex groupings diminishes significantly in adolescence, and the ways in which children define gender roles tends to become less rigid and stereotypic. Gender isn't predetermined, but the fact that females give birth and nurse and males don't has always imposed certain limitations on the roles that men and women played in a given society. There is great variation among societies, however, in the extent of these limitations.[15] Cultures and historical eras differ in how gender is defined. Just as the word "shoe" is masculine in Spanish (*el zapato*) and feminine in French (*la chaussure*), different professions, activities, and attributes—depending on the time and place—have been predominately male, predominately female, or gender neutral. In the 1870s, for example, there were fewer than ten women working as secretaries in the United States: In order to use a typewriter, a woman needed a physician to certify that she was physically and mentally able to withstand the pressure of the job. By 1980, 95 percent of secretaries in the United States were women.[16]

Cultural definitions combine with "microcultural" parental influences and are superimposed on a child's unique temperament to create the way in which she eventually comes to define her gender identity, including how closely she will conform to gender stereotypes. She learns by example, by observing what men and women do. If her father helps with the housework and cooks, for instance, a child is more likely to identify cooking and cleaning as unisex or even masculine activities.[17]

Parents and peers also give kids direct instruction on gender roles. I am still surprised, for example, by parents who try to dissuade their sons from playing with dolls or wrangle their tomboy daughters into dresses. It's all too easy as parents to slip into wanting or expecting our children to grow up to reflect what we feel *we* want them to become. We need to love our children for who they are, but, ultimately, to get out of the way. We need to "let go" as our children age and allow them to separate from us and be themselves, particularly during adolescence, when they grapple with how they feel about religion, politics, their sexuality, and the kind of roles they want to play in the world.

～

During adolescence, psychologists think that separation and connection play key roles. Freud argued that our personalities are pretty much set in stone before puberty. Developmental psychologists now think that adolescence begins an intense period of identity formation, or, more accurately, *re*-formation, in which, typically, the child's connection with her parents is considerably reduced, or at least suspended, as she looks to friends and mentors to form her *own* identity.

The eminent psychologist Erik Erikson—the man who coined the term "identity crisis"—theorized that the main task for a teenager is to become more independent, more autonomous. This independence is propelled by a separation from parental attitudes, values, and morality. Adolescents often explore aspects of identity, perhaps a religious or sexual orientation, which make their parents uncomfortable.[18]

The general thinking in psychology is that it is usually healthiest for an adolescent to go through a period of exploration, trying on different roles and experimenting with ideas about who to become before fully committing to a personal identity. Not all teens do this, however. Some do very little exploration and quickly foreclose their quest for a separate identity by recommitting to parental values. Others explore their options but never commit, and still others drift without truly exploring or committing.[19]

Dan Kindlon, PhD

Empirical research has confirmed Erikson's theories. Adolescents who have more masculine traits—more autonomy, a less enmeshed relationship with parents and friends—tend to have a more successful course of identity development. They separate easily from parents, explore options, and make choices about who to be, what career path to follow, and the kind of person they want to marry.[20] This ability to be independent, autonomous, and separate—to consider one's own needs to the exclusion of others—has, in the past, been thought to be far more common among boys than girls.

It should be noted that Erikson's ideas are applicable to Western societies and relatively affluent adolescents. The process of becoming an adult and the qualities of autonomy Erikson championed don't play themselves out in other societies in the same way, or even in our culture in the milieu of poor urban children, many of whom are forced into adult roles at a younger age than their more affluent peers and who may not see themselves as having the luxury to explore their options and find themselves.

By the middle of the 1980s, the new psychology of women had cohered, acquired its shape, and been applied to adolescent girls. The feminists all came to the same conclusion: Girls are not inferior or psychologically damaged, they are victims of an oppressive male-dominated culture, which has foisted upon them low self-esteem, depression, eating disorders, pernicious self-doubt, and diminished expectations. The following full quote from Peggy Orenstein, the author of *SchoolGirls*, which appeared in the book's introduction, encapsulated the feminist concern for what was happening to teenage girls.

"For a girl," Ornstein wrote, "the passage into adolescence is not just marked by menarche or a few new curves. It is marked by a loss of confidence in herself and her abilities, especially in math and science. It is marked by a scathingly critical attitude toward her body and a blossoming sense of personal inadequacy."[21]

These claims were substantiated by empirical research, particularly a well-publicized national study commissioned by the American Association of University Women (AAUW). The study concluded: "As girls and boys grow older, both experience a significant loss of self-esteem in a variety of areas. However, the loss is most dramatic and has the most long-lasting effects for girls."[22]

An example of one of the key findings on which the report's conclusions were based was that girls, especially once they entered middle school, appeared less satisfied with themselves. After elementary school, "Girls self-esteem falls 31 percentage points, with only 29 percent of the girls describing the statement 'I'm happy the way I am' as always true. Almost half of the high school boys (46 percent) retain their high self-esteem. Thus the gender gap had grown from seven points [in elementary school] to 17 points."[23]

Self-esteem is, at its core, an overall evaluation of oneself, whether people see themselves in generally positive or negative light., People often perceive different aspects of themselves more positively than others. We might, for example, have a positive view of our moral character. We might view ourselves as honest, trustworthy, loyal, and helpful. At the same time, we might a negative self-perception of our intelligence, social skills, sexual attractiveness, or athleticism.

Dan Kindlon, PhD

The AAUW relied primarily on a simplistic index of self-esteem that was based on the average rating of five items:

I like the way I look

I like most things about myself

I'm happy the way I am

Sometimes I don't like myself that much

I wish I were somebody else

In our study we used the Rosenberg Self-Esteem Scale, which is what most researchers use. The Rosenberg questionnaire contains 10 items, which students rate on a scale from 1–4: strongly disagree to strongly agree. The items with the asterisks are reverse-scored.

I feel that I'm a person of worth, at least on an equal plane with others.
I feel that I have a number of good qualities.
All in all, I am inclined to feel that I am a failure.**
I am able to do things as well as most other people.
I feel I do not have much to be proud of.**
I take a positive attitude toward myself.
On the whole, I am satisfied with myself.
I wish I could have more respect for myself.**
I certainly feel useless at times.**
At times I think I am no good at all.**

According to the AAUW, girls had lower self-esteem than boys because of subtle sexism in the classroom. This sexism took a variety of forms. Boys were given higher-quality instruction than girls and were chosen more often to answer questions in front of the class and then given more time to formulate a response. Moreover, the report said: "[S]chools collude in this process by systematically cheating girls of classroom attention, by stressing competition rather than cooperative learning."

Thus, the interpretation of the causes of adolescent girls' drop in self-esteem was firmly anchored in the context of the new psychology of women—especially the assumption that girls, with their greater need to be connected to others, were harmed when school instruction was based on a "male model" of competitive learning. "Is it any wonder," the report said, "that many girls consequently become women who aim lower and achieve less than they should?"

Many psychologists—whether or not they were feminists—were alarmed at the AAUW findings because they were a harbinger of more dire psychological problems for girls. The main reason that psychologists care so much about low self-esteem is that it is tightly linked to depression.[24]

Psychologists were well aware that depression in nearly all its forms is far more common among girls and women than boys and men, but not until girls are at precisely the age—13 to 15 years old— when the AAUW study indicates that their self-esteem plummets. It wasn't much of a leap to suppose that the cause for the drop in self-esteem was the same as the cause of the large gap in rates of depression for boys and girls.

The AAUW report also said popular culture helped deflate girls' self-esteem by "marginalizing women and stereotyping their roles, presenting texts and lessons devoid of women as role models and reinforcing negative stereotypes about girl's abilities, especially in math and science."[25]

Male-dominated society had established different expectations for men and women, different gender roles that in the final analysis were unhealthy for girls. When girls reached puberty, these expectations became more salient. Girlhood was over. There was a new set of rules and increased pressure on girls to conform to phallocentric cultural expectations of what it is to be a woman, pressures which were thought to lead girls to adopt personality characteristics deemed appropriate for their gender. This process was termed *gender intensification*.[26] The aspects of gender that get intensified are, from the feminist point of view, mostly unhealthy. Girls are supposed to become self-sacrificing, sexy, and submissive.

Gilligan and others said that beginning in adolescence many females compromise their authenticity. Their postpubertal role called for them to be good women and put others' needs ahead of their own. As a result, many girls sacrificed their "true selves" to preserve connectedness to others. Speaking their minds might lead to alienation and hurt feelings, end a relationship, and sever an important connection. Thus, Gilligan feels that adolescent girls choose to minimize the risk of rejection by masking their true selves, a solution that for many is accompanied by conflict and distress.

Sacrificing one's "true self" and depending on others' approval for self-esteem is a recipe for depression. Feminists like Miller contended that, in many cases, female depression is a "relational disorder" caused by a loss of connection to others. Because girls and women purportedly define themselves by their relationships, when one is threatened or disrupted, it is "*not* just a loss of a relationship but something closer to a total loss of self."[27]

After puberty, boys and men treat girls differently. Clothing stores offer bare midriffs, tank tops, and short shorts in 12-year-old sizes. Parents may begin to encourage their young teenage daughters to pay more attention to their appearance. If a girl wasn't aware before puberty of the power and powerlessness that accompanies sexual attractiveness, she is now. If she is attractive, she becomes a sex object whether she likes it or not. If she isn't, she can be ignored or shunned—made to feel that she is an outsider or even that she doesn't exist for the opposite sex.

Puberty brings more than intensified gender expectations. It also brings about dramatic physical change. During puberty, the average girl grows about 10 inches and puts on around 25 pounds of new weight.[28] Boys gain weight, too, but in contrast to girls, boys' weight gain is in lean muscle and skeletal mass rather than in body fat. Boys generally like what happens to their bodies during puberty. They become sexier. Girls dislike the weight gain and the loss of the skinny prepubescent look that is idealized in modern fashion. Adolescent girls' dissatisfaction with their bodies—brought on by the combination of gender intensification and increased fat—is a blow to their self-esteem and may lead to depression.[29]

The psychological disorders of depression or anxiety were reinforced by a culture that taught girls that passivity and helplessness were acceptable, indeed desirable, feminine qualities. A girl was told to follow, not to lead. She felt pressure to subsume whatever ambitions she had and become a "connected" nurturer. The professions open to her were the connected professions of nursing, teaching, and secretarial duties, which recreated her domestic role in the world of work. She was expected to be modest rather than assertive. She was supposed to sacrifice her personal ambitions to her husband, family, or society. Her interior was shaped—first by her relationship with her mother and then by society—to maintain harmony within the web of human relationships before asserting her individual needs.

Dan Kindlon, PhD

The adolescent girl was cunningly inculcated with messages that said that her life was not in her own hands, that the only way she could ever hope to be in control was through using her looks and sexuality. Her "feminine wiles" were the way to get what she wanted. And she was told in no uncertain terms that what she should want was a husband and family. As if that wasn't bad enough, she was also taught that because of her hormones or her indelible feminine nature she was a creature swayed by emotion rather than reason and that it was culturally acceptable for her to be histrionic and impressionable. Instead of proactive problem solving, she tended to cope with anxiety through helplessness and confusion, an inability to make decisions, and an irrational belief that "things will turn out just fine." Psychologists characterized this as an "impressionistic" cognitive style that lacked analytic rigor and sustained intellectual concentration.

Anxiety. Depression. Helplessness. Confusion. Eating disorders. Low self-esteem. Diminished expectations. Passivity. Hysteria. This was the psychological mess that was supposed to be the adolescent girl. No wonder she crumpled inward and withdrew, turning from a vibrant creature full of confidence into a withdrawn, anxious shadow of her former self.

The late 1990s and the first years of our new millennia added to this embattled view of teenage girls. Books like Rosalind Wiseman's *Queen Bees and Wannabees* and Rachael Simmons' *Odd Girl Out* described a culture of adolescent femininity that consisted of snipingly cruel cliques and rigid hierarchies that conferred on girls either an insider or outsider status. All in all, writers on girls' psychology painted a grim picture. Their bleak renderings gripped the public mind. It doesn't surprise me that in the schools where I speak, parents are often on edge, worried that their daughters are in danger.

The women-as-connected view that was the bedrock of the feminists' "new psychology of women" does not adequately capture the psychology of American girls—especially the alpha girl—as I have come to know her. Alpha girls are *both* separate and connected. They are able to balance the different aspects of the self: the "connected" self that is subsumed by the web of her relationships with loved ones and the "separate" self that is more autonomous and selfish.

This new balance has created a girl with more psychological strength than her forerunners, who is not as prone to some of the problems that have accompanied the classically connected female personality. The psychology of alphas confers on them the possibility of a new freedom to be able to evaluate their options and choose the kind of life they want to live, unfettered by many of the insidious assumptions about what it was to be a woman that have plagued girls—shaping who they thought they were and how they have felt about themselves—in the past.

Dan Kindlon, PhD

CHAPTER FOUR

THE PSYCHOLOGY OF EMANCIPATION

"I am completely free to choose how I want to live my life.
I can't see what will hold me back, except a lack of energy or ambition.
If there are still inequities in society, I will change them."

–Justine, 20, Vassar College sophomore

Our alpha interviewees challenged almost all of the assumptions that psychologists had routinely made about girls. Most of the girls we interviewed were emotionally healthy, positively assertive, and self-confident. They certainly didn't feel in any way disadvantaged in the classroom.

This may be because classroom discrimination against girls has been largely addressed. Teachers with whom we spoke in coed schools felt that a new awareness, at least in many classrooms, was challenging whatever inequities had existed in the past. The staffs in the schools where we interviewed said that they were seeing new levels of confidence and ambition in their students in all areas, including math and science. The *bring it on* attitude was ubiquitous.

Some teachers wondered about how realistic the dark view of adolescent girls had been to begin with and whether mood disorders and shaky self-esteem were specific to teenage girls or *all* teenagers, boys included. Some teachers and administrators, while they still felt protective of girls, had begun to shed their reflexive habit of treating the adolescent female as if she was a fragile victim of oppression poised to implode. Still, there were other educators who struggled with my take on the robust psychology of contemporary girls.

Ellen, a middle school head at a coed prep school in Westchester County, New York, cut her professional teeth on Gilligan, Pipher, and Orenstein. I was interested in how Ellen dealt with the apparent dissonance between Gilligan and company's view of teenaged girls and the students who filled her classrooms. She was not ready to give up the idea that female adolescents were at risk for the kinds of problems we've discussed. Still, she admitted that her school attracted some pretty amazing girls—girls who were smart, talented, and brimming with confidence.

Ellen's office had big south-facing windows that let in light but were high enough above the quad to ensure anonymity to anyone inside. The only indication that she had a life outside school was a picture of her two young daughters draped over Ellen's partner, Melanie, their other mother, a former corporate lawyer who Ellen said was relishing her new role as a full-time stay-at-home mom.

Had Ellen seen a loss of voice and low self-esteem among the girls she mentors? "I'm coach of the girl's field hockey team," she said. "Boys can dive around on the floor for a basketball. It's *okay* for them to be aggressive. But you really have to encourage most girls to let that out of themselves. I have to teach girls to hit the ball *hard*, to use their whole body. I have to show them how good it feels to hear that ball *whack* into the wood at the back of the practice net."

"It doesn't take too long to rid a girl of her ball-whacking inhibitions," I said, describing my Tiger experiences.

Dan Kindlon, PhD

"I'm glad to hear that," she replied, unconvinced.

I briefly considered telling Ellen about Lynda, an alpha girl I met in Alabama, who, after winning the girls' state championship in golf as a junior, played for her school's boy's team. Lynda played from the same tee position as the boys and drove the ball farther than many of them. It is customary in golf, when men and women compete, to move the women's tees up the fairway, so that women begin each hole closer to the green than their male opponents. Lynda neither needed nor wanted this handicap.

Ellen and I agreed to disagree on our differing perceptions of girls and sports. "Do you try to teach girls to be assertive in the classroom as well as on the playing field?" I asked.

"We groom kids here for leadership roles. For better or worse, we teach them about the culture of power and success as it is defined in present-day America. For example, we teach them how to give a firm handshake and look people in eye. As a result, we are doing a much better job teaching girls some historically male skills and character-istics."

"Is it working?"

"Girls do learn to speak forcefully. They don't bump up against the female icon of what a girl should be—shy, demure, well coifed. That icon has been blown out of the water, which is incredibly healthy for girls."

"You seem to be saying that some girls still show unhealthy aspects of traditional femininity, at least in field hockey. But you've also given me examples of some of the amazing, assertive, self-confident girls here. Let's cut to the chase. Do most girls who have had a lot of social and intellectual advantages still face obstacles to success? Lim-itations on what they want to do in life?"

"I don't see obstacles for the population of girls that this school serves," Ellen said. "They're surrounded by women in leadership positions. The head of the school is a man. But I'm running the middle school, and a woman runs the admissions department. The director of communications and dean of the faculty are both women. No matter what they decide to do, what field they enter, no girl here will need to be a pioneer."

The data from our survey confirmed Ellen's perception that the girls she currently teaches have more confidence, at least in some areas, than girls of the past. Our survey showed that there wasn't a drop in self-esteem during puberty, which traditional women's psychology had taught us to expect. And that was true not just for alphas but for all girls.

Self-esteem remained relatively stable for girls from sixth through twelfth grade. Although there is a slight drop for girls between sixth and seventh grade, they quickly recover. By tenth grade, girls have higher self-esteem than boys and continue to maintain parity with them through the rest of high school.[i]

There were no differences in measured self-esteem between alpha girls and boys at any grade level.[1] Our finding stands in stark contrast to the AAUW findings that after elementary school, girls' self-esteem falls sharply, even relative to boys, and remains low throughout high school[2] (see Figure 4-1).

Rosenberg self-esteem scores were adjusted for socioeconomic status, race/ethnicity, and school in multiple regression models.

Our survey results were consistent with a growing number of

---

[i] Alpha girls had significantly higher self-esteem than non–alpha girls in grades nine, eleven, and twelve. See endnote 2 for details.

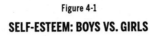

Figure 4-1

SELF-ESTEEM: BOYS VS. GIRLS

■ Boys　　■ Girls

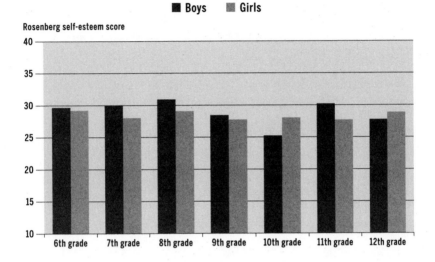

Rosenberg self-esteem score

studies that indicate that the pessimistic portrait of adolescent girl's psychological health is obsolete. Several other recent research projects have found negligible sex differences in self-esteem[3] and no difference in assertiveness between boys and girls.[4] Girls speak up for themselves in most situations; loss of voice is largely a thing of the past. Girls today have higher self-esteem due, in large part, to changes in the family, the culture at large, and because classrooms have become places where a generation of confident girls can now "speak forcefully," thanks to dedicated women like Ellen.

Is what Ellen describes—a cohort of confident girls ready to take on the world—confined to privileged children? Is the assertive, confident, liberated alpha a product of her economic class rather than the embodiment of a new, pervasive psychology of the feminine?

Although American society is increasingly egalitarian with respect to gender, there are glaring social divisions between the haves and the have-nots.

Girls who grow up without the many advantages that Ellen's students enjoy are starting out life at least a few steps behind their more privileged peers—and their self-esteem scores reflected that disadvantage. Children from the lowest social strata in our sample—whose parents lacked the education that leads to higher-paying jobs—were more likely to have low levels of self-esteem, irrespective of their race or ethnicity.[5]

Alpha psychology may be more prevalent among girls in the middle and upper classes. But it also exists among girls who come from less advantaged backgrounds. I was particularly impressed by some of the girls we interviewed who came from poorer homes. The relative distance they had traveled was even greater than their more privileged peers. They had surmounted greater obstacles than your average alpha girl.

Inner city alphas had their own culture, as I found out when I interviewed at an urban charter school in Hartford, Connecticut, that I'll call CATCH. The school had 180 students in grades nine through twelve. It recruited kids from the public schools in the poorest parts of the city. The school's classes were small and set up for individual instruction. The point of the program was to prepare students for successful college careers, and each student at CATCH had to take one AP class and two college level classes before graduation. Candidates for CATCH were accepted into the school by lottery, and its student body was 91 percent African American or Hispanic. Girls far outnumbered boys. They were more likely to enter the lottery pool and were therefore picked more often in the drawings. Once at CATCH, they outperformed the boys academically. This finding was not confined to Hartford: It was true for many urban public school districts, such as Boston, where 80 percent of the valedictorians in 2004 were girls.[6]

I asked girls at CATCH why they got better grades than boys and why more girls than boys enter the school lottery. The girls were unanimous in their perception in the academic differences between the sexes.

"Boys are scared to be smart," said Natasha, a CATCH senior with a 3.7 GPA who had been accepted at Duke. "They have so many other issues. Like that they have to be tough. Or that they have to make it in the streets. They still have the mentality that women should do this and that for them."

"You mean a woman will support them?"

"That's right. They don't feel the need to be smart or achieve."

"How would you characterize yourself?"

"I'm outspoken, outgoing, not afraid to speak my mind."

"Why do you think you were chosen by the school to be interviewed? Are you a leader?"

"I do well academically. I try to connect to everyone. I get down on people when I feel that they're not being themselves."

"What do you want to be when you grow up?"

Natasha laughed. "I want to go into pediatric nursing. I love, love, *love* kids."

"Why not be a pediatrician? A doctor?"

"What's wrong with being a nurse?"

"Doctors have more prestige. Make more money."

"Well, I don't know . . . No way would I allow myself to fail. It [being a doctor] is a lot of responsibility. And money isn't that important to me."

Like many of the alpha girls we interviewed, Natasha seemed to like hanging out with boys.

"I'd rather hang out with boys than girls," she said. "Boys think so differently. I'm fascinated by their reasoning."

"For example?"

"Like why they go off on the side."

"What do you mean?"

"Why does a boy have to have one girl for this and another girl for that? If he did that to me, I wouldn't be mad but I would dump him."

"Why wouldn't you be mad?"

"That's how boys are. I wouldn't be surprised."

Outgoing, outspoken, assertive, high achieving—I came away with the impression that Natasha was a typical alpha girl. Although she came from an economically less advantaged background than many of the other alphas I had talked to, she obviously knew what she wanted and knew her own mind. She had made the effort to get herself into CATCH so she could get a better education than would have been available to her at her local public school.

I found it interesting that an alpha girl with similar interests from a more privileged background would probably have her sights set on being a doctor. Race and class may have been factors in Natasha's projection of herself into a stereotypic gender role. Nonetheless, Natasha was ambitious and driven. She felt that she would succeed no matter and that she would overcome whatever obstacles were placed in her path.

"I don't rule out being a doctor," she said. "We'll see."

~

It is wonderful to see how unfettered and filled with possibility many girls feel. They don't *feel* inferior. They're not afraid to succeed or assert themselves. They are not afraid to alienate people if they think it's in their own best interest. Theirs is a psychology of emancipation.

The drive for emancipation has shaped Western civilization. The word comes to us from *emancipare,* which in Roman law was the freeing of a wife or child from the *patria potestas,* the father's dominion. Over the last 500 years in the West, the greatest social upheavals—the Protestant Reformation, the French, American, and Russian Revolutions, the American Civil War—have come when the powerless have freed themselves from their tyrannical institutional "fathers." It's not just a little ironic that the alpha girls' emancipated psychology has in part come about because of the championing of her cause by her *pater familias.*

It's important for mothers to recognize that their daughters are psychologically different from them. If a mother projects her own psychology onto her daughter, she runs the risk of alienating her, making her feel isolated and misunderstood. (Your daughter may feel that you're clueless—and why add yet another item to the list of things you are clueless about?)

This point was driven home to me as I talked to Alexis and Sara, two dynamic 15-year-old Canadian girls, and Julie, their 28-year-old

French teacher, about their school's history curriculum. The girls said that they were sick of hearing about "women's history" and the battles of the women's movement.

"We *get* it," said Sara, with that eye-rolling look of exasperation that teenagers work so hard to perfect. "But it doesn't really apply to us."

Julie said that she sees a "big difference" between women from her generation and the high school girls that she teaches. "They're right," she said about the two girls. "They don't see themselves as oppressed. They don't see the world in the same way we did."

As a child psychologist, it's clear to me that many girls today sense that they put their own psychological health in danger by accepting the view that women are oppressed. When Alexis and Sara say that they are tired of hearing about "women's history," they aren't simply saying they are bored. I think they know—perhaps only unconsciously—that the role of the oppressed robs them of their "internal locus of control," the conviction that they are largely the masters of their own fates and that they are responsible for their successes and failures.

If we want our daughters to be leaders, if we truly want them to be able to command positions of real power and influence in society, it is essential that we clearly communicate our expectation that they are up to the challenge. Children are keenly aware of our anxiety and our doubts, the moments when we fear that they will be devastated by failure. As I discussed at length in an earlier book, *Tough Times, Strong Children*,[7] one of the most fundamental roles a parent must play is the "confident coach." If our kids sense that we think they can succeed, it's far more likely that they will.

Children never quite outgrow their need for our reassurance. After a toddler falls down, her first move is to look up at her parent as if to ask, "Am I hurt?" The parent whose look communicates her conviction that the toddler has the strength to bounce back from adversity is setting her on the path to emotional maturity, resilience, and, ultimately, success.

That is clearly 20-year-old Vassar junior Justine's perception of herself and her future. Justine's ambition is to go into business and make a lot of money. I interviewed her in the Vassar café, housed in one of the college's brick buildings that has been designated as a National Historical Landmark, on a breezy May afternoon when the immaculately maintained campus was in bloom.

Spring term was over and students in shorts, flip-flops, and T-shirts were decamping for their summer break. Parents in sleek sedans collected them, or they were readying to drive themselves, stuffing their old wrecks with a motley assortment of gear: clothes, computers, stereo equipment, and the odd piece of furniture that to my eye looked like it should been consigned long ago to the junkyard.

Justine drank bottled water. "Are you worried that you're going to bump up against the glass ceiling?" I asked her.

"I won't accept that a man will make more money than me for the same job," she said. "I will get what I want because I am aggressive. I am not afraid to stand up for myself. My self-esteem does not come from what other people think of me. Sure, people say you can't be a CEO because you're a woman. Why not? I'm not buying it."

"Do you think your confidence comes, at least in part, because you haven't yet had to confront a sexist society?"

Justine became impatient. "I am completely free to choose how I want to live my life. I can't see what will hold me back, except a lack of energy or ambition. If there are still inequities in society, I will change them."

Justine made me think of other Vassar alumni: anthropologist Margaret Mead, poet Elizabeth Bishop, and the brilliant writer Mary McCarthy, author of *The Group*, a novel about the lives of eight Vassar graduates in the early 1930s.

In *The Group*, almost all of McCarthy's female characters largely define themselves through their relationships with men and recognize that if they want careers they will need to work in fields that were socially acceptable at the time: nursing, teaching, secretarial, and publishing. But the idea that women could have *both* a career and a marriage was new in the 1930s.

One of the book's most sympathetic characters, Dottie, patiently explains to her mother that women in her generation don't have to choose between a career and marriage: "That was in your day, Mother . . . Nobody has to chose between getting married and being a teacher. If they ever did. It was the homeliest members of your class who became teachers—admit it. . . . Sacrifice is a dated idea. A superstition, really, Mother, like burning widows in India. What society is aiming at now is the full development of the individual."[8]

Dottie embodies what at the time was an emancipated psychology of women. Dottie knows, along with her peers, that her Vassar experience has equipped her for useful work, which is not just about sacrificing herself and her ambitions to inevitable domesticity. In this sense, she stands, historically, at a midpoint between Jo March in *Little Women* and Justine.

"In the 1860s," said Justine, "the men who designed the corridors at Vassar made them extra wide. Do you know why they did that? They were worried that too much blood would go to the girls' heads

Dan Kindlon, PhD

when they studied and not enough would go to their reproductive systems. They built wide hallways so that girls moving through them between classes would have room to exercise and not impair their reproductive potential. Have you ever heard of anything so ridiculous!"

We want our daughters to be like Justine, full of moxie. We want them to be courageous. Resilient. Ready to take on the world.

The weight of research-based, statistical evidence clearly indicates that girls have changed. The passive, voiceless, self-hating teenage girl appears to be an endangered species, slowly disappearing from the face of North America. But before I pronounced her extinct, I wanted to hear from the source of much of the fanfare surrounding what was perceived as the crisis among adolescent girls of the 1980s and 1990s.

Susan McGee Bailey, director of the Wellesley Centers for Women,[9] was the lead author of *How Schools Shortchange Girls—The AAUW Report*—an extension of the AAUW's *Shortchanging Girls, Shortchanging America*. Unlike the prior AAUW report, Bailey's did not focus on girls' self-esteem but took a broader look at biases in educational curricula, testing, and teacher behavior that affect girls' academic achievement.[10]

Bailey heads one of the world's largest research think tanks on women's issues. From her spacious office (one of the nicest on campus, she tells me) in a rambling white Victorian house, she directs the activity of dozens of social scientists, who are conducting research on a wide range of issues of importance to girls and women in areas such as gender equitable education, child care, intimate partner violence, work and family balance, and, of course, the psychological development of women.

To my surprise, Bailey didn't jump to defend the original AAUW report when I said that I didn't think many girls today had low self-esteem. Instead, she said that people had simplified the issue and that her report had been skewed in the press and elsewhere. "Most people only read the executive summary," said Bailey. "Hardly anyone read the full report."

"Are girls still not being served well by schools?" I asked.

"You'll find a lot of variability from school to school in how girls are treated," she said. "Race, class, culture—they're all important and often overlooked. And don't think that just because women have made progress that it can't be reversed. I'm especially worried that with some of the decisions the Bush administration is making and the cultural shift in this country towards conservatism and fundamentalism, that there will be a move toward 'putting women back in our place.'"

She certainly had a point there. In March 2005, the U.S. Congress passed a measure weakening Title IX,[11] and in early 2006 Samuel Alito was confirmed as a Supreme Court justice; many believe he will tip the balance of the court and help overturn *Roe v. Wade*. Conservative think tanks such as the American Enterprise Institute have argued for a return to a kind of 1950s thinking (and federal policy) about the "natural" roles that men and women should play in society.[12] There are books such as *The Politically Incorrect Wife: God's Plan for Marriage Still Works Today*. The book asserts that submitting to a husband's will is part of "God's scriptural job description for wives."[13]

Bailey, like most social scientists with a respect for solid research, hedges her bets when asked to give definitive answers. While she agreed that girls have made progress in education in the past decade and a half, she reminds me that there is also research indicating that problems remain. She suggested that I take a look at Dr. Karen Arnold's work on self-esteem among college women. So I did.

Arnold directed the Illinois Valedictorian Project that, for 10 years, followed 81 valedictorians (46 girls and 35 boys) who had graduated from a range of high schools in Illinois in 1981. In her book, *Lives of Promise: What Becomes of High School Valedictorians*, Arnold wrote: "Women—but not men—showed a sharp decline in their self-estimated intelligence between high school graduation and their sophomore year of college."[14] This language sounded to me like a repetition of the AAUW findings, except that the age of the participants had been shifted from middle school to the middle of college. Gloria Steinem used Arnold's research in her widely read book, *Revolution from Within: A Book of Self-Esteem*, arguing that colleges do not support women, which Steinem said caused women to lower estimates of their own intelligence.[15]

I was skeptical. Perhaps, I thought, these college women suffered from crises of confidence because de Beauvoir's inner metamorphosis was still gestating in 1983. It was hard to imagine alphas being cowed in college. The alpha college students who I interviewed all seemed to be thriving as undergraduates. Audrey, the MIT freshman with an interest in artificial intelligence whom you met earlier, didn't appear to have a diminished sense of her own intelligence or capacities. In fact, she seemed to think that the amount of work expected of her and its difficulty were not quite challenging enough!

"I have about five hours of homework a night," she said. "It's really not more than I was doing in high school. It might be good if it was *more* challenging or difficult. I kinda feel like I'm cruising."

June, another MIT freshman we interviewed who is interested in engineering, was similarly unfazed by MIT's workload. When asked whether her course work was difficult, she replied, "not particularly." Like Audrey, she sounded disappointed.

Alex, a sophomore at Williams College, told me that her hardest class was Arabic, which she was taking because she wanted to join the CIA after college. She did three hours of Arabic homework each night. "It's not too bad," she said in a blasé tone. "Nothing I can't handle."

One of Arnold's valedictorians, Beth, came across Steinem's book with its reference to Arnold's work and wrote Arnold a fascinating e-mail: "I am one of those women who was less likely to assess myself as being 'far above average' in intellect as I got older and progressed further in the educational system. Frankly, I consider that more a sign of maturity than low self-esteem. What I find more alarming is that the men's percentages don't change at all. . . . So I just find myself questioning Steinem's implicit assumption that the male trend was 'healthy' whereas the female trend was 'unhealthy.'"[16]

Beth was suggesting that some of the boys who said that they were "far above average" intellectually were overvaluing them-selves—much like the executives at Enron who spuriously inflated the value of the company's stock.

Having devoted a great deal of time to studying boys, it was

Dan Kindlon, PhD

apparent to me that boys often boast and underreport problems. Isn't that part of the male code? Never admit weakness. Any woman will tell you that many men have a skewed view of reality: They are simply not as good as they think they are. Is this "healthy" self-esteem, which is what Steinem, Gilligan, and Arnold would have us believe? The AAUW had reported that that fewer girls than boys said that they were "always happy with themselves the way they are." People who are *always* happy with themselves are either saints or deluded. Many men I know fit the latter description; none, the former.[17]

Justine was one of many alphas who were clearly assertive—a trait they can summon to handle problems and get what they want. Assertiveness will help alphas stand up for their rights and succeed in whatever arena they will eventually choose to exercise their energy and intelligence. Alphas like Justine are already whole people: They are "individuated" in the sense used by psychologist Carl Jung.

Jung felt that the primary psychological task in life is individuation, the process of getting in touch with and synthesizing the various components of the psyche. Among other aspects of our personalities, Jung thought that the *animus* and *anima*—the male and female aspects of our selves—*both* needed to be recognized, expressed, and, most importantly, integrated for a person to be psychologically healthy.

Justine and many girls like her have integrated their *anima* and *animus*. Justine is in touch with the male side of herself. Many of the other girls we interviewed had incorporated traditionally male attributes into their personalities. They were able to balance the traditionally female "feeling" parts of themselves with what have been viewed as the male "thinking" parts. Their hybrid selves integrated the intuitive and rational, the tender and hardheaded, the self-sacrificing and self-serving.

The alphas emancipated psychology reflects our times in the same way as Chodorow and Freud's psychology of women reflected their eras and milieus. Freud's focus on the father's role in a child's life stemmed, in part, from the fact that the father dominated the family of late nineteenth-century Vienna. Children were afraid of them. Little boys wanted to be strong, stoic, and separate like their dads, while their penis-lacking daughters reluctantly resigned themselves to second-sex status. Chodorow's critique of Freud was based partly on her observation that in the middle of the twentieth century, mothers were the primary parent. They were the dominant force in a family when it came to child rearing. With the early mother-daughter bond as the primary shaper of a girl's personality, Chodorow argued, daughters grew up connected.

One of the most useful ways to describe the changes that have occurred in the psychology of girls today is by "role theory,"[18] which posits that much of human behavior, especially how we behave in social situations, can be described by the roles we play.

Role theory states that people play the social roles that are expected of them. These role expectations may be formalized into rigid conventions in some societies. For example, in ancient China, Confucius described six primary relationships (husband-wife, parent-child, older brother-younger brother, etc.) and the inflexible rules that

Dan Kindlon, PhD

govern them. (In the husband-wife relationship, for example, the husband must show benevolence; the wife, obedience.)

The father of role theory, Erving Gottesman, who wrote in the 1950s, gave the example of a common role that "young American middle class girls" adopt—"playing dumb for the benefit of her boyfriend."[19] He said that her boyfriend likes her because she's being submissive, placing him in the dominant role. She is confused, lost, waiting for his direction. This makes him feel powerful. Potent. Gottesman said the girlfriend who acts dumb is going along with a role that she knows she's supposed to play, but that it feels real and right to her. He writes about reality and contrivance and how the roles we play seem real to us. We know that we're actors, but we become caught up and believe in our own dramas. Gottesman recognized that there are some roles we want to play, but that others are foisted on us. Feelings of obligation, however, don't invalidate the verisimilitude of our performance.

Ellen, the middle school head, recalled that when she was in high school in the 1980s, the "athletic" girl was still not an accepted gender role. "Today," Ellen said, "a girl can be beautiful and sexy and popular and athletic, and the athleticism adds to the sexiness and beauty and popularity. When I was growing up, if you were an athlete you had to work really hard to not be automatically [labeled] a dyke."

In the past, women could be caretakers, housewives, and homemakers. Now, among other roles, they can be soldiers, athletes, scholars, politicians, and businesswomen.

Girls who have a diverse set of roles at their disposal will be healthier and more resilient than girls who have had fewer choices about the roles that they're allowed to play. Girls who can play masculine or androgynous roles are at a distinct psychological advantage. Recall that previously we discussed how the passive feminine role is related to depression and low self-esteem. It doesn't matter if you're a man or woman—if you take charge of your life, if you don't feel helpless in the face of adversity, you are at much lower risk for mental health problems.[20]

When we looked at the most "masculine" group of girls in our sample, the salutatory effects of being able to adopt a more assertive, autonomous role was confirmed. The girls in this group were the top quartile of scorers on the Bem Sex Role Inventory—that is, those most likely to strongly agree with traditionally male sentiments such as "When I play games I like to win" and "I would rather do things on my own than ask others for help." Compared to their less androgynous counterparts, these girls were less likely to be anxious or self-conscious and less likely to say they often worried about things. They had higher self-esteem. It was interesting that they didn't tend toward substance use or promiscuous sex—behavior problems more often seen in males than females.[21, 22]

As a clinician who has worked with disturbed kids, I was particularly impressed that the alphas we interviewed who had some of the classic risk factors for low self-esteem and mood disorders seemed to be doing fine because there were more roles available to them. Alphas have protective buffers that help ameliorate or reduce the risk of mood disorders—buffers such as doing well in school, enthusiastic involvement in athletics, and the support of family or friends.[23]

Amy was a case in point; I interviewed her at St. Ann's. The immaculately kept school grounds impressed me. It never ceases to amaze me that we lavish the kind of attention and care on our chil-

Dan Kindlon, PhD

dren that schools like St. Ann's provide. Our schools are a reflection of what we value as a society. In too few of our public schools, but in many of our private schools, we've created great environments for learning—schools with small classes, committed teachers, and incredible facilities.

The evening before I met with Amy, I spoke to parents in St. Ann's comfortable auditorium about the conflicts so many of us seem to have with authority and discipline as our kids move through adolescence. I was struck, as I often am, by how many fathers attended. Would this have been the case 10 or 20 years ago? Some men were there alone or with another man, without their wives, or perhaps as single parents.

I was also struck (again, as is often case) by how harshly we evaluate ourselves as parents. Some of the questions that I fielded after the talk had a self-castigating tone, as though the parents who asked them felt that they could be doing a better job, that they were in some way lacking. Part of what the popular psychological literature on adolescence has done is make parents feel that they are somehow to blame for everything. I try to tell parents that you can only do so much. Bad parents raise good kids and good parents can raise bad kids. We want our children to be perfect, and that's an unfair, not to mention an unrealistic, expectation.

St. Ann's principal had selected the alpha girls I interviewed the following day. Amy was my last interview. She had come to the interview straight from volleyball practice.

"What grade are you in?" I asked.

"Seventh," she replied. Her voice carried a hint of "I know that's hard to believe." Amy said she had been 5'8" since fifth grade. Her older and younger brothers had also had early growth spurts. Amy was the star "spiker" on St. Ann's middle school volleyball team. She had also been nationally ranked as a speed skater when she was 10, but now there were more girls her size with whom she had to compete.

I was curious about how Amy had been affected by her physical appearance. Research says that early-maturing girls are particularly at risk for low self-esteem and depression.

"Is it a pain to be tall?" I asked.

"Not really. When I was younger, it was the best thing to be tall."

I went through my standard list of mental health questions. "Are you depressed? Do you get sad?"

"No."

"Are you nervous or anxious?"

"I used to get nervous at swim meets, but I don't anymore."

"Do you have ADD? Do you ever have trouble concentrating?"

"No."

"What kinds of grades to you get?"

"Mostly As and Bs."

"If you had to describe yourself with three adjectives, which would you choose?"

"Loud!" said Amy, laughing. "I'm outgoing, and I laugh a lot."

"It sounds like you're generally happy."

"Yes, sir."

"You're a psychologist's dream-come-true. Tell me this—what would you change about your life if you could?"

"I don't know, really. . . . I have good friends."

"Are you satisfied with the way you look?"

"I guess I am . . ."

Dan Kindlon, PhD

I pressed Amy because she has key risk factors for depression—early puberty and a "big-boned" figure. But as far as I could tell, she was mentally healthy. As I asked her about her life, it turned out she had buffers against pressure and disappointment. She was close to her family, religious (which, for most people, is a source of support during tough times[24]), and she was an accomplished athlete. Because she goes to an all-girls school, her deviance from the media ideal of a "pre-pubescent look" isn't as much of a day-to-day issue for her as, perhaps, it would have been if she were in coed environment. Still, I wondered if she was as psychologically balanced as she appeared.

"Are you interested in boys?" I asked. She nodded and blushed. "Do you have a boyfriend?"

"No. Lots of my friends do."

"Does your size make it difficult?"

"The boys in my grade are, like, two inches tall."

Amy did seem sad when we discussed boys, as if she was starting to realize the consequences of not being one of the girls in her class who boys want to date. I wondered how she would do when she was older. Whatever direction her life took, I would guess that she will be at a lower risk for feelings of inadequacy or insecurity as an alpha girl in the twenty-first century than she would have been if she had been born a generation ago. Her self-esteem was clearly not dependent solely on her body image. In addition to church, friends, and family, it was tied to athletics and academic performance—and in those areas she felt good about herself.

I also interviewed Holly Prentice, a Harvard sophomore, another alpha girl who I thought was a prime candidate for various psychological disorders because of her troubled family background, but who seemed to be emerging from adolescence in fairly good shape. She was one of the few alpha girls who I interviewed who had had mental health problems.

I met her on a late fall day on the quad in Harvard Square. Holly and I walked from the quad into Harvard Square proper. The Square is a part of the campus that was once bohemian but has yuppified in recent years. Students were going out to lunch, buying magazines at kiosks, and hopping on the Red Line for a trip into Boston. We passed several of the Square's many bookstores. There are probably more bookstores per square foot in Harvard Square than in any other place in America. There are also no video stores in the Square, which is not really a square at all. It is a place where cow paths used to run that is now a maze of narrow streets which curve and converge.

We brunched at the Charles Hotel's restaurant, among faculty, business people, and parents visiting their kids. Holly ordered a burger and fries.

"I had a really, like, rough adolescence that involved, um . . . mild anorexia and a lot of depression," said Holly. "These days I'm generally in a good mood, but I do have depressive, like, moments."

Holly was admitted to Harvard after having had a typical alpha girl experience at an all-girls private prep school in a New Orleans suburb. She had graduated at the top of her class, played the cello, and edited the school's literary magazine.

So what had caused her depression? On the surface, one could interpret her case as a typical Ophelia-in-need-of-revival.

Holly's first experience with patriarchy was unpleasant. Her father, who had grown up in the South, had a traditional view of child rearing and expected unquestioning obedience.

"My father was very controlling," she said. "He has a dominant temperament that borders on the abusive. Physically, no. But emotionally? Absolutely."

"What does he do for a living?"

"He is a very good businessman and happens to have a lot of money. Because he's got money and power, he has never had to function at an emotionally mature level. He has the emotional intelligence of an 8-year-old."

"There are some girls who have domineering fathers but who manage to get approval from their dads by flirting—by being cute, funny, and coy. Other girls want to show their fathers that they're smart or capable . . . "

"My dad loves that."

"The smart part?"

"No. The flirty part. He loves it. I've learned how and when to use that because it makes things so much easier. But it's disingenuous and it feels kind of, like, yucky."

"Does your father have high expectations for you?"

"I don't know. We'll be driving around. My dad's an architect by trade. He's a technically interested guy. He likes water plants and paper plants and powery things. We'll be driving and pass a powery thing, and he'll go to my brother, 'Wendell, Wendell, look at that!' And it would never occur to him to say, 'Holly, look at that!' Despite the fact that I do better in school than my little brother and am more mechanically minded than him."

"Do you try to impress your father with your smarts? Your abilities?"

"Well, yeah."

"Does it work?"

"No. It scares him. My dad has always been threatened by my ability to communicate. We've fought since I was old enough to hold down my end of an argument. I have become adept at sidestepping his anger. I know when he wants to fight, and I can get around it."

"It sounds like a difficult relationship. That must have been hard on you growing up."

"It created a lot of stress. There was a problem that I had. I tried to attain a bodily ideal."

"The anorexia? What triggered it? Were you overweight?"

"No. But I remember lying about my weight. I went to an all-girls school. You learn by the time you are in fourth or fifth grade that boys exist and maybe you should, like, do something about it. There are girls who are skinny and pretty from birth. You become aware of the way people respond to that type of girl, and you're, like, 'whoa, interesting!' I remember lying about how much I weighed when I was eighty pounds. I would say seventy-five. I wasn't fat, but I was roundish, and I wore glasses and a retainer. And I've always been sort of—not the nerdy type exactly—I always considered myself more socially competent than a nerd, by definition."

"How do you feel about yourself now?"

"In what way?"

"Your looks."

"Oh, I think they're fine now."

"What about your mother? Where is she in all this?"

"She has been diagnosed as bipolar. My father, too, is depressive. He may not be an alcoholic, but he has three or more beers every night. It's not optional."

"You mentioned before that your father was abusive. Did your mother try to protect you from him?"

"She couldn't protect me. She was out of it. When I said my father wasn't physically abusive, that is almost entirely true. But he did spank me until I was 13. At which point I told him in no uncertain terms that that could be construed as sexual abuse."

"Yes."

"And if he didn't stop, I would call the police. He was furious, but he never spanked me again."

"Did your Mom know that this was going on?"

"Yes. I'd say, 'Mom, this is not okay.' And she'd be, like, 'Well, I don't want to get between you and your father.' She's still that way."

"With all this difficulty, how did you manage to survive? Even thrive?"

"I had wonderful teachers. I worked very hard to please them. They became god-like figures for me. And then in sixth grade . . . oh, God, I had a very classically traumatic adolescence. In sixth grade, I was best friends with a girl who was a few years older than I was. And she turned out to be lesbian and told me that she was in love with me."

"How did you respond?"

"I didn't know what to do. She was my best friend, and I thought she was pretty and cool."

"Was the relationship sexual?"

"Well, kinda. We talked on the phone almost every night. Sometimes we'd make out. It didn't go much past that."

"Do you have a girlfriend or boyfriend now?"

Molly laughed. "She was my only woman. My first kiss! Which is always a fun story to tell at parties. It's been all guys since. But no, I'm not dating now. I was with a really great guy last year. We broke up for the summer. In September, I said, 'Phil, let's date again.' And he said, 'Never.'"

"Why?"

"He said there was too much tension in the relationship. Too many problems. I knew that was true, but I was willing to try to make it work. I've never been, like, shot down so hard. I was gutted emotionally."

"But you're doing okay now?"

"Yes. I'm focused on my schoolwork, my friends. What life has to offer."

It's always risky to hypothesize, but as with Amy's case, I think there would have been a much better chance that Holly would have been a mess a generation ago. Holly's problems didn't keep her from excelling in school. She obviously had teachers who encouraged her and provided ballast in her complex and difficult relationship with her parents.

Both Amy and Holly support the research that indicates that if boys have higher self-esteem than girls, the difference is negligible. What has been interpreted as lower self-esteem in girls may be partially explained by the ways in which they are more honest and mature than their male counterparts. There was an openness and emotionally vulnerable quality to Amy and Holly that you would be hard pressed to find in their male peers.

There were a handful of high-achieving middle school girls we interviewed who appeared to exemplify the Gilligan dynamic. They gave the kind of "I don't know" answers to questions that Gilligan says are characteristic of girls who have lost their voice.

Betsy was a memorable example of this type of girl. An eighth grader from a wealthy family near Charlottesville, Virginia, Betsy attended a competitive private school in Massachusetts. Unlike most of my interviewees, Betsy was in no hurry to list her accomplishments. She had just come from volleyball practice. I asked her whether she was one of the better players on the team. "Not really," she answered. Another member of the team had spontaneously told me in a separate interview that Betsy was the team's best player. Similarly, when asked what kinds of grades she gets, Betsy answered, "Good grades, I guess." When pressed, she acknowledged that she earned straight As.

"Do you think you're smart?" I asked.

Betsy nervously laughed. "I guess. I don't know."

"What three adjectives would you use to describe yourself?" This was a question I thought she would have no trouble answering because it was asked of each student at the beginning of the year in a school-wide class exercise.

"I don't really know," Betsy responded.

One could view Betsy's behavior through the lens of the old psychology and say Betsy had "lost her voice." But had Betsy changed? Had she been a confident, outspoken sixth grader, full of ideas and opinions? Had she been faced with the dilemma of trying to fit into the role of Gilligan's "good woman?" Is that why she was withdrawn and inarticulate? She didn't report any significant symptoms of depression or anxiety, which one would expect from a teenager who had lost her voice.[25] My clinical impression was not that she was hiding something, or was conflicted about what to say. She simply wasn't introspective. She was young and her thinking was still concrete. Some teenagers haven't reached the stage where they can articulate abstract propositions about themselves. These adolescents are not yet self-aware.

It remains to be seen how the psychology of adolescent alpha girls will play out as they mature, go out in the world, and have families of their own. Will they become more exclusively connected than they are now? Will they forgo some of their more selfish inclinations and become more sensitive to the web of human relationships? When we become parents, we lose a degree of autonomy, although as men assume more of the childcare burden, the separateness that they have traditionally been thought to maintain through adulthood may be compromised—conveyed to or wrested from them by their partners or wives.

Independence. Autonomy. Self-sufficiency. Ambition. Competence. A desire to be challenged and engaged. These are some of the characteristics of the psychology of emancipation that is embodied by alpha girls. The following table sums up the differences we saw between what has been the traditional view of girls' psychology and the new psychology that so many of the girls we interviewed display.

TRADITIONAL CONCEPTIONS OF GIRLS' PSYCHOLOGY	ALPHA GIRLS' PSYCHOLOGY
Low self-esteem	High self-esteem
Girl's self-esteem plummets in early adolescence when she realizes that the patriarchy is in control and that to be valued she must be beautiful. Her low self-esteem is often accompanied by anxiety or depression and is occasionally accompanied by body image/eating disorders. Moreover, low self-esteem leads girls to undervalue their abilities and may limit their life success.	Recent research, including our own, shows that teen girls' self-esteem does not take a precipitous drop in middle school and is essentially equal to that of boys. These new findings suggest that more positive role models, less gender discrimination in schools, and fathers' changing attitudes toward their daughters make it easier for girls to value more aspects of their identities, leading to higher self-esteem.

Dan Kindlon, PhD

TRADITIONAL CONCEPTIONS OF GIRLS' PSYCHOLOGY	ALPHA GIRLS' PSYCHOLOGY
Mood disorders (depression/anxiety)	**Greater psychological health**
It has been a psychiatric truism that teenage girls and women have much higher rates of anxiety and depression than boys and men. Theories about why this is vary. Some are biologically based (sex hormones); others focus on social or cultural causes. One influential cultural explanation, which is supported by empirical research, is that feminine sex role identification, which may include more expressed emotion and a more helpless or passive coping style, is a risk factor for depression/anxiety among girls. Another explanation is that early onset of puberty is associated with mood disorders in girls because it can lead to stronger identification with the feminine sex role, and because the increase in weight that usually accompanies pubertal development is linked with greater body dissatisfaction.	Alpha girls should have a lower lifetime risk for mood disorders. First, as discussed previously, a close father-daughter bond may help delay the onset of puberty. Second, alpha girls should be less identified with a *passive* feminine sex role. Because a critical mass of alpha girls has appeared only recently, there are no large-scale studies that can determine if rates of clinical depression/anxiety are falling among adolescent girls. In our sample there were no sex differences in rates of "depression" based on a composite of measured self-esteem and anxiety. Consistent with previous research, girls in our sample were more likely than boys to show the highest rates of anxiety.[26]
"Other-oriented" values	**"Self-oriented" values**
Throughout human history, at least since the Pleistocene, patriarchal social systems have predominated. Men have had more social standing, owned or controlled most of the wealth, and occupied the important leadership positions. In contrast, women have performed domestic roles and done the lion's share of child care. The patriarchy influenced, or in some cases, determined a girl's choice of occupation. In her work life, she was most often constrained to a domestic role or low-paying "women's work," such as teaching, nursing, or secretarial duties, which recreated her domestic role in the world of work. Consistent with her role expectations, self-centered values such as ambition, assertiveness, and hedonism were subservient to values such as subjugation, modesty, and self-sacrifice.	Studies of younger female executives find that they are less likely than their older female counterparts to worry about "tooting their own horn" or being perceived as aggressive.[27] In addition, recent polls show that a graduating high school girl is three times as likely to place a high value on "having a lot of money" as were her counterparts in 1972. In short, alpha girls tend to have a range of values that encompass both self-orientation and other-orientation. Although these value systems can sometimes conflict, self-oriented values are often important for career advancement.

TRADITIONAL CONCEPTIONS OF GIRLS' PSYCHOLOGY	ALPHA GIRLS' PSYCHOLOGY
Connected orientation Strong, almost symbiotic attachment to mothers leads girls to perceive themselves less as independent entities and more as a part of a web of relationships; maintaining harmony within the web takes precedence over individual needs.	**Separate and connected orientations** With fathers taking a more active role in rearing daughters, both connected and separate styles of relating to the world are instilled in girls. Girls are becoming more psychologically flexible and better adapted to a world in which it will be effective to have both orientations (President Bush's unilateral action against Iraq, for example, is consistent with separate or agentic values and motives; a more communal leader would have worked harder to establish a coalition).
Emotional style Each person tends to respond to stress/anxiety in characteristic ways. A highly emotional, histrionic, or hysterical adaptational style has traditionally been viewed as the most common style employed by women, in part because it was culturally acceptable in ways that other, more masculine styles, were not. While extreme examples of this style—such as Blanche DuBois in *A Streetcar Named Desire*—are well known, in most cases hysterical personality styles function to protect their users from anxiety by keeping reality at bay through repression and an irrational sense that "things will turn out just fine." The hysterical cognitive style is impressionistic, impressionable, and generally lacking in the ability to sustain intellectual concentration.	**Rational style** Girls may now adopt a more rational, "masculine" style. This style involves a quest for control, hard thought, and the development of detailed factual memories, accompanied by a suppression/denial of emotion. While not necessarily "healthier" than the more emotional/hysterical style, this typically masculine style is more adaptive in the sciences, engineering, and business. More importantly, people who have more flexibility in their psychological defense against anxiety will be more able to tailor their adaptation to the situation at hand.

Dan Kindlon, PhD

CHAPTER FIVE

THE FEMININE BRAIN

"I guess my experience with my 2½-year-old twin daughters
who were not given dolls and who were given trucks,
and found themselves saying to each other, look, daddy truck
is carrying the baby truck, tells me something."

—Dr. Larry Summers, President, Harvard University, January, 14, 2005

On a cold, gray January day in 2005, Harvard University president
Larry Summers addressed a luncheon crowd of accomplished scholars from around the country who had gathered in Cambridge, Massachusetts, for a meeting of the National Bureau of Economic
Research—the nation's leading nonprofit economic research organization. The issue on the table was the economic impact of the under-
representation of women in top science jobs.[i] In 2005, women held

---

[i] When we talk about "top" jobs in science, engineering, and math, we are
mostly talking about faculty positions at major colleges and universities.
The very top jobs are faculty positions with tenure, which means the
faculty member has been accepted to work at an institution permanently.
Usually, faculty members are hired into a "tenure-track" position, which
requires them to work for the institution for five to seven years. At this
time, a committee evaluates the faculty member's productiveness (grants
received, research conducted, scientific papers published) and contribution to the university community (teaching, advising, serving as a
member of committees, etc.). The committee decides whether the
faculty member should receive tenure. Usually, if a faculty member does
not receive tenure, she or he leaves the institution (voluntarily or by
official termination of the position) and seeks a tenure-track position at
another institution.

* This chapter was written in collaboration with Amy Sapp.

only about 20 percent of faculty appointments in science, math, and engineering departments nationwide, and they held only a fraction of senior positions.[1]

Summers had been invited to address the group on the reasons for this.[2] He admitted that he was no expert on the subject, but said that he had read and thought about the issue and offered three possible reasons for the dearth of women in top science and engineering jobs:

1. Discrimination—bias against girls and women in these fields
2. Motherhood—women with children may be less willing to put in the 80-hour workweeks that would make them competitive with their male peers
3. "Intrinsic aptitude"—men may have greater natural ability in the sciences that leads them to outperform women at the top end of these professions

Summers emphasized the last of these points, intrinsic aptitude, in his remarks, citing evidence that indicates that at the extreme end of ability distribution—the 99.9 percentile of math ability for example—there are many more men than women. He said that recent research indicates that the reason for this difference is genetic.[ii]

[ii] Two relevant quotes from the transcript of Summers remarks are: 1) "I'm focusing on something that would seek to answer the question of why is the pattern different in science and engineering, and why is the representation even lower and more problematic in science and engineering than it is in other fields. And here, you can get a fair distance, it seems to me, looking at a relatively simple hypothesis. It does appear that on many, many different human attributes—height, weight, propensity for criminality, overall IQ, mathematical ability, scientific ability—there is relatively clear evidence that whatever the difference in

Dan Kindlon, PhD

Discipline	Career level (percent women)			
	PhD Degree	Assistant Professor	Associate Professor	Full/Tenured Professor
Astronomy	22.9%	20.2%	15.7%	9.8%
Biology	45.9%	30.2%	24.9%	14.8%
Chemical	25.0%	21.4%	19.2%	4.4%
Chemistry	33.4%	21.5%	20.5%	7.6%
Civil	17.9%	22.3%	11.5%	3.5%
Computer Science	15.3%	10.8%	14.4%	8.3%
Electrical	12.1%	10.9%	9.8%	3.9%
Engineering	15.3%	16.9%	11.2%	3.7%
Math & Statistics	26.9%	19.6%	13.2%	4.6%
Mechanical	10.9%	15.7%	8.9%	3.2%
Physical Science	24.7%	16.1%	14.2%	6.4%
Physics	14.8%	11.2%	9.4%	5.2%

WOMEN PHDS AND FACULTY, TOP 50 DEPARTMENTS IN SELECTED DISCIPLINES

Source: Handelsman, J. (2005) "More Women in Science," *Science,* 19, pp. 1190–1191.

Not everyone at the meeting agreed with Summers' remarks. Not by a long shot. In fact, before Summers spoke, several speakers had

means—which can be debated—there is a difference in the standard deviation, and variability of a male and a female population." 2) "My point was simply that the field of behavioral genetics had a revolution in the last 15 years, and the principal thrust of that revolution was the discovery that a large number of things that people thought were due to socialization weren't, and were in fact due to more intrinsic human nature, and that set of discoveries, it seemed to me, ought to influence the way one thought about other areas where there was a perception of the importance of socialization."

presented research that stood in stark contrast to his views. As Denise Denton, former dean of the College of Engineering at the University of Washington and the head of UC Santa Cruz, put it: "Here was this economist lecturing pompously [to] this room full of the country's most accomplished scholars on women's issues in science and engineering, and he kept saying things we had refuted in the first half of the day.[3]

One conference attendee, Nancy Hopkins, a biology professor at the Massachusetts Institute of Technology (MIT) who had graduated from Harvard, walked out during Summers' speech with what she described as a physical sense of disgust. Afterward, she was quoted as saying: "It's one thing for an ordinary person to shoot his mouth off like that, but quite another for a top educational leader. That's the kind of insidious, destructive, un-thought-through attitude that causes a lot of harm."[4]

Many Harvard faculty members expressed their dismay at Summers' lack of intellectual rigor, his insensitivity to women (particularly those who were undergraduate majors in math and the sciences at Harvard), and his bull-in-a-china-shop approach to public relations. Some felt particular dismay because under Summers' leadership, through January 2005, tenure appointments of women at Harvard had declined each year. Only four of the university's last 32 appointments had been women; there were no senior female math professors; and in a department of 18 chemistry professors, only one senior position was held by a woman.[5]

By week's end, Summers' comments had made front-page news and touched off a media firestorm. Alumni were threatening to withhold donations. Professors demanded apologies; some even called for Summers' resignation.[6]

Summers seemed genuinely surprised at the uproar. He downplayed the significance of his comments, noting that he had been *asked* to be speculative and provocative and was merely trying to fulfill his assignment. But the issue wouldn't die. By mid-February, after several, often contentious, meetings with faculty groups, Summers issued a formal letter of apology to the faculty: "[I]f I could turn back the clock," he wrote, "I would have spoken differently on matters so complex. Though my . . . remarks were explicitly speculative, and noted that 'I may be all wrong,' I should have left such speculation to those more expert in the relevant fields."

Furthermore, Summers retreated from his position about the primacy of biology over socialization as the cause of the under-representation of women in university science faculties. He said that his January remarks had "substantially understated the impact of socialization and discrimination, including implicit attitudes—patterns of thought to which all of us are unconsciously subject. The issue of gender difference is far more complex than comes through in my comments and my remarks about variability [that there are more men than women at the high end of the ability distribution] went beyond what the research has established."[7]

Summers didn't stop there. He adopted a "stop the clock" policy, which extended the time to earn tenure for professors expecting or adopting a child. Faculty members (men or women) wouldn't be penalized if they stopped or slowed their output of professional publications during the early part of their academic careers. Next, as the icing on the cake, Summers[iii] pledged that Harvard would spend an extra $50 million to promote the hiring of women and minorities at the university.[8]

[iii] In late February 2006, Larry Summers announced his resignation, effective June 30.

We have seen in earlier chapters how an alpha girl's social environment and her relationship with her parents shape her psychology. But are there limits to this? How far can experience go in shaping her personality? Are there not, after all, major biological differences between men and women? Doesn't a girl's double-X genetic makeup influence who she is and limit who she can become?

As Summers pointed out, our knowledge of genetics is exploding. Topics such as genome mapping, cloning, stem cells, and brain imaging that 25 years ago would have sounded to most people like science fiction are now part of everyday language. Because this new science is so mind-boggling and so difficult for the non-biologist to really understand, we tend, too often, to swallow new biological findings uncritically. This is certainly true when it comes to biological research on sex differences, particularly complicated imaging studies that describe ways in which the structure and functioning of men and women's brains appear to differ.

Neuroscientists have just begun to penetrate the brain's secrets. Anne Fausto-Sterling, Professor of Biology and Women's Studies at Brown University, cautions us against jumping to conclusions: " . . . despite the many recent insights of brain research," she writes, "this organ remains a vast unknown, a perfect medium on which to project, even unwittingly, assumptions about gender."[9]

Part of the reason that we like to focus on differences in brain function between men and women (rather than the similarities) is that this fits our preconceived notions that men and women *are* fundamentally different—in fact, they're from different planets.

Dan Kindlon, PhD

For alpha girls, what was probably most important about the brouhaha caused by Summers' remarks was the *intensity* of the reaction to what he said. In the society in which alphas are coming of age, assertions of male superiority are under attack. Woe to any man, as Summers discovered, who dares to suggest that men are innately more capable than women—especially that they're smarter.

One alpha mother, Genette, a fundraiser for an Ivy League college, said, "I personally found Summers' remarks repellent, and I was glad to see they were subjected to such intense scrutiny. I have spent my professional life working in universities. I know how hard it's been—and still *is*—for women in all fields, not only in math and science, to rise to top positions."

"How did your daughter respond to Summers' remarks?" I asked.

Genette laughed. "We discussed them at some length. They did not seem to bother my daughter, Sybil, in the least."

Sybil, a junior at a coed private high school who described herself as "obsessed with Shakespeare," commented: "I wasn't surprised that my mother got so bent out of shape about the Summers thing. I mean, maybe on the freaky end of math and science ability there may be some genetic difference between the sexes. But I can tell you that in my math and science classes everybody knows it's ridiculous to think that boys are smarter than girls."

Sybil's reaction is typical of the teenaged alpha girls we interviewed. To Sybil and her peers, the Summers controversy is a nonissue: they don't feel as though they need to defend their equal status; they take it for granted.

Sybil's view that, overall, girls are at least as smart as boys is supported by science:[10]

→ Memory: There are many different aspects to memory: memory for events or experiences versus memory for something spatially based—where you left your keys, for example. Regardless of what area is measured, however, a female advantage in memory is found across a variety of ages and tasks.

→ Perceptual speed: Women are much faster in general than men at many tasks in this domain, such as scanning long lists of letters and circling only the letter A.

→ Verbal abilities: When sex differences in verbal abilities are found, they almost always show female superiority.

→ Spatial ability: This is one area where men tend to do better than women. Men are clearly better when it comes to mentally rotating two-or three-dimensional shapes.

It is this last finding that lends credence to the claim that there may, after all, be a genetic difference in the math abilities of the two sexes. The roots of mathematics have to do with spatial relationships. The earliest mathematicians—Babylonians and Egyptians—used math to approximate spatial quantities. Early Egyptian surveyors, for example, re-established land boundaries each year after the Nile floodwaters receded. In a later period of their history, the Egyptians relied on mathematical representations of spatial relationships when they built the apexes of the pyramids at Giza to line up with the stars that form Orion's belt. Many areas of higher math, such as geometry and trigonometry, involve being able to understand, characterize, and analyze aspects of spatial relationships.[11]

It turns out, however, that the consistent finding of male superiority in mental rotation does not translate into superiority in all or even most other areas of spatial abilities. Dr. Elizabeth Spelke, a psychology professor at Harvard, published an article in the prestigious academic journal *American Psychologist* titled: "Sex Differences in Intrinsic Aptitude for Math and Science: A Critical Review."[12] I talked with Spelke in her 13th-floor office, which overlooks the Harvard campus. Spelke knows sex-differences research the way Roger Ebert knows movies.

The day we talked, Spelke was irate about some sloppy science by Simon Baron-Cohen, a British psychologist who has argued that there are stark differences between male and female brains. Baron-Cohen's primary interest is in autism, especially the fact that there seem to be up to five times as many boys with autism as girls.[13] Baron-Cohen reasons that the "autistic brain" is an extreme example of the "male brain." As evidence, he points to the fascination with objects that many autistic children have, a male rather than female trait, according to his research. Baron-Cohen showed newborns a series of pictures—some of people, some of objects. Boys tended to look more at objects, girls at people.[14] Extrapolating from this finding, Baron-Cohen hypothesizes that boys and girls are preprogrammed: males to learn about objects and their mechanical relationships and girls to focus on emotions and human relationships.

Spelke notes that Baron-Cohen ignores a long history of findings that contradict his own. She also said that although it is clear from research that boys consistently show superiority in mental rotation, there are many other aspects of spatial ability in which there is no appreciable difference between girls and boys and still others in which girls outperform boys.[15]

It was interesting that many of the alpha girls we talked to seemed to think that boys *were* inherently smarter than girls when it came to math. Audrey, the engineering student you met earlier who is a freshman at MIT, where many of the most brilliant math students congregate, said she thought that it is quite possible that men are inherently better at math than women. "I think there are different areas where—just because of the way the brain is set up—that males will excel," she said. "I've found that a lot of females have spatial problems."

"You really believe that?" I asked. "That there are hardwired differences?"

"Yeah. I think it causes advantages or disadvantages depending on what you're doing."

Audrey added that in her coed study group *she* is considered to be the "math person," but she felt that she was an anomaly. She didn't think, however, that differences between the sexes meant that women were necessarily at a disadvantage. "When you're working on a project," she said, "you need people with all kinds of abilities, or else it won't get done. One kind of ability isn't more important than the others."

To get a boy's perspective on sex differences in math ability, I talked to Levon, a sophomore math major at a prestigious liberal arts college. He said that he saw absolutely no difference between the abilities of girls and boys through high school. He had gone to a large public high school in a suburb of Boston and noted that his school's math team and the teams they competed against were almost equally composed of girls and boys. If there was a difference in representation of the sexes on the math team or in his classes, he added, that difference had "evaporated" in college.

Levon was familiar with the point of view that said that men were smarter than women in math, especially in areas that had to do with spatial rotation. "I just took a topology class," Levon said, "where we mapped surfaces—just the kind of the kind of thing where men have been thought to be more capable in than women. As a mathematician, I don't like to draw general conclusions from my own personal experience, but I will say that the class was split 50-50 between girls and boys and that the better presentations were all by females, and all fell into the realm of what men are supposed to be better at."

Levon said he didn't think that "inherent abilities" change from one generation to another, but he said that among his peers he's definitely seen girls who were confident of their ability to compete with boys in areas where boys in prior generations would have been clearly dominant.

Juliette, a gifted math student, was Levon's best friend through high school and now attends MIT. I asked her if she thought that there were inherent differences in math aptitude between men and women. She sent this reply by e-mail: "I think it is important to make a distinction between ability and performance . . . I do not believe there is any inherent difference between the analytical capabilities of men and women, and I have certainly met enough brilliant women in my life to be confident in saying this.

"Social factors can dictate the extent to which these abilities are expressed, however. Strong math and science ability may be inherent, but it is also a product of concentration, effort, interest, and motivation."

Juliette's point is well taken. Regardless of whether boys have greater intrinsic aptitude for math, girls get better math grades.[16] I queried my 11-year-old daughter, whose favorite subject is math, about this phenomena. "Are girls just smarter than boys?" I asked, giving her the latitude to slam the sex of those who, she complains, too often disrupt her classes with their fooling around. She surprised me with her answer. "No," she said, after a thoughtful pause. "Girls aren't smarter than boys, but they have more stamina."

Some of the teachers and school administrators I interviewed for this book saw wisdom in my daughter's analysis. Even if girls have less intrinsic math aptitude than boys—so this line of thinking goes—they get better grades because they are diligent. As Robert, a high school senior boy at Sybil's school who had been accepted into an Ivy League college, somewhat derisively observed, "I don't know any guys who do all their homework, but all the girls do. They're not smarter—they're just grinds."

I asked Flora, an alpha girl who most enjoys her English classes but is also getting an A in AP Physics, about Robert's characterization of high-achieving girls as "grinds."

"That is a definite possibility," she said. "There is pressure on girls to be likeable and popular. There is a pressure to fit in and a pressure to excel. Overall, I'd like to preserve the distinction between men and women. Differences are not really a bad thing. It's obvious there *are* differences. Men are physically stronger [than women], but women consistently do better on national reading exams. I do think men are better in math. Maybe this is a southern thing. If I was living in New York City I'd be singing a different tune."

Nan, a Canadian attorney whose 17-year-old daughter was one of our alpha interviewees, said that she thinks, given her own experience with her kids and their friends, that there may, indeed, be biological differences in the ways that girls' and boys' minds work, but that those differences don't have to do with math and science ability.

"My older daughter, Janet," said Nan, "is 20 and studying engineering at university. She's a math and science whiz. Her field is mechanical engineering, which is great around the house when it comes to fixing the car or programming the VCR. So, in my experience, I don't see that boys are smarter than girls in these areas. What I see, however, is that in our "techie" society boys are more interested in computer games than girls. Our 13-year-old son can play on the computer for hours. But that's not social enough for girls. Social interaction is far more important to them. I think the same could be said of women—they need their relationships with friends and other women. I think there's a biological component in that."

~

The Summers story didn't end with his apology. Not everyone had taken issue with what he had said; in fact, many people in the public eye had applauded him. George Will, the conservative *Washington Post* columnist, called Nancy Hopkins—the MIT professor who disgustedly walked out of Summers' speech—"hysterical," adding that her critical comments of Summers were "a sample of America's campus-based indignation industry, which churns out operatic reactions to imagined slights."[17]

In one of the most visible pro-Summers editorials, Charles Murray, a political scientist and research fellow at the conservative think tank the American Enterprise Institute,[18] attacked Summers' critics for being small-minded and stifling debate.

Murray is best known as the coauthor of *The Bell Curve: Intelligence and Class Structure in American Life*, the controversial 1994 book that argued that black-white IQ differences are due to genetics rather than discrimination or socialization.[19] Following that book's publication, Murray was the target of the same kinds of criticism leveled at Summers.[20]

In the wake of Summers' remarks, Murray extended his line of reasoning from the genetic inferiority of blacks to the genetic inferiority of girls in math and science. Murray even referred to Simon Baron-Cohen's research on the "male brain" as "a grand unified theory of male and female cognition that may well be a historic breakthrough."[21]

Murray weighed in on the Summer's debate not because he was interested in biology, but because of his public policy agenda: the elimination of affirmative action programs and other anti-discrimination laws that are costly for many of the major sponsors of the AEI, which include corporations such as Coors, Exxon-Mobile, and Amoco.[22]

The conservative response of Murray and others who oppose affirmative action is ideological as well as economic. Affirmative action interferes with corporate hiring policies, which conservatives think of as unnecessary and detrimental government meddling in the private sector—an anathema to free-market capitalism.[23]

Murray is up front about his view that different groups—such as blacks and whites and gays and straights—are *intrinsically* dissimilar. He extends this view to women as well, writing in the September 2005 *Commentary Magazine*: "Title IX of the Educational Amendments of 1972 assumes that women are no different from men in their attraction to sports. Affirmative action in all its forms assumes there are no innate differences between any of the groups it seeks to help and everyone else. The assumption of no innate differences among groups suffuses American social policy. That assumption is wrong."

Dan Kindlon, PhD

Some conservative religious groups support a separate and unequal doctrine because they believe that it reflects God's will. Consider this quote from ConservativeTruth.org: "Indeed, God made man in his image—as God made woman in his image. But he gave each a different skill set. Men are warriors and providers; women are stabilizers and nurturers. Men think more than they feel; women feel more than they think. While some crossover occurs—no man lives in an emotional vacuum, and most women can stand up and fight for themselves when necessary—it is to these roles that men and women have been created. Both will always feel most satisfied when they are performing these primary duties."[24]

Regardless of the effectiveness of conservative politics in the United States at the beginning of the twenty-first century, the alpha generation is coming into adulthood in a world where discrimination against women is not tolerated in the way it once was. Again, we have to look no farther than reaction to Summers' comments to see that there is a motivated, vocal opposition by *both* men and women to sex discrimination.

Neil French, a well-known Canadian advertising director, recently learned just how powerful the opposition to discrimination is. During an address to a group of advertising executives, he was asked by an audience member why there weren't more women at the top levels of the creative departments of advertising firms. French replied that women "don't make it to the top because they don't deserve to." He added that their roles as caregivers and child bearers prevented them from succeeding in top positions. The flap that ensued was so intense that French was forced to resign.[25]

Wall Street has learned that it's expensive to discriminate. Merrill Lynch was ordered by a three-member arbitration panel in an unusual public hearing held in San Antonio in 2003[26] to pay $2.2 million to Hydie Sumner, a female broker. She alleged that she had not been given the same amount of work as male colleagues and that her manager at the San Antonio office had sexually harassed her. Ms. Sumner further alleged that when she complained about the harassment, her supervisor retaliated against her, distributing around the office copies of a magazine article titled "Stop Whining" that warned that "constant complaining can cost you your job."

Two million and change may seem like a drop in bucket to the company that's "bullish on America," but the panel's award to Sumner stemmed from a class action lawsuit for systemic sexual discrimination that was filed against Merrill Lynch in 1997. Thirty-nine other cases from that lawsuit are still pending.

These are only two examples of judgments made in the many cases that are being filed alleging sexual discrimination. When Murray claimed in his *Times* op-ed piece that a liberal bias was stifling the truth about the Summers controversy, he was, at least in part, responding to the power of the disenfranchised to seek redress in the courts.

"To judge from the subsequent furor," wrote Murray about the response to Summers' remarks, "one might conclude that Mr. Summers was advancing a radical idea backed only by personal anecdotes and a fringe of cranks. In truth, it's the other way around. If you were to query all the scholars who deal professionally with data about the cognitive repertoires of men and women, all but a fringe would accept that the sexes are different, and that genes are clearly implicated."

Murray added that research on "the environmental sources of male-female differences tend to be stale," while "scholarship about innate male-female differences has the vibrancy and excitement of an important new field gaining momentum."

～

Summers remarks became the flashpoint for two great cultural armies to clash over "intrinsic aptitude" in the sexes. The war of which this battle is a part is not only about a scientific disagreement—like most wars it is, at its core, also about power and money.

On one side of the conflict are Summers' critics, who believe that there are no important biological differences between women and men when it comes to making social policy. On the other side are people like Murray who claim that there are important biological differences between the sexes, which should be kept in mind when formulating social policies, whether those policies address the underrepresentation of tenured women scientists at Harvard or the relative financial needs of men's and women's collegiate ice hockey teams.

Science is the high ground in this conflict: both armies know that to control the scientific "truth" is to control the battlefield. But is there any way to get at this "truth?" Is there objective evidence for genetic differences between men and women? What is the practical significance of the differences if they do exist? Do they matter in any meaningful way?

When we compare males and females on almost any trait, even if a large difference is found, this alone is not sufficient evidence to conclude that the difference is due to genetics. This caveat even applies to *structural* differences in the shape or size of different parts of male and female brains. Why? Because our environment shapes the structure of our brains. In fact, of the trillions of neural connections that the billions of neurons in an infant's brain will eventually make, the overwhelming majority are determined by his or her early experience.[27]

There are critical periods in a child's development when its brain expects to receive specific kinds of input. During the first few years of life, for example, our brains are primed to develop language. We need to hear language during this period for normal speech to develop. If language input occurs later, say at 6 years of age, some speech may develop, but it will never be as complete as it would have been had the child heard spoken language during the earlier, more critical period of development.[28]

This is why native speakers of Japanese often confuse the sounds made by the letters *r* and *l* in English: those sounds do not exist in Japanese.[29] The large differences between Japanese and English speakers in their abilities to pronounce the letter *r* is not based on genetic differences, but occurs because their early environments differed in an important way during a critical period of development. Male superiority in spatial abilities, therefore, might be similarly explained. Perhaps more boys than girls were given a set of blocks on their third birthday, for example.

On a closely related issue, research shows that there are substantial verbal IQ differences between rich and poor children. Using this finding, one could infer that genetically smarter people make more money and that they pass their smarts on to their kids. But when environmental differences in language exposure are studied, it becomes clear that heredity is not the whole story by a long shot. One study found considerable class differences in the amount of parental speech addressed per hour to 13- to 36-month-olds: 2,100 words per hour in the average professional family; 1,200 in the average working-class family; 600 in the average welfare family.[30]

When genetic differences have been found between the sexes, they tend to be small—and even for the largest of these differences, there are always many exceptions. An obvious example of this overlap is the height difference between men and women, which is one of the largest sex differences—the average height of men in the U.S. is 5 feet, 9.4 inches, the average woman, 5 feet, 4 inches. We all know, however, men who are shorter than most women and women who are taller than most men.[31]

Although Murray was right when he said that all but a lunatic fringe of social scientists would contend that there are *no* genetic differences between men and women, he was wrong in his implication that most social science research highlights the differences between the sexes rather than the similarities.

Janet Sibley Hyde, a psychologist at the University of Wisconsin, undertook the enormous job of cataloging and summarizing all of the available studies on the psychology of sex differences, publishing her findings in the professional journal of record, *American Psychologist*, in August 2005.[32] Her review encompassed six main areas:

1. Cognitive abilities (including math and spatial relationships)
2. Communication styles (talkativeness, a tendency to interrupt)
3. Personality (leadership ability and aggression, among other traits)
4. Psychological well-being (including self-esteem and coping skills)

5. Physical and motor skills (throwing speed, activity level, etc.)

6. Miscellaneous (the way the two sexes reach moral decisions, for example, or their abilities to delay gratification)

Hyde's results showed that 78 percent of the studies found gender differences that were "small or close to zero." But there were differences.

The biggest areas of differences were, as you would expect, in physical skills. Men, on average, can throw a ball faster and farther than women. There are also differences, although they are much smaller, in sprinting speed and activity level, but there are almost no sex differences in balance or flexibility. Are these differences important or meaningful? While a woman will have a difficult time playing her way onto a major league baseball roster, the differences that Hyde found shouldn't keep her out of Harvard's chemistry department. Are sex differences in throwing accuracy and speed due to genes? To some extent, yes, even to a large extent when it comes to throwing speed, but throwing accuracy is also clearly affected by practice.

Aside from strength and quickness, there are other physical differences between men and women. Women, almost across the board, have sharper senses than men:[33]

➤ Smell: Women can perceive, categorize, identify, and remember odors better than men.

➤ Hearing: Men begin to lose their hearing at an earlier age; women are better at detecting pure tones.

Dan Kindlon, PhD

→ Vision: Males under forty are better at detecting movement; vision loss occurs earlier in women than men.

→ Touch: Women are more sensitive to touch than men (except, for some reason, on the nose).

→ Taste: Women can detect tastes (sweet, bitter, salty, etc.) more easily than men.

Are these differences genetic? The answer is yes, at least in part: perceptual differences between the sexes can be observed within the first few months of life. Are these differences important? You won't see lawsuits, angry editorials, or contentious faculty meetings about whether men's noses are really more sensitive than women's or whether the best "smellers" in the world are men or women.

You might ask whether women as a group have higher IQs than men? The IQ test is, after all, the best that psychological science has to offer as a single measure of intelligence. The most widely used IQ tests contain a dozen subsections that measure a range of abilities, such as verbal, visual-spatial, memory, and speed of information processing.

IQ tests are designed specifically, however, so that men and women, or boys and girls, will, on average, have the same IQ. Test items on which one sex tends to do significantly better than the other don't make the final cut. There are intelligence tests that are not purposely sex-balanced, but even these reveal few sex differences.[34]

The Summers controversy wasn't, however, about average intelligence; it was about whether men outnumbered women at the highest levels of math and science ability (leaving aside the question whether or not it is possible to accurately measure the multiple abilities necessary to excel in these areas). Summers and Murray are correct when they say that on tests such as the math SAT, the highest scorers do tend to be boys. Among college-bound seniors who took the math SATs in 2001, for example, nearly twice as many boys as girls scored over 700, and the ratio skews ever more male the closer one gets to the top score of 800.[35]

Figure 5-1, which shows the distribution of math SAT scores for boys and girls, illustrates this disparity. Although there is a lot of overlap between the two sets of scores, boys, on average, get higher scores than girls, and there are more boys at the highest end of the distribution.

Figure 5-1
DISTRIBUTION OF MATH SAT SCORES, 2003

—— Boys —— Girls

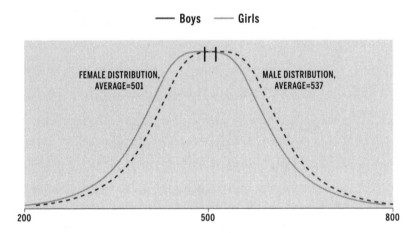

On first glance, this would seem to be incontrovertible proof for Summers' original statements. Unfortunately, even this apparently straightforward finding is more complicated than it first appears. The first problem is with the SAT itself. Similar tests, such the ACT[36]—the other "big" college admissions exam—don't show the same gender gap.[37] Moreover, the items on the SAT don't necessarily reflect an objective standard for math ability. The items on the SAT (as is true for most IQ tests) are selected, in part, to balance the overall scores for boys and girls.[38] The Educational Testing Service has, in the past, altered the verbal portion of the test to increase scores for boys by adding new questions on sports, business, and politics. The ETS has not, however, deemed it necessary to alter the test to increase math scores for girls.[39]

If one wanted to be completely fair, a panel of "experts" would have to start from scratch and devise a test based on an agreed-upon pool of items that measure mathematical ability.[40]

A second problem with the SAT-Math is that it doesn't do its job in a gender-equitable way. A primary purpose of the SAT is to predict college grades. This is why it is used as an admissions test. It gives colleges better odds of accepting only high schoolers who will do well in college. If it is doing its job, students who have the highest SAT scores should also get the best grades in college; to some extent this is true, but not equally true for boys and girls, especially at the high end of the test. Although most of the high scorers on the SAT-M are male, the highest-performing math majors at U.S. colleges are not.[41] Evidence such as this is part of what prompted Summers' apology.

Finally, if genetic differences account for the overrepresentation of boys at the high end of the math ability spectrum, then one would expect to see this difference across all cultures and at all times. This, however, is not the case. Consider the following:[iv]

[iv] Data are from Programme for International Student Assessment, which is sponsored by the Organization for Economic Co-operation and Development (OECD) and tests 15-year-olds around the world on reading, math, and science every three years.

➼ Among 29,899 ninth and tenth graders living in the U.S., the U.K., and Australia in 2000, 47 percent of the highest achievers in math and science were girls.[42]

➼ In only five of the OECD-member countries, not including the U.S., were there any differences between male and female students in performance on the problem-solving portion of the math exam.[43] In all five countries where there were differences (Iceland, Norway, Sweden, Australia, and Germany), the female students did better.

➼ In Iceland, girls outscored boys by a significant margin on all parts of 2003 math portion of the exam.[44]

➼ On the other hand, while Japan showed a near-equality between the sexes in three of the five portions of the exam, there was a significant gender gap favoring boys for both the "uncertainty" (14.0 points) and "space and shape" (8.9 points) sections. Gaps in the other exam sections, again favoring boys, were 6.3 for "change and relationships," 3.1 for "quantity." Girls came out ahead 2.4 points in "problem-solving." The U.S. has comparable gender gap scores: 15.2 for "space and shape," 5.6 for "change and relationships," 4.2 for "quantity," 3.2 for "uncertainty," and -0.9 for "problem-solving."

Girls living in England have recently started to do better than boys on the A-level exams (taken by students who plan to apply to university) in nearly all subject areas, including math, chemistry, biology, computer science, economics, physics, and business studies.[45] SAT-Math items that showed a large gender difference in American students showed no such difference in Chinese students.[46]

In addition, the preponderance of high-scoring males taking the SAT has declined substantially over the last 20 years in U.S. samples. In the early 1980s, there were 13 boys for every girl who scored over 700 on the math SAT. Now the ratio is only 2.8 to 1, a precipitous drop that is underreported.[47]

⌒

Let's briefly look inside the kind of work that's being done today on sex differences in brain function to get a sense of how complex it is and why its findings are ambiguous. In a typical study, Dr. Ruben C. Gur, a distinguished neuroscientist, and his colleagues at the Brain Behavior Laboratory, University of Pennsylvania Medical School, posted an ad, soliciting volunteers for a brain imaging study using MRI[v] and PET[vi] scans. The purpose: to see if men and women differ

[v] MRI—Magnetic Resonance Imaging, a technique that uses strong magnetic fields and radio waves to see (image) structures inside the human body. Unlike an X-ray, which is primarily useful in imaging dense areas such as bones, an MRI can provide detailed images of soft tissue such as the brain or other organs. In research on sex differences, MRI is often used to detect male-female differences in the size or shape of different brain areas.

[vi] PET—Positron emission tomography is kind of like an inside-out X-ray. Instead of shooting radiation (X-rays) into the body, the person ingests a radioactive substance that is usually attached or "tagged" to an energy source, such as the simple sugar glucose. When the body uses the tagged glucose as fuel, the radiation is released and can be detected by the PET machine. In brain research, PET scans are often used to see which brain areas are most active (and thus burning glucose) when a person performs a task such as mental arithmetic, memorizing word lists, or is simply at rest.

in terms of which areas of their brains are most active while they are doing nothing.[48]

Thirty-seven men and 24 women who answered the ad fasted all night; in the morning each had an IV inserted in his or her arm and had a radioactive isotope tagged to glucose dripped into their radial artery. Both the men and women in the study were, on average, in their late twenties and had completed two years of college.

The subjects sat in a dimly lit room and were told to relax without falling asleep. The PET scans did show some sex differences in which parts of the brain were more active, but also many similarities. There were no differences in the overall activity level of the male and female brains. Each sex burned the same amount of radioactive sugar while "idling." This finding agreed with some earlier studies, but not with others that had shown female brains to be the more active under these kinds of circumstances. The areas of the brains showing the least amount of activity (the corpus callosum) and the most activity (the basal ganglia) were also the same for both the male and the female subjects.

The finding concerning the corpus callosum, a bundle of white matter with 200 million to 800 million nerve fibers that connects the two hemispheres of the brain, was particularly noteworthy because that is a part of the brain that some people have speculated accounts for sex differences in performance of certain tasks—higher mathematics, for example.

The debate over the corpus callosum began with a 1982 article in the journal *Science* suggesting that women have a slightly wider or more bulbous corpus callosum than men. *Time, Newsweek*, and other popular media reported that this anatomical difference was the

Dan Kindlon, PhD

source of "women's intuition" or girls' inferiority in math. Neuroscientists continue to hotly debate whether there actually are sex differences in the callosum's size (it's really difficult to measure accurately), and, if so, how such differences affect how we think.[49]

Gur and his colleagues reported that men and women showed the same level of brain activity (or, more accurately, metabolism) in all areas of the cerebral cortex, the parts of the brain that have evolved more recently, than the areas in which he did find some sex differences—older brain structures that are most involved with coordinating movements and some aspects of emotions.[vii]

Finally, these researchers found that most, but not all, men and women showed a brain profile that was characteristic of their sex. Thirteen of the 34 men (about 38 percent) had metabolism patterns that were not "male typical," and four of the 24 women (roughly 17 percent) did not show the "female typical" pattern.

I leave you to interpret these findings. My guess is that if you are predisposed to believe that there are meaningful biological differences underlying male and female thought patterns, Gur's research will support that belief. If you're not so predisposed, his findings will not impress you.

One more example that is a bit easier to grasp because it doesn't

---

[vii] The relevant passage from the article is: "The groups had identical relative metabolism in all nonlimbic frontal, parietal, and occipital regions, but sex differences were prevalent in temporal-limbic regions, basal ganglia, brainstem, and cerebellum. Whereas men had higher relative metabolism in lateral and ventro-medial aspects of temporal lobe regions, they had lower relative metabolism in the middle and posterior cingulate gyrus. The raw absolute metabolic rates were only higher in men than in women for the occipital temporal region, temporal pole, hippocampus, amygdala, and orbital frontal cortex."

rely on sophisticated imaging techniques and focuses on the whole brain rather than its myriad substructures, is the work of Dr. Sandra Witelson, who recruited more than 100 terminally-ill cancer patients, gave them IQ tests, and then measured their brain weights after they died.

This was the first direct test of the "bigger is better" hypothesis. Several previous studies had compared IQ and head size; there was a very small indication that the bigger the head, the higher the IQ.[50] On average, men have bigger brains than women (perhaps even when difference in body size is taken into account—it depends which studies you accept).

Witelson studied the two major components of IQ tests, verbal intelligence and performance intelligence. The former is tested by assessing verbal abilities such as vocabulary and verbal reasoning. Performance IQ, sometimes called visual-spatial ability, measures nonverbal tasks such as puzzle building and putting a sequence of pictures in a logical order, the kinds of spatial abilities that boys are supposed to be better at.

Oddly, Witelson doesn't mention whether she found an association between brain volume and overall IQ in her analysis. The article does, however, state that she found a relationship between brain volume and verbal IQ—but not for left-handed men. Furthermore, she had to adjust her analysis for the subject's age in order to account for the fact that your brain shrinks as you get older. Or mine does anyway, because I'm a man. Men's brains shrink by about 50 ml per decade. Women's brains tend not to shrink very much at all, only about six ml per decade.

Does a bigger brain mean higher performance IQ? Yes, but the association is much weaker, and it is only true for women. For men,

Dan Kindlon, PhD

there was even a suggestion that higher performance IQ is associated with *smaller* brains.

I have taken you through the complexities and ambiguities of this research in order to suggest that if there are structural or functional differences between male and female brains, they're not as easy to spot as other anatomical differences between the sexes. Which is something that Summers is well aware of by now.

~

We're not sure yet what genetic and brain imaging studies tell us about inherent ability. What we do know is that the role of discrimination and socialization dramatically affects male-female aptitude and performance. Numerous studies show the impact of socialization on girls when it comes to math and science ability. Prime among these are what psychologists call "gender biases"—our collective *assumption* that men are better than women at science and math. Whether or not genetic differences actually impact math and science performance, there's clearly something else going on to inhibit the large number of women math and science majors from continuing on in those fields.

Claude Steele's work on gender differences in learning gives solid rather than impressionistic grounding to the concern that comments like Summers' are exactly what work against the continuing advancement of women. Steele, a professor of social psychology at Stanford, has studied the way stereotypes affect performance. When women are told that a test is going to measure cognitive differences between genders, Steele found, they tend to score much lower than men.

Women tend to perform as well as men, however, when they're told a test is gender-blind.

Steele calls this phenomenon "stereotype threat," and he has proven that it impairs performance. The amazing thing is, as Steele convincingly argues, "stereotype threat" most affects women at the *high end* of the spectrum in math and science. Why? Because they're the ones who are the most identified with the field and have the most to lose as they move upward and are increasingly identified as, say, a *female* engineer or airline pilot. They have internalized the assumption that they're not as capable as their male peers—that they are inferior, anomalies, and, perhaps, even frauds. The alpha girls we interviewed seemed remarkably free, at least consciously, of the kinds of assumptions that can subtly undermine and erode confidence and performance. But they weren't, of course, invested in careers. They were optimistic adolescents with their whole lives ahead of them.

Steele's studies provide evidence that socialization is a weighty factor in the gender disparities at the top levels of male-dominated occupations, including faculty at colleges and universities. According to the American Association of University Women, less than one-third of tenured faculty at four-year institutions are women. As we saw in the table at the beginning of the chapter, data show that the small number of women who reach the highest levels of academia—tenured professors at the leading research universities—does not reflect the large number of women who receive bachelors, masters, and PhD degrees in science, math, and engineering. This is significant in a number of ways, not the least of which is that college professors will be role models for the alpha generation as they decide how to live their lives.

Steele's research exposes subtle forms of internalized discrimination, but our society is still riddled with *overt* prejudice: Women are still excluded from what are perceived as male preserves.

Mia says she learned about overt discrimination when she was in the graduate chemistry program at a large Midwestern university. Mia, who is now in her late twenties, described herself as a "math kind of girl" who was specializing in physical chemistry.

"It was, and is, a predominantly male area," she said. "Physical chemistry analyzes where all the theoretical constructs in the field come from. It has a close relationship to physics and chemical engineering. There's a lot of math."

Mia, whose stepfather is a chemist, says she always excelled at math and science and grew up in a "science household." She says that she thought she was going to do the "med school thing," but discovered that she enjoyed the "analytic end" of the sciences. When she decided to leave the graduate program in physical chemistry, her professors assumed it was because she had a boyfriend in New York and that she had decided to forgo her career to go be with him.

"That wasn't at all the reason," she said. "It was common knowledge in the department that I was involved in a long-distance relationship, and they just *assumed* because I was a woman that I was going to be with my boyfriend. I was one of only two women in the department, and they thought that I wasn't taking my career seriously."

Mia said that her male colleagues in graduate school also assumed that she was the weakest student in the department. In fact, says Mia, she was told when she was awarded a teaching fellowship that she was the program's best student. "Part of the reason they thought I wasn't up to par was because I had done my undergraduate work at Bard College, where the undergraduate science department is hardly what you would call cutthroat. In fact, it was a hugely supportive environment. Not at all what I found in grad school."

Mia is now the editor of a trade science publication. She says she might have gone on into research and an academic track if she had felt that the environment wasn't tilted against her as a woman.

This kind of undermining attitude can discourage gifted students like Mia and squelch careers before they even get started. Until recently, a clear example of this was the highly competitive world of professional music. Until blind auditions were held for national orchestras, women were radically underrepresented. Professional male musicians argued that women had less wind power and were biologically incapable of performance at highest levels on many instruments. Since blind auditions have been held, however, the participation of women in national orchestras has risen precipitously—evidence that it was almost entirely discrimination that was keeping women out.[51] In any event, it's clear that the alpha generation is well aware that success in any career depends on far more that one's IQ, SAT score, or grades. Motivation, social skills, assertiveness, leadership ability, patience, negotiation style, conscientiousness, and perseverance are at least as important as intrinsic aptitude. Research on sex differences in these areas reveals that there are no appreciable differences between men and women.

Sybil, the alpha girl who is "obsessed" with Shakespeare, says she wants to go into law. "I think you can use femininity in the workplace," she says. "Women have their own analytic style. They tend to be good on detail. They're focused. They are often able to gauge how people will respond. Part of the personality of many women is that they're used to being in tune with emotions, and they can use that professionally."

Our personalities are a combination of our genes and the environment we grow up in. When we look at personality, the biggest difference between men and women has to do with their sexuality. Men masturbate more and have more positive attitudes towards casual sex. Neither sex, according to most research, has an edge when it comes to being sexually satisfied.[52]

Studies also consistently find that boys and men are more physically aggressive than girls, but the findings are less clear for indirect, nonphysical, "relational aggression" (the catty, cliquey type of aggression portrayed in the movie *Mean Girls*). Some studies have found that girls are the more relationally aggressive sex, but not all studies of this trait find sex differences.[53]

Slight differences favoring females in trust and "tender-mindedness" have also been found. Women have been more tender-minded than men for as long as this trait has been measured. In 1936, a major study of male and female personality revealed some interesting findings.[54] On a word association test, when a researcher said war, men were more likely to reply "soldiers;" women, "hate." For "hunt," men said "shoot;" women, "find." This research found that women were more afraid of ghosts; men, of old age. Women, as an example of their tender-mindedness, were far more likely than men to agree with the statement: "The largest fortunes should be seized by the government and divided among the poor."

The possibility that genetically based differences may account for the gender disparities in top academic positions *should* be discussed. But in our age of genome mapping, people hear "genetics" and draw broad, ill-considered conclusions—even well-informed columnists like Robert Samuelson, who concluded that "many women probably reject science and engineering for another reason: They simply don't find the work appealing, just as they generally don't like football." (In fact, 43 percent of the NFL fan base is women,[55] but perhaps scientists are about to find the male football gene.)

Politics plays a role in the gender and genes debate no matter which side you're on. Is it coincidental that nearly all of the research cited that emphasizes the similarities rather than the differences between men's and women's cognitive abilities have been conducted by women university professors, invariably psychologists, who may well have a personal stake in showing that women and men are equally talented and capable?

In the ongoing nurture versus nature debate, neither side is right. When we look at who we are—and, as alpha girls are doing now, who we may become—we need to take into account both biology *and* our environment. What *is* clear is that men and women are far more alike than they are different. Even when the narrowest of cases is examined—such as the predominance of men with the highest math aptitude—the evidence is skewed by the socialization of girls away from math and science and the continued discrimination against women. In order for a scientist to determine whether the genetic differences between men and women matter, she would need to approximate the quintessential experiment: to plant two different varieties of seeds in the same soil and make sure they get the same amount of

Dan Kindlon, PhD

water, sun, and nutrients. If one variety of plant grew taller, she could infer that genetic differences between the seeds were the cause. When it comes to the real world, whether we're looking at Harvard or Wall Street, men and women do not develop in the same soil. Until they do, the significance of genetic differences between the sexes will remain an open question.

CHAPTER SIX

THE DESCENT OF MEN

"There are more girls in college now than guys—
which from my point of view is great!"

—Sam, 18, freshman at UC Santa Cruz

When it comes to chimps, scientists have found that, as my daughters were fond of saying when they were in kindergarten, "girls rule and boys drool."

Researchers have observed that young female chimpanzees in the Gombe National Park in Tanzania are smarter than young male chimps, at least when it comes to learning how to fish for termites. Young female chimps watch carefully as their mothers select the right size stick to dip into the termite mound and quickly learn to imitate them. The young males, on the other hand, pay their mothers no mind. They are inattentive, rolling around in the dirt and generally slacking off. The young females start fishing for termites on their own at a much earlier age than the males—on average over two years earlier—and they remain more proficient fishers as adults. The study's authors conclude that given "[a] similar disparity in the ability of young males and females has been demonstrated in human children, sex-based learning differences may therefore date back at least to the last common ancestor of chimpanzees and humans."[1]

This picture of young female chimps as focused, receptive learners fits well with our portrait of academically accomplished girls. I haven't spent much time discussing their male peers and the psychological challenges and difficulties they face, but boys are obviously part of the equation when it comes to understanding the alpha girl generation and its future impact on society.

As girls move into positions of power and prominence, what will happen to boys? Will their penchant for figuratively horsing around while their female peers master important life skills mean that they are going to become increasingly irrelevant? Are our boys headed in the direction of Johnny Lechner, who, at the age of 29, is still a college undergraduate and has spent his last 12 years as a frat boy?

Lechner has appeared on *Good Morning America* and *Letterman*. He has an agent at William Morris who is trying to get him television and book deals and product endorsements. His brand image, according to the *New York Times*, where his story made front page news, will be linked to his "record of debauchery . . . a roisterous college life of beer and merrymaking." Fame, however, has come with a price. The *Times* quotes Lechner: "I'm really stressed out. All the money, the book deals, the agents. It's crazy."[2]

While not all our boys are doomed to careers as frat house party animals, it's self-evident that as girls fill more of the challenging and desirable positions in the workforce, the opportunities and positions open to men will shrink. Not all the academic and occupational gains achieved by women in recent years have come at the expense of men—but some have.

In the case of college admissions, the more spots that are given to

Figure 6-1

NUMBER OF BACHELOR'S DEGREES AWARDED TO MALES AND FEMALES, PROJECTED TO 2050

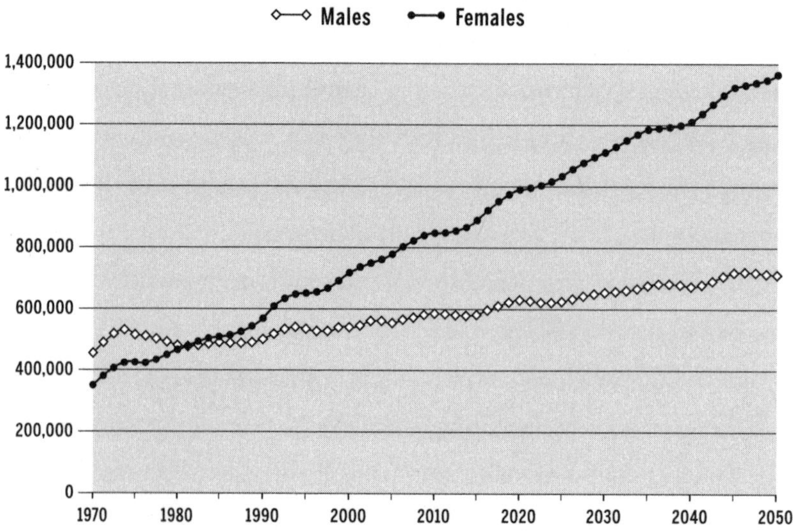

Source data (1970–2003): U.S. Department of Education, National Center for Education Statistics[4] Projected data (2004–2050): see Appendix B.

girls, the fewer will be available for boys.[i] Similarly, if the board of directors at a Fortune 500 company is limited to ten members, if five are women, only five can be men. There is no simple equation, however, that will tell us which sex will be better off following the kinds of gender role changes we can expect in the coming years.

As we start to look forward into the future, we see a number of significant trends. The first is the dominance of women in higher education. As we've noted, in 2005, nearly 59 percent of undergraduate degrees were granted to women. The degree gap is growing.[3] The

---

[i] Some colleges and universities are starting to admit what has been known among admissions officers for years: that they sometimes use affirmative action standards in order to increase the number of male enrollees. See Britz, J.D. "To all the girls I've rejected," *New York Times*, OP-ED, Thursday, March 23, 2006.

　　　　　　　　　　　　　　　Dan Kindlon, PhD

chart opposite (Figure 6-1) projects the changing sex-ratio in colleges into the next decade and beyond.

We see the same trend for advanced degrees. Over the next 10 years, the number of degrees awarded in medicine, law, dentistry, and the theological professions is projected to increase 16 percent for men and 26 percent for women. For doctorate degrees (PhDs), the results are even more startling. As Figure 6-2 shows, in 2050, *fewer* men will receive PhDs than they did in 2000, while the number of doctorates awarded to women will continue to sharply rise. These degree-gap trends hold true across racial and ethnic groups. For the foreseeable future, white, black, Latina, and Asian women will all be receiving more college degrees than their male counterparts.[5]

Figure 6-2

NUMBER OF DOCTORATE DEGREES AWARDED TO MALES AND FEMALES, PROJECTED TO 2050

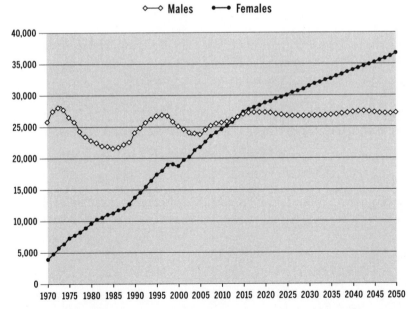

Source data (1970–2003): U.S. Department of Education, National Center for Education Statistics[6] Projected data (2004–2050): see Appendix B.

What are the implications of these trends? An oddly analogous situation has occurred in China. When China instituted its One-Child Policy in 1979, male babies had long been considered the more desirable pregnancy outcome in China, a preference that only became more pronounced when couples were told by the state that they could only have one child. One upshot of the policy was that girl babies were more likely to be aborted or become victims of infanticide and medical neglect. Some parents took advantage of a loophole in the law that allowed a couple to have a second child if their first was disabled or female.

As a result, the birth ratio in China began to change. As many as 1.3 boys were born for each girl in rural areas such as Qinghai province.[7] Now that the first members of the One-Child Policy generation are well into marriageable and childbearing age, there are around 80 million men, according to one source, who can't find partners.[8]

A similar trend is emerging—although reversed—in the U.S. when we look at the mating dance open to college graduates. The degree gap between men and women is similar to the birth ratio in Qinghai.

NUMBER OF BACHELOR'S DEGREES AWARDED BY SEX AND RACE/ETHNICITY, 2004 AND 2025 (PROJECTED)								
	White		Black		Hispanic		Asian	
	2004	2025	2004	2025	2004	2025	2004	2025
Males	405,409	438,492	39,256	65,338	32,697	70,057	37,073	59,557
Females	533,899	692,740	76,379	158,292	49,423	113,844	44,955	107,541
Ratio F : M	1.3	1.6	1.9	2.4	1.5	1.6	1.2	1.8

Source data (2004): U.S. Department of Education, National Center for Education Statistics.[9] Projected data (2025): see Appendix B.

Figure 6-3

PERCENTAGE OF U.S. POPULATION AGED 25+ WITH A
BACHELOR'S DEGREE OR HIGHER, PROJECTED TO 2040

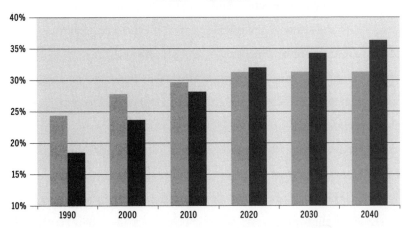

Source data: U.S. Census Bureau. Current Population Survey 2003.[10] Projected data: see Appendix B.

With each passing year the ratio of college-educated women to college-educated men will grow. There will be an increasing number of college-educated women who will not be able to marry or partner with a college-educated man (see Figure 6-3).

In a few years, the population of the United States will have more living women college graduates than men college graduates. This preponderance of women among the "educated class" will be an event that is unprecedented in human history and promises to have far-reaching implications. Women will begin to appear in greater numbers among the applicants for prestigious, highly paid jobs. A college degree currently yields nearly one million dollars more over the course of a working life than a high school degree. A PhD is estimated to return $1.5 million more, and professional degrees in medicine or law over $2.5 million more in lifetime salary than a bachelor's degree.[11] To the extent that money is power, women who obtain advanced degrees and enter the workforce will have more of it than they have in the past.

Much of what motivated feminists in the 1960s and 1970s was a reaction to the relative powerlessness of American housewives in the 1950s. At the root of nearly all of the myriad meanings of power is the concept of control. If you have power, you have the ability to influence events rather than be influenced by them. To control rather than be controlled.

Women traditionally were dependent on their husbands for financial support; many of them had few, if any, job skills. But if the current trends in higher education continue, men are going to have to share or relinquish some of their power because their wives will control the proverbial purse strings.

One consequence of women moving into highly paid jobs is that more of the men they marry and bear children with will earn less than they do. One out of every four women today earns more than her husband; by 2050, it is projected that almost one in two will (see Figure 6-4).

Even if a married woman doesn't earn *more* than her husband, if she earns enough to live on or has the status and job skills that come from being better educated, she will have more control over her life. In cases of divorce or abandonment, she won't be at the mercy of her ex-husband's goodwill or a court's ability to enforce child support or alimony laws. Better education and higher earnings provide a financial safety net for women today that dependent housewives in the 1950s didn't have.

The distribution of power in a couple's relationship does not, how-

Dan Kindlon, PhD

Figure 6-4

PERCENT OF MARRIED COUPLES WITH WIVES EARNING MORE THAN HUSBANDS, PROJECTED TO 2050

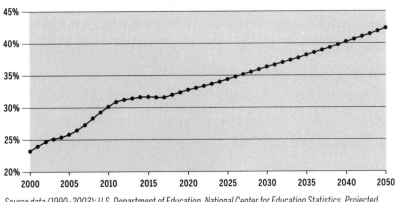

Source data (1990–2003): U.S. Department of Education, National Center for Education Statistics. Projected data (2004–2040): see Appendix B.

ever, have to be a battle. Many men are happy to share power. In the future, the following scenario will become more common. Jim Krawieki, 47, and his younger wife, Carroll, work on the Needham, Massachusetts, police force. Carroll, a sergeant, is Jim's boss, a cause for mirth among his fellow patrolmen. Despite being a political conservative, not a traditionally feminist group, Jim says, "The easiest way to deal with it is just accept it." It was Jim who originally encouraged Carroll to quit waitressing, join the force, and take the tests necessary for promotion. Jim didn't want to climb the career ladder himself because of all the "paperwork."

The couple's first child is soon due. Carroll plans to return to work after her maternity leave. Her shift runs midnight to eight and Jim works days, so they'll divvy up child care.[12]

Jim and Carroll's story illustrates the degree to which gender roles are changing. Carroll is thriving in a non-traditional occupation for women, and her older, politically conservative husband, whom she outranks, not only accepts the situation, he helped create it.

Is Jim an anomaly? Will most men accept the eclipse of their traditional role as breadwinners? Or will there be a backlash against the emancipation of women fueled by wounded male pride? At least two important factors argue against backlash.

First, cultural trends suggest that men are less intent on wearing the pants in the family. In many cases, they do not feel threatened, demeaned, or emasculated by being married to a woman who is more successful than they are. Men are also more amenable to sharing household duties, particularly child care. In fact, young men hunger for more time with their kids. This is the case with Trevor, 25, and his wife, Lindsay, who is pregnant with their first child. Trevor's adolescence was spent rolling around on the proverbial termite mound. Although he has a high IQ, he barely graduated from high school. "I couldn't stand school and my teachers couldn't stand me," he said. After high school, he delivered pizzas, installed carpeting, and did custodial work at a community airport. He eventually drifted back to school, taking a few classes at a community college, then tried his hand at flight school, and completed a 12-week course in car stereo installation. When Lindsay became pregnant, Trevor had recently left a sales job that had the potential for rapid advancement. "I couldn't see myself selling boxes for the rest of my life," he said. "It wasn't going to work out for either me or the company."

Lindsay graduated from a local college and became a middle manager at a small company. Her work provides the couple with a moderate salary and decent benefits. Trevor is looking forward to doing the bulk of the child care when the baby comes. "My wife makes more than I do. I hope she always does. I'd love to stay home with the kids. Are you kidding me, it'd be a blast."

Trevor is not the only man who wants to stay home with the kids. *Business Week* magazine reports that working men born between 1965 and 1979 now spend about 3.5 hours a day with their kids—the same amount as working women. Seventy percent of men said they would take a pay cut to spend more time with their family, and almost half would turn down a promotion if it meant less family time. The article states:

"The shift in attitudes among male workers is evident to veteran staffers such as Betty Purkey, who manages work-life strategies at Texas Instruments. Not only are men, who make up seventy percent of the chipmaker's employee base, clamoring for more flexibility, but they frequently crowd into the company's classes for new parents. 'They really want to spend more time with their families,' marvels Purkey, who finds a pronounced difference among younger employees."[13]

Men are better suited in many ways to be contemporary home-makers. Start with the most robust biological differences between men and women—size and strength. One of the only aspects of contemporary urban and suburban life that requires physical strength is household tasks—carrying a baby and two bags of groceries in from the car, for example. Domestic duties are one of the few remaining areas in which men's physical strength is an advantage. In addition, many men are fascinated by gadgets, tools, and machinery; these men should love hanging around the house doing minor car repairs, fixing a leaky faucet, programming the VCR, installing an electric garage door opener—all jobs for a handyman!

The large majority of boys in our survey group said that they felt that working mothers were not detrimental to their children's development,[ii] and, more important, many boys wanted to participate in child rearing. Close to 25 percent said that they expected to be a stay-at-home parent at some point in their lives.

~

In the schools where we interviewed, many of the boys were aware that they were in the company of a new generation of high-achieving, empowered females. Nowhere was this more the case than in JUMP, a charter high school of around 500 students in Newark, New Jersey, that draws many of its students from the poorer areas of the city.

We interviewed a mix of boys and girls at JUMP. Honor student Charise, a senior, whose father is Puerto Rican and whose mother is Algerian, characterized herself as "extremely competitive." She had been accepted at Penn State and was interested in psychology. Next to her sat Jason, an African-American senior, also an honor student, who had been raised by his grandmother. Jason wanted to go into "communications" and become an entrepreneur; he hoped to attend Rutgers in the fall.

Jason roundly agreed with the statement that girls are on the ascent. "I'm the only boy in the top 10 percent of my graduating class," he said. "I'm only one of three boys in this school who are in the National Honors Society. I'm the only boy working on the student newspaper. I like to write."

"What kinds of things do you like to write?" I asked.

[ii] 77.72 percent of boys agreed or strongly agreed with the statement "Working mothers can have relationships with their children that are just as warm and secure as mothers who do not work."

Dan Kindlon, PhD

Jason dropped his eyes and squirmed. "Well, you know, I like to keep a journal—don't you go telling anyone about this, Charise! I swear, if you do . . ."

Charise raised her hands in a placating gesture, but it was clear from her irrepressible smile and the gleam in her eyes that she was enjoying Jason's discomfort.

Jason recovered quickly. "Girls," he continued, "they will, like, *allow* me my opinion. When I have something to say, it's like 'okay, whatever.' Boys say that they can make it without college. But girls are more ambitious. They're more competitive. If they want something, they're going to get it."

"Do you think girls are more competitive than boys?" I asked Charise.

"I think girls are competitive," she said. "I know I am. My older sister and I compete about everything—grades, swimming, who does more housework, cooking. Everything."

"You two compete over who does more housework?" Both Jason and I considered this.

"Yes, we do."

"Is your sister in college?"

"She's studying law at Rutgers."

"But she still lives at home?"

"Yeah. Both my parents work, so she's usually around when I get home from school." Charise gave Jason a covert sideways glance, but he was restless and bit unfocused and didn't register it.

"What do your parents do?" I asked Charise.

"My mom's a nurse. My dad's a therapist for drug addicts inside a prison."

"What do your parents do, Jason?" I asked.

"They sit on their ass."

"Who makes more money, your mom or dad?" I asked Charise.

"My mom."

"How does that affect their relationship?"

"Well, I hear them talking. I know that making more money makes my mom *feel* that it gives her more power."

"Would you feel that way?"

"It wouldn't matter to me. Either way is fine."

At this point, Jason could no longer contain himself. "Don't you be saying that, Charise!" he exclaimed. "I work at Burger King and you work as a lifeguard. You're already making more money than me. And when we're older, you're the one gonna be bringing home the bacon, and I'm gonna be cooking it."

When I asked Jason if that prospect bothered him, he replied: "I don't know about that one way or another. But what I do know is that's the way it's gonna be. These girls—they want to get noticed. In their careers. In the way they look and dress. They want to flash it. They say, I've done this, and I've done that. What have *you* done? Girls dominate. They rule."

Conservative groups such as the Heritage Foundation[14] bemoan the fact the women are becoming more powerful and less economically dependent on men. They point out that the movement of more married women into the workforce that began in the 1960s was accompanied by a rise in the divorce rate. Women who earn more than their husbands are more likely to get divorced than those who don't. In general, marriages are less likely to end in divorce the more a husband earns relative to his wife. In fact, the more women earn, the less attractive marriage appears to be.[15] This may be true, at least in part, because marriage is generally more beneficial to men than women.

➤ Once married, men are much less likely to engage in risky behaviors such as drinking heavily, driving dangerously, or using drugs. They are also more likely to work regularly, help others more, volunteer more, and attend religious services more frequently. [16, 17]

➤ The sociologist Emile Durkheim argued that these changes occur because marriage integrates men into social groups of likeminded others, establishing acceptable boundaries around their behavior. Other sociologists have made similar arguments: marriage "domesticates" men by fostering a sense of responsibility for their families, orienting them toward the future, and making them sensitive to the long-term consequences of their actions. Wives offer advice, schedule medical appointments, and encourage social behavior. Both partners' mental health appears to benefit from the support and understanding they share. [18]

➤ Married men are more successful in work, getting promoted more often and receiving higher performance appraisals. They also miss work or arrive late less often than single men. [19, 20]

➤ Married men may have better immune systems, either from support or because their wives nag them to monitor blood pressure, cholesterol, and weight, etc. [21]

➤ Married men are half as likely to commit suicide as single men and one-third as likely as divorced men. Widowed men under 45 are nine times more likely to commit suicide as married men. [22]

➤ Cohabiting seems to be beneficial to men's mental health and less beneficial to women's mental health. Recent research found that women who stayed single all their lives seemed to have rather good mental health, while men who stayed single all their lives did not. "Choosing to be single seems to be good for women but not so good for men," the study notes.[23]

With girls on the ascent, educators and policy makers have begun to worry about boys. In 2004, First Lady Laura Bush said: "I feel like, in the United States, that we've sort of shifted our gaze away from boys for the last several decades, and that we've neglected boys."[24]

But even if we started to focus more on boys, they would just keep rolling around on the termite mound, said Barry Sheeman, a member of the British Parliament, in a 2004 BBC interview. He was discussing the news that girls had done better than boys in nearly all subject areas on the British A-Level exams. Sheeman said that there is a danger of being obsessed with how boys are doing at school. "My own personal view is that women are brighter than men," commented the MP. "We should celebrate this, shouldn't we? The brightest kids are coming through and they happen to be women."[25]

Some marriages may be more stable when there is a large power differential between the partners and marital roles are clear. One person leads; the other follows. Many women want that kind of control, and increasing numbers of men are voluntarily ceding power to their wives or significant others. Boys of the alpha generation are watching this happen and it's confusing for some of them. They are unsure what society expects of them as men, they feel a pressure to

Dan Kindlon, PhD

figure out new kinds of masculine identity, and they are anxious about how girls are responding to their quest.

Daniel, a senior at a small private boarding school in Massachusetts, says that he is part of a "men's group" at his school. He and five other guys get together after lights-out in his dorm to discuss, among other things, gender issues.

"The girls at our school feel empowered," Daniel said. "No doubt about it. They feel their voice will be heard. As boys, I think we're curious about their attitudes and opinions, but not threatened by them. In my men's group, we often talk about the cumbersome expectations that society puts on us to be men—about how men feel pressured to go out and compete and put bread on the table. I don't think that I'd get anything out of competing. It wouldn't bother me if the woman I was with made more money than I did—if I stayed home and did painting or photography. I guess that I see this as a real possibility, because my brother was married to a high-powered lawyer; he stayed home and painted. He'd be dressed in an apron and joke that he was the housewife."

"Do you think that may be part of why the marriage didn't last?" I asked. "That a high-powered woman needs a man who can match her energy and intensity?"

"I don't know," he replied. "But I do think it's strange that the most independent and strongly feminist girls at school—the ones who are always wearing pants, who *always* stand up about being equal to guys—have all bought used wedding dresses, which they wear on Sunday night when we all dress up. When we do our dances."

"When they're in their dresses, do you feel a pressure to propose?"

"Not directly. But they're all very up-front about wanting to get married and have kids. They're the ones who also tend to go for the really masculine guys—the ones with chest hair showing, who dress in Carhart."

Sam, an 18-year-old freshman at the University of California, Santa Cruz, who plans to major in marine biology, said that in his high school the "girls certainly cared more about their work than the boys [did]. I never saw guys get upset about a bad grade. We had a French teacher who was a real jerk. Most of the dudes in class stopped caring. But the girls got pissed off. They went to the administration and complained and got him fired."

I asked Sam what he thought of the young women he was meeting at college.

"I've noticed that I'm surrounded by *really* smart girls," he said. "A lot of them respect guys as equals. But I would say about one-sixth of them have a disparaging attitude about guys, about how smart we are and our ability to make decisions. God knows what they're looking for in a guy. They're pushy intellectually. In recent times, guys have gone from a position of superiority to equality. I don't think it's going to drop more from there." Sam paused for a moment. "Although there are more girls in college now than guys—which, from my point of view, is great!"

Not all guys, of course, have such a high opinion of female intelligence. There are certainly boys (and men, for that matter) out there who think that girls can be overly emotional and concerned with their looks. No doubt some alphas would fit this description, at least in the eyes of their male peers. But my experience has shown me that most adolescent boys recognize that they are dealing with a generation of girls that is high achieving and assertive.

Dan Kindlon, PhD

As Daniel and Sam show us, both men and women are trying to sort out their feelings about what is desirable in a mate. According to evolutionary psychologists, men most desired physical attractiveness in a woman. They wanted a wife who was young and healthy enough to bear high-quality young. (Men, of course, often looked for other traits as well: loyalty, intelligence, domestic skills, and maternal instinct, to name a few.) Women, on the other hand, wanted a mate who was a good provider. A man's desirability lay in the amount of "resource display." A fancy car, nice clothes, and the ability to be able to pay for a luxurious date—these were as important, or perhaps even more important, to a woman's choice of who to marry than physical attractiveness.

These "rules of attractiveness" are no longer necessarily the norm. One would think, following this reasoning, that women who have their own resources are more likely to exhibit a traditional male pattern, focusing on non-material traits such as a sense of humor, kindness, and maybe a good complexion in a potential mate. Perhaps, like Madonna, they will in one form or another marry their "trainers." I think the other side of the equation is clearer: many more men may begin to develop the traditionally female pattern, finding greater attractiveness in women who are able—by virtue of their higher education and occupational status—to bring substantial resources into the home.

In the coming world of the alpha generation, our sons will be forced to confront some of the core psychological attributes of traditional masculinity. Modern boys will need to go through their own "inner metamorphosis" and make similar changes in their personal psychology to those that have been made by the daughters of the feminist revolution. In particular, boys will need to strike a better balance between separation and connection, dominance and submission. As their sisters have, boys will need to incorporate elements of both their fathers and their mothers into their personalities.

As Michael Thompson and I discussed in our 1999 book *Raising Cain: Protecting the Emotional Life of Boys*,[26] the historical domination of men over women has come with a price. Boys have long been socialized not only to dominate and control others, especially women, but also to control themselves. They have been told that they have to control their "weaker" emotions. They have been pushed to be autonomous, to remain separate from others and self-sufficient. They have been taught never to ask for help.

Michael and I discussed the findings of the groundbreaking National Survey of Adolescent Males (NSAM). We were struck by the fact that boys who approved of more rigid gender roles were, in the survey's word, "hypermasculine" and at greater risk for a host of problems, including school suspension, date rape, and drug and alcohol use.[27] Boys who tend towards hypermasculinity also tend be dominant in their relationships with girls. They are less likely to wear a condom during sex, for example.

In our sample, the boys with the most traditionally masculine attitudes were, similar to the NSAM findings, more likely to have had sex at an earlier age and to have more sexual partners. They were also more likely to have had sex in a non-monogamous "casual" relationship. They watch more hours of television and have more body image problems than boys with less traditionally masculine attitudes. On the flip side, they rated themselves as more dependable.

Unfortunately, boys don't have the abundance of positive media role models that girls have had in recent years. The hypermasculine male is still very much present on television. Studies by media watch-

Dan Kindlon, PhD

dog groups find that men and boys on television rarely show signs of vulnerability, and almost three-quarters of young adult male characters use antisocial behaviors to solve problems.[28] A remarkable long-term study showed that boys who watched more violent television when they were in early elementary school were more likely as young adults to physically assault their spouses and respond to an insult with physical force. They were also three times as likely to have been convicted of a crime.[29]

In subtle and not-so-subtle ways, our culture gives boys the message that they should behave like the men the see on TV or else. In one recent television commercial, a hapless young man is crushed by a giant can of beer that falls from the sky when he displays feminine tendencies. "Men should act like men," the ad's announcer intones, giving fair warning to the boys in the audience. These are amusing commercials, but they push boys in unhealthy ways; they are part of an onslaught of media that is encouraging hypermasculinity.

When I speak to audiences about boys' psychology, I often ask parents to try to think of three male characters on television that they would like their son to emulate. Parents are surprised by how difficult this is. Male characters on prime-time television tend to be buffoons, while their female counterparts are increasingly clever and capable.

⟨～⟩

Education, wealth, and social status are not the only areas where men are in decline. Boys have a myriad of biological vulnerabilities that affect their health, cognitive abilities, and personalities. Many of the biological vulnerabilities that afflict boys are a result of simply being boys—they have a Y chromosome, while girls don't.

Chromosomes come in 23 pairs. This redundancy is important when we inherit damaged genes on one of these pairs, as we all do to some extent, because we have an undamaged backup copy. Both males and females benefit from this redundancy, but for only 22 of the 23 chromosome pairs. When it comes to the 23rd—the chromosomes that determine sex—only girls, by virtue of their double-X genotype, have a spare copy of every gene on the X chromosome. If a boy's single X is damaged in some way—as is the case in hemophilia, color blindness, and Duchene Muscular Dystrophy—they have no backup, which is why all these disorders are far more common among males.[30]

The single male Y has been handed down over millennia, and its inability to repair itself has caused it to degenerate. Geneticists believe that the X and Y chromosomes probably started out hundreds of millions of years ago as an equal set, each with about 1,500 genes. At that time, X and Y had nothing to do with sex differentiation: The splitting of organisms into male and female didn't occur until about a billion years after life emerged on earth. As X and Y evolved into sex chromosomes, Y became specialized to make "maleness." The X has retained its full compliment of 1,500 genes, while the lone Y has been shrinking, down to a mere 78 genes that do relatively little genetic work other than to produce boy babies.[31]

The boy babies that these Y chromosomes produce are, as a group, more fragile than their double-X sisters. Boys are at greater risk than girls not only for the previously mentioned sex-linked problems, but also for many kinds of mental disorders. Four times as many boys as girls are diagnosed with autism,[32] and two to five times as many boys have Attention Deficit Hyperactivity Disorder and reading disabilities.[33] Fragile X syndrome, the most common form of inherited mental retardation (passed from mothers to sons in the same way as hemophilia), affects approximately one in every 1,000 to 2,000 males.[34]

With advances in genetic research and genome mapping, scientists now know that the X chromosome has many genes that code for proteins important to higher brain functions, at least two of which have been linked to autism.[35] In fact, some geneticists believe that it is likely that these X chromosome genes are what differentiate human mental functioning from that of other mammals.[36] With no backup copy, boys with damage to their single X will always exhibit the defect it causes. For a girl, with two Xs to distribute among her cells, only the damaged member of the pair will malfunction, thereby eliminating the disability or reducing its severity.[37]

Men are not only at greater risk for various forms of organic disorders than women—they don't live as long. Men's lives are, on average, five years shorter than women's.[38] Economic disadvantage and low social status are major risk factors for higher mortality. The poor have a much shorter life expectancy than the rich, due to higher stress levels, unequal access to medical care, and greater exposure to pathogens,[39] but even adjusting for income, women live longer. On average, the poorest women outlive the richest men.[40] Men, it seems, are just not built to last.

As bad as this news is for individual men, there is also some evidence that the *population* of men is slowly disappearing. There has been a slow but steady decline in the proportion of men to women born each year since 1950 in the United States, Denmark, Wales, England, Canada, the Netherlands, Germany, Finland, Norway, and

Figure 6-5

SEX RATIO AT BIRTH AND JOINPOINT SEGMENTS, 1940–2002

—— Joinpoint sex ratio trend   ········ Observed sex ratio trend

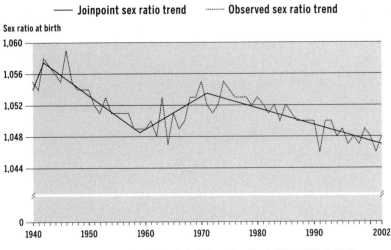

*NOTES: Sex ratio at birth is the number of male births divided by the number of female births multiplied by 1,000.

Source: Matthews, T. J. and Hamilton, B. E. (2005) "Trend analysis of the sex ratio at birth in the United States." National Vital Statistics Reports, V. 53 no. 20, June 14, 2005. Centers for Disease Control and Prevention.

Sweden[41] (see Figure 6-5). Even at this lower rate, there are still more boys than girls being born (about 105 boys for every 100 girls), but the slow decline is persistent and noteworthy, especially when one considers its possible causes. Two stand out: increased psychological stress and environmental pollution.

Recent evidence shows that during economic hardship or following natural disasters, fewer boys are born. A recent study from Sweden, covering the years 1862 to 1991, found that the sex ratio at birth varied with the economic health of the nation.[42] When times were good, more boys were born. Similarly, in the early 1990s, when East Germany was foundering, the number of male versus female births fell there.[43]

The reason for this appears to be that stress causes sperm to swim more slowly. Normally sperm carrying the male Y chromosome have

Dan Kindlon, PhD

an advantage in their race to fertilize an egg, since the Y chromosome, with its fewer genes, is lighter and thus these sperm swim faster than their double-X female counterparts. The slower swimming speed of all sperm that follows stressful experiences appears to negate the Y sperm's normal advantage.[44] These results suggest that if stress levels increase around the world (as they may with global warming, terrorist attacks, or a flu pandemic), fewer and fewer male babies will be born.

The stress-induced decline in male births is a fairly subtle effect, especially when compared to the effects of environmental pollutants, which, in some areas, have cut the ratio of male birth to female births in half in less than a decade.[45] This is what has happened to the Chippewa people on the Aamjiwnaang First Nation Reserve in Canada, just across the border from Port Huron, Michigan.[46] The reserve is located in an area so dense in petrochemical factories and petroleum storage tanks that it is known locally as "Chemical Valley."

Several years ago, the Chippewa became concerned about possible pollution from the factories. Tests of the surrounding area revealed elevated levels of dioxin, PCBs, pesticides, and heavy metals, including arsenic, cadmium, lead, and mercury. The community was aware that it was giving birth to many more girls than boys. Although scientists have been unable to determine the exact cause for this, they are fairly certain that it's due to the introduction of an endocrine-disrupting pollutant into the area in the early 1990s.

Endocrine disrupters, as scientists call them, not only affect how many boys are born: they may cause severe disruption of boys' fundamental maleness. For the past 60 years, all of us have been subjects in an enormous uncontrolled chemistry experiment; thousands upon thousands of bioactive chemicals have been manufactured and released into the environment by the megaton, bathing every living creature. Many of these chemicals have endocrine-disrupting properties: they adversely affect the normal functioning of hormones, in particular the female sex hormone estrogen. These pollutants include pesticides, PCBs,[iii] dioxins,[iv] and chemicals used in the manufacture of common plastics. All have estrogen-mimicking actions that disrupt normal male sexual development.

Even very low doses of endocrine-disrupting chemicals (EDCs)

[iii] Polychlorinated biphenyls (PCBs) have been used as coolants and lubricants in transformers, capacitors, and other electrical equipment because they don't burn easily and are good insulators. The manufacture of PCBs was stopped in the U.S. in 1977 because of evidence that they build up in the environment and can cause harmful health effects. PCBs have been found in at least 500 of the 1,598 National Priorities List sites identified by the Environmental Protection Agency (EPA). Source: Centers for Disease Control and Prevention Web site: www.atsdr.cdc. gov/tfacts17.html.

[iv] Dioxin is the common name used to refer to the chemical 2,3,7,8-tetrachlorodibenzo-p-dioxin, or TCDD. In addition to dioxin itself, there are other compounds, such as the polychlorinated dibenzodioxins (PCDDs), polychlorinated dibenzofurans (PCDFs), and some polychlorinated biphenyls (PCBs) that have similar structures and activity as dioxin. These are often commonly referred to as dioxin-like compounds or "dioxins." The way in which dioxin affects cells is similar in some way to the way in which hormones such as estrogen work. Dioxin enters a cell and binds to a protein present in cells known as the Ah receptor. The receptor when bound to dioxin can then bind to DNA and alter the expression of some genes. This can lead to alterations in the level of specific proteins and enzymes in the cell. While it is not known exactly how changes in the levels of these different proteins cause the toxicity of dioxin, it is believed by most scientists that the initial binding of dioxin the Ah receptor is the first step. Source: National Institutes of Health: www.niehs.nih.gov/oc/factsheets/dioxin.htm.

Dan Kindlon, PhD

can have powerful effects if the exposure occurs during fetal development.[47] And because some of the effects of these chemical pollutants can mimic estrogen, the most powerful effects of these chemicals are often seen in the way they appear to have "feminized" males.

The gender-bending effects of EDC pollutants were first noticed in birds that lived along the Great Lakes. This region was, for many years, an uncontrolled dumping ground for endocrine disrupters like DDT and DDE.[v] Naturalists studying Great Lakes bird populations noticed that twice the normal number of eggs had started to appear in the nests of herring gulls. They found that the majority of these eggs were unfertilized. They were even more surprised to find that the two gulls that were tending these double-egged nests were usually both female.

Eventually scientists were able to determine that EDCs were to blame. Male gulls exposed to estrogen-mimicking chemicals had lost interest in mating with females. In response, the females made the best out of a bad situation, pooled their eggs, and, in a kind of ornithological Boston marriage, set up housekeeping together.

Other examples from the animal world illustrate the effects of EDCs. Male rats exposed to high amounts of the insecticide DDE as pups have delayed puberty. Male rabbits exposed *in utero* to EDC have no sexual interest in female rabbits. There are instances of

---

[v] DDT (dichlorodiphenyltrichloroethane) is a pesticide once widely used to control insects in agriculture and insects that carry diseases such as malaria. Its use in the U.S. was banned in 1972 because of damage to wildlife, but it is still used in some countries. DDE (dichlorodiphenyldichloroethylene) and DDD (dichlorodiphenyldichloroethane) are chemicals similar to DDT that contaminate commercial DDT preparations. DDT, and especially DDE, build up in plants and in fatty tissues of fish, birds, and other animals. Source: Center for Disease Control and Prevention: www.atsdr.cdc.gov/tfacts35.html.

"inter-sex" fish, such as male trout that were exposed to the EDCs contained in detergents and have eggs in their testes.[48]

Women of childbearing ages 20 to 40 may have disproportionately high levels of phthalates (a class of EDCs) in their bodies, according to a 1999 Center for Disease Control study. The study found that these women had significantly higher levels of monobutyl phthalate in their bodies than other age or gender groups.[49] The relatively high use of cosmetic products by women of childbearing age is hypothesized to be the reason for this. This may be impacting their male progeny. It is now generally accepted that the quality of a man's sperm is largely set by the time he is born, and there are grave concerns about the prenatal effects of female hormones on male fertility.[50] These concerns are warranted because sperm quality is already in rapid decline. A number of recent studies have shown that sperm counts have been falling steadily since 1940.[51]

An editorial in the *British Medical Journal* sounds the alarm: "Such examples, and our growing understanding of the vulnerability of the male reproductive system to environmental factors, highlight the need for vigilance. Regulatory and research agencies need to determine the most appropriate methods of assessing the actions of agents on the reproductive system and should undertake whatever studies are necessary to confirm or refute the emerging hypotheses. Delay may compromise the fertility of future generations."[52]

The biological research into gender-bending chemicals raises major health concerns. Less understood, however, is whether increased

Dan Kindlon, PhD

exposure to estrogen-mimicking chemicals has also changed male behavior. Although there are some intriguing findings from animal research (male herring gulls that had lost all interest in mating with females), there hasn't yet been enough research on humans to conclude whether anything similar is going on. Perhaps some enterprising scientist has a study underway that is retrospectively characterizing the uterine EDC exposures of metrosexual men,[vi] searching for a biological cause for their unabashed embrace of day spas, manicures, and facials. Whether the new visibility of feminized men is the result of chemical pollutants or social changes (or both), there certainly seem to be more boys around who are concerned with traditionally feminine pursuits.

Not all alpha girls find this new kind of male appealing. Natalie, an intense eighth grader who attends a public school in northern New Jersey, is a high voltage, take-no-prisoners alpha. "I'm a very competitive person," she said. "No one can compete with me. Everyone else just stands back. I love to argue and debate. I never lose an argument at school. So law is an option [as a profession]. I'm like my dad: I'm argumentative, competitive in debating, and I have his social skills. He is aggressive, and you can tell he's mean—he walks into a room to close a deal and the people know there's no debating about it; they just sign the papers. Although guys like me, I don't have a boyfriend. Boys have cooties. Having a boyfriend isn't important to me, especially because all the guys here are metrosexual and obsessed with the way they look. They'll spend $500 on one outfit."

[vi] The online Urban Dictionary defines metrosexual as: A straight man who embraces the homosexual lifestyle; i.e. refined tastes in clothing, excessive use of designer hygiene products, etc. Usually is on the brink of homosexuality. See: www.urbandictionary.com/define.php?term=metrosexual.

When we look at the decline of men, it is easy to become alarmed. But perhaps the coming generations of feminized men may be happier than men of the past. The onus of running the world, the endless problems and headaches—let alpha women have a crack at them; we'll see if they can do better! It's clear that there is much room for improvement.

Perhaps in a world run by women, men will live longer, less stress-filled lives. They will cultivate hitherto underdeveloped aspects of their masculinity; they will allow the full flowering of the tenderer, nurturing aspects of being a "good provider." They will raise the kids and keep house. Men will reassert the role as their children's primary mentor and guide that they held in agrarian America.[53] They will finally fulfill the great hope that has been the dream behind all our wealth and technology—a society where we have the leisure to enjoy one another and appreciate the simple joy of being alive. Men will be able to drop some of the burden of maleness and become more loving. The alphas will provide—fishing for termites, bringing home the bacon—while men will have more of a chance to indulge themselves in sublimely pointless play.

Dan Kindlon, PhD

CHAPTER SEVEN

ALPHAS AT WORK

"If I don't fit into GE or Ford or IBM that's not my problem.
That's their problem."

What does the future hold for alpha girls? How many of them will have dynamic, fulfilling careers? What kind of impact will they have on our society? It will be fascinating to watch how their inner revolution will manifest in the world as our daughters come of age.

Many alphas assume that limitless opportunities await them; if there are glass ceilings in place, they will shatter them. My impression is that they have the talent, ambition, and self-confidence to do just that.

One of the deepest impressions the alphas left me with was how hard they work—how intent they are on putting their abundant energy to good use. They are determined, resolute, and tenacious, yet they are also touchingly eager. I was struck by how many alphas were adaptable—how gracefully they played both traditionally masculine and feminine roles. Audrey, the MIT engineering student you met

* This chapter was written in collaboration with Amy Sapp.

earlier, is adept with both an eggbeater and a circular saw. The alphas are strong, resilient, brilliantly adapted hybrids who have taken the best from their mothers and their fathers.

In their rock-solid work ethic, in their energy and optimism, they embody the best in the American character. They are pragmatic and idealistic. They are individualistic and egalitarian, broad in their range of interests and open to the possibilities of what life has to offer. Their psychology is a powerful expression of the drive toward emancipation that is so much a part of our history, our raison d'etre.

Most alphas had a clear idea of the kind of career they wanted. A few even had *written* itineraries that mapped the years ahead, with stops at college, graduate school, their first job, marriage, and the names they were going to give their children.

Many alphas had strong altruistic inclinations—they wanted to improve social conditions and fight injustice. One out of every three alphas said having a job in which she could help people was extremely important to her; this was as important to only 18 percent of her non-alpha peers.

Helen, 17, president of her school's Ecology Club, is active in environmental causes. She wants to make a difference, even if it means that she won't make much money. "My fear is that I'll be a poor person who works for a nonprofit. But my dream career is to be an environmental activist . . . I like to get into the middle of things. I want to make products more environmentally friendly and encourage people to stop consuming what they don't need. Like shoes. I only have three pairs."

While money wasn't important to 10 percent of alphas (not yet, anyway), nearly a third were determined to become rich. "I want three houses," said Justine, the Vassar sophomore you met earlier. "I aim high. I want one place on the Jersey shore and one place overseas. Greece is nice. Then I want a Manhattan penthouse. I'm giving myself 10 years to get to that point. My friends and I are always talking about ways to get rich quick."

The current generation of young people is far more concerned with wealth than previous generations, as I discussed in a prior book, *Too Much of a Good Thing*. In 1972, the most common reason high school seniors gave for going to college was to "develop a meaningful philosophy of life." Granted, many of the respondents to that survey were stoned when they gave their answers. Nonetheless, there is a stark contrast between that era's idealism and "to become very well-off financially,"[1] the most common response given by today's kids.

In the past, money was more important to boys than girls. While this is still true, the gap is narrowing. In our sample, 36 percent of boys and 24 percent of girls said that it was "extremely important" for them to have lucrative work.

The alphas with wealth uppermost in their minds didn't want to do just anything to get rich: they wanted work that would challenge and absorb them.[i] Becky, a 16-year-old varsity tennis star and junior class president, described herself as hardworking, outgoing, and ambitious—attributes that fit most alphas. "I want to do something that I'll have fun with," she said, "something I won't get tired of. I don't want to live a settled life in the suburbs. I want to travel. Money is important. If I want to be at the top, I know I'll have to work real hard. I know my potential and I feel that I should fulfill that potential."

[i] 81 percent of these money-seeking alpha girls also said that having an interesting job was extremely important.

Many alphas had astutely assessed the realities of the marketplace; they knew what it took to make ends meet. They were far more practical than their baby boomer parents were at their age. Lindsay would love to be an actress, but she is focusing her energy elsewhere. "I want to be able to send my kids to college," she said. "If I didn't have to worry about money, I'd definitely be an actress, but I may end up as a lawyer or psychologist."

Almost all the alphas we interviewed assumed that whatever financial security they achieved would be independently accomplished. Many told us they didn't want to have to rely on husbands or significant others to pay their way or even help support their children! Just as there was a strong assumption of gender equality among alphas, there was also the assumption of independence and self-sufficiency. (We'll discuss alpha girls' attitudes toward love, marriage, and family and their views on balancing family and work in the next chapter.)

Alpha girls placed a slightly higher value than non-alpha girls on being successful in their careers.[2] They were also intent on becoming "experts" in their fields, as evidenced by their responses to the question:

"How important is it for you to become an expert in your future occupational field?"

	Non–Alpha Girls	Alpha Girls
Not important	1.8 %	0.7 %
A little important	3.3 %	3.7 %
Somewhat important	25.6 %	12.5 %
Very important	38.0 %	37.5 %
Extremely important	31.4 %	45.6 %

Alpha girls are significantly more likely than non–alpha girls to place greater importance on becoming an expert in their future occupational field (in multiple regression analysis adjusting for socioeconomic status, grade in school, and race/ethnicity).

Dan Kindlon, PhD

All in all, the alphas were already looking forward to brilliant careers where they could make a difference as well as a killing. They had energy and drive. They were in it for the long haul. They gave the impression of endurance, stamina, and fortitude. I got the sense of long-distance runners who weren't carrying any extra weight. The lack of constraint emanating from them is palpable—a result of their emancipated psychology. There is nothing inside them that is holding them back.

While it is always tricky to make predictions about how an individual, let alone a whole generation, will act in the future, most of the alphas I interviewed seemed to have a fairly clear sense of what they want out of life. That may change, of course, as they get older. But I think one would be hard put to argue that the clear social trends that are empowering women, which we have already discussed and will describe in greater detail below, are going into remission any time soon.

~

There have always been girls with talent, drive, and dreams of a brilliant career. Most of those dreams were never realized. In the 1920s, Lewis Terman conducted the "Genius Studies," the first scientific research on the life history of talented girls. Terman, a psychologist at Stanford University,[3] had studied with Frenchman Alfred Binet, who designed the original IQ test.

Terman identified over 1,000 California elementary school children with very high IQs. He hypothesized that the vast majority of them would go on to lead productive lives.[ii] Despite being an early proponent of eugenics (a position he repudiated after the Nazis embraced the field), Terman was not sexist. He was disappointed when the female Termites, as his subjects came to call themselves, didn't realize their potential.

Most of Terman's girls, 86 percent, had enrolled in college; 67 percent had graduated, similar to the rates for the boys in the study: 90 percent had enrolled in college and 70 percent had graduated. But the similarity ended there. More of the men went on to graduate school and about two-thirds of them landed high-status jobs, while almost none of the women did.[4] By the time they were in their mid-thirties, 50 percent of Terman's women listed their occupation as housewife. Terman concluded that their lives had been undermined by a lack of opportunity and discrimination against women.[iii]

Terman's research was followed by another telling study of gifted women that began in the late 1950s, after the Soviets launched Sputnik 1 and Sputnik 2, the first satellites. Barbara Kerr was one of 30 gifted children (15 of whom were girls) from eight elementary schools in St. Louis who were plucked from fourth grade, bussed to a special building, and given an accelerated curriculum that was designed to help their genius flower. This program, called Track A-1,

---

[ii] This was not a common view of gifted children in the 1920s. The prevailing wisdom about precocious children was "early ripe, early rot."

[iii] "Intelligence tests, for example, have demonstrated for all time the falsity of the once widely prevalent belief that women as a class are appreciably or at all inferior to men in the major aspects of intellect. The essential equality of the sexes has further been shown by psychometric methods to obtain also in various special fields, such as musical ability, artistic ability, mathematical ability, and even mechanical ability." Quote from page 1 of Terman, L.M. and Miles, C.C., *Sex and Personality: Studies in Masculinity and Femininity.* New York: McGraw-Hill (1936).

Dan Kindlon, PhD

was one of many that were started in the late 1950s to foster talent to compete with what was perceived as the Soviets' superiority in the sciences.[5]

Kerr continued on Track A-1 through high school. She eventually became a psychologist and decided to study her fellow female A-1 alumnae. She expected to find classmates who were stars in physics, chemistry, and math; instead, she discovered a third of the A-1s were housewives, a quarter had never graduated from college, and most of those who were employed worked in traditionally feminine fields such as nursing or elementary education.

Kerr concluded that her female classmates had never really believed that they were intellectually gifted. In some cases, they had assumed that they had been chosen for A-1 by mistake. Many of their parents hadn't supported their intellectual abilities. One set of parents had told their A-1 daughter that her abilities "were nothing to brag about." Insecurity and the lack of parental support caused many A-1 girls to lower their sights. Kerr also noted that many of the A-1s' careers were aborted when they married and had children, especially if they did so when they were in their early or mid-twenties.

Termite and A-1 girls came of age before the feminist revolution of the 1960s and '70s began to abolish the psychological and legal obstacles to career advancement for women. The mid 1970s were a tipping point for feminism: the 1972 passage of Title IX and the founding of *Ms.* magazine; the U.S. Supreme Court ruling on *Roe v. Wade* in 1973; the admission of women to the army and navy military academies in 1976. The number of women who started to pursue professional careers exploded. Between 1970 and 1980, the percentage of women who earned medical degrees nearly tripled, and the number of women completing law school increased nearly six-fold.[6]

Gifted girls who entered high school after the mid 1970s had a markedly different pattern of career development than the Termites or the A-1s. Dr. Karen Arnold's Illinois Valedictorian Project (which we mentioned briefly in Chapter 4[7]) followed valedictorians randomly selected from the class of 1981 for 15 years and watched their lives unfold. Arnold became especially interested in the career choices of the 46 female valedictorians in her group.

By the time they had turned 30, Arnold classified about 40 percent of these women as "top-career achievers . . . physicians, attorneys, professors, scientists, and business executives."[8] About a third were housewives or working in low-prestige jobs. Despite these apparent advances, Arnold felt that the women she studied still faced significant barriers that had caused them to give up or limit their careers in order to raise families. Others, according to Arnold, were rattled by subtle sex discrimination in college and had lost confidence in themselves, exactly what had happened to the A-1s.

What have the career trajectories been for women in countries where gender equity has been more of a priority than it has been in the U.S.? In 2005, the World Economic Forum (WEF)[9] published a ranking of 58 nations[iv] based on the size of their gender gap.[10] The U.S. ranked 17th, ahead of Costa Rica (18) but behind the former

[iv] The 58 participating nations included 30 (OECD) developed nations with democratic governments and market economies plus "28 emerging markets" (e.g. Latvia, Bangladesh, China, Colombia, South Africa). Due to data limitations, Jordan and Egypt were the only two Arab world countries that were included in the WEF report.

Soviet republics of Estonia (15), Latvia (12), Lithuania (11),[v] and New Zealand, Canada, the U.K., and Australia, which finished, respectively, in 6th, 7th, 8th, and 10th place.

These rankings were based on the following five-point index:[11]

→ Economic participation—wage equality between women and men for similar work

→ Economic opportunity—the extent of government-provided childcare and the percentage of women professionals in the workforce

→ Political empowerment—the percentage of parliamentary or congressional seats held by women

→ Educational attainment—the male-female gap in average years of school

→ Health and well-being—this included the maternal mortality rate per 100,000 live births

The U.S. made the top ten (8) for educational attainment for women, but it ranked near the bottom in terms of economic opportunity (46) and health and well-being (42). Meager maternity leave and maternity benefits and the lack of government-provided childcare are the reasons for our low rank for economic opportunity. High maternal mortality and our relatively high rate of teenage pregnancy compromise our women's health and well-being.

Sweden, Norway, Iceland, Denmark, and Finland hold the top five spots in the WEF report. Although these countries have not

---

[v] To my knowledge, there are no Cold War-ish U.S. government programs in place to reduce this gender-gap gap.

completely eliminated the gender gap, they have made more progress than we have.

Much of the relative equality of women in Norway is the result of strong affirmative action programs, particularly the 1978 Gender Equality Act, which was adopted around the same time that the similarly-worded Equal Rights Amendment was dying a slow death in U.S. state legislatures. The Act stipulated: "Women and men shall be given equal opportunities in education, employment and cultural and professional advancement." It established the office of a Gender Equity Ombudsman and a national Gender Equality Center. A 1988 amendment to the Act established a gender quota system for all publicly appointed committees, boards, and councils, mandating that in all such bodies each gender should have a minimum representation of 40 percent.

Radical laws enacted recently by the Norwegian government require that by 2008 the boards of *private* sector corporations that have publicly traded stock must also have a minimum of 40 percent women or face being disbanded. In anticipation of the deadline and in spite of strong opposition from the male-dominated business community, Norwegian companies have increased female representation on corporate boards, but most are still well shy of the legal quota.[12]

In 1986, Gro Harlem Brundtland,[vi] Norway's first female prime minister, appointed a government (similar to cabinet posts in the U.S.) that was made up of a record number of women. Since then, all

[vi] Dr. Brundtland is a physician, former student at the Harvard School of Public Health (where I currently teach), and the current director of the World Health Organization. See the WHO Web site for more information: www.who.int/dg/brundtland/bruntland/en.

Dan Kindlon, PhD

governments in Norway have been formed with 40 percent or more women.

Norwegian women currently hold 37 percent of the seats in parliament (in 2005 in the U.S., women were represented at a rate of 16 percent in the House and 14 percent in the Senate). Three out of five university students are women. Male and female employment rates are similar and the salary gap is smaller than in the U.S.: Norwegian women earn 85 cents for each dollar a man earns, compared to 77 cents in the U.S.

Still, glaring inequities persist between men and women in Norway. Women are primarily employed in the public sector. Two out of every three government workers are women, but they hold less than half the managerial jobs. In the private sector, one of three middle managers is female, but women are only 3 percent of board chairpersons. Eighty-three percent of municipal executives (mayors) are men. In short, men in Norway are still far more likely to be the boss.

Norwegian women tend to choose the typically "nurturing" professions of teaching and health care, while men gravitate towards science and technology. The average Norwegian woman still does more around the house: about two hours a day compared to a man's fifty minutes.

The picture for Swedish women is somewhat rosier. Unlike Larry Summers and Charles Murray, the Swedish government doesn't put much stock in the importance of genetic differences between men and women. Consider this excerpt from the government publication *Women and Men in Sweden*: "The concepts of feminine and masculine are social constructions, which means that gender patterns are the result of upbringing, culture, the economic framework, power structures and political ideologies . . . This is why the Swedish

Government has decided that work on gender equality should have a feminist focus that consciously tackles this structure."[13]

A major reason that Sweden ranks number one in the WEF report is that it grants the longest maternity leave of any country on the planet. And it's paid! Full leave for both parents at 80 percent salary is guaranteed *for 18 months*.[14] Once a parent returns to work in Sweden, there is subsidized childcare: two-thirds of children under age six attend municipal day care centers. In contrast, the U.S. has no legal requirement for private companies or government employers to offer paid maternity leave, although the Family Medical Leave Act mandates that companies with over 50 employees provide 12 weeks of *unpaid* leave in any 12-month period after a birth or adoption.[15]

Gender inequalities still exist in Sweden, however. The only three occupations with a roughly equal percentage of men and women are secondary school teachers, accountants, and cooks. Ninety-eight percent of office secretaries are women. Fifty-six percent of the managers in the public sector are women, but only 19 percent in the private sector. Women do occupy 45 percent of the seats in parliament.

Despite mandated gender equality in Scandinavian countries, it hasn't quite happened. Still, the Nordic countries are called "the Petri dish of equality," said Laura Liswood, one of the cofounders of the Council of Women World Leaders and a partner at Goldman Sachs.

"They are homogenous societies that have historically been fishing cultures," she said. "The men were off at sea for nine to twelve months at a time. This gave women the chance to run things at home. You saw the same thing in New England when the economy was whaling- and fishing-based."

Liswood said that "incumbency" is pushing against gender equal-

Dan Kindlon, PhD

ity in the U.S. today: "Historically, it's extremely difficult to overturn those who already hold power. It just so happens that today in our world that tends to be white American males. In parliamentary political systems, you can obtain power with a smaller percentage of the overall vote. Our political system of winner take all is historically unfriendly to out-of-power groups."

Liswood said that she would be fascinated to see how the empowered alpha girls, with their assumption of equality, fare as they entered the workforce. But she was concerned that they didn't have the "revolutionary skills" needed to finish the job her generation had started.

"Let's check them in five or ten years," she said. "They need to develop their organizing skills, their anger skills. We're not done. Not by a long shot. I recently asked the women in an MBA graduating class how many of the CEOs in this country are women. They said 25 percent. That makes me worry that girls are living in a fantasy world."

These were the words of a seasoned warrior. Liswood said that although women had made a lot of progress, 20 years ago she would have expected women to be further along than they are now. "Our expectations haven't been met," she said. "All these women went through professional schools. But where are they in the senior leadership of law firms? Why are we 69th in the world in female elected representatives? Why have we never had a woman vice president or had a woman on the joint chiefs? You have to look at where the power is."

Our First Lady would seem to disagree. She thinks a woman is poised to become the most powerful person on earth! In January of 2006, Laura Bush predicted that the United States would soon have a woman president. "I think it will happen probably in the next few terms of the presidency in the United States," she said to reporters. Her predictions just might be accurate. While Nancy Pelosi has recently been elected Speaker of the House, Hillary Clinton is a lead contender for the 2008 presidential election. In a telling twist, our former president might become the first "first husband."

Bush said she thought Condoleezza Rice—who was a prototype for today's alphas, entering the University of Denver at the age of 16—would be a good candidate for the presidency. "I'd love to see her run," Mrs. Bush said. "She's terrific."[16]

<hr />

Although women haven't yet reached the ultimate pinnacle of power in the United States, they are entering the professions of medicine, business, and law in record numbers. Almost half our alphas said they were most likely to work in these fields[vii] (see Figure 7-1).

Medicine was the most popular alpha choice and indicative of a larger trend. Although only one out of every four practicing physicians is a woman,[17] half the students in medical school are. Medicine will eventually reflect this 50–50 split. As Figure 7-2 illustrates, however, we believe that the change will be more dramatic. Even using relatively conservative estimates, in less than 50 years, 70 percent of the medical school graduates will be women. Women will dominate medicine in the way they now dominate the field of clinical psychology, where over 70 percent of the new PhDs are women.[18, viii]

[vii] Other popular occupational choices for alpha girls were: Art/Music—13 percent; and Other—19 percent.

[viii] See Appendix B for projection methodology.

Dan Kindlon, PhD

Figure 7-1

ALPHA GIRLS' RESPONSE TO: "INDICATE THE FIELD IN WHICH YOU WOULD MOST LIKE TO WORK SOMEDAY."

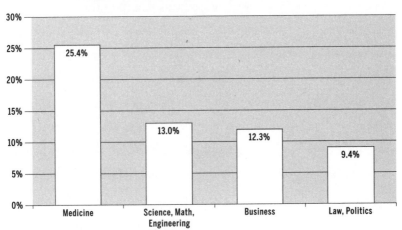

Figure 7-2

MEDICAL SCHOOL GRADUATES—PERCENT FEMALE, PROJECTED TO 2050

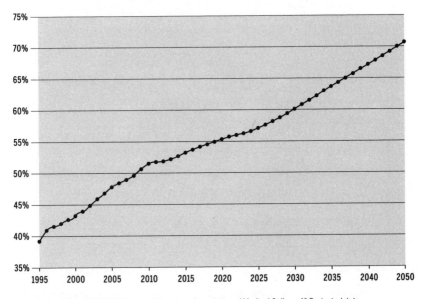

Source data (1995–2005): M.D. degrees. American Association of Medical Colleges[19] Projected data (2006–2050): see Appendix B.

Women are changing the way medicine is practiced. About 20 years ago, before Harvard's reference materials had been digitized and become available on my laptop, I was haunting the subbasement of Countway Medical Library. In a bleak room full of old journals, the cover of one magazine, *Doctor's Wife,* caught my eye. It was an illustration of a pretty, neatly dressed housewife, standing on tiptoe in black high heels to place an ornament high up on a large Christmas tree in a well-appointed living room. She has paused in mid-movement to watch her husband, the doctor, running out the door, black medical bag in hand. Her expression is a mixture of resignation and pride. The picture seemed to say: "You are a doctor's wife. These are the burdens you must bear. It is part of the price you pay for your beautiful home and lovely tree ornaments. It is the price your husband has to pay for being a doctor."

That was the 1950s, and doctors made house calls 24/7. Today, Americans are increasingly unwilling to accept this kind of life. As more women have become physicians, they have opted to work shorter hours, mainly because they want to spend time with their kids, and medicine is changing as a result. Female physicians are more likely to work part-time than their male counterparts. Twenty-five percent of women doctors work less than 40 hours per week and this trend toward part-time work is greatest among younger women. Hospitals, private clinics, and HMOs are starting to offer work schedules that are more flexible than they have been in the past. [20, 21]

Women most often choose to enter the medical subspecialties that are flexible—pediatrics, OB-GYN, and dermatology. (The joke among doctors is that dermatology is the perfect specialty: you're never on call, your patients never die, and they never get better.) The residency attracting the least number of women is surgery: Only one of four residents is female.[22]

FEMALE MEDICAL RESIDENTS GRADUATING FROM U.S. ACGME-ACCREDITED AND COMBINED SPECIALTY PROGRAMS, 2003	
Residency Programs	Percent of female residents
Anesthesiology	28.0 %
Dermatology	57.0 %
Family medicine	49.1 %
Obstetrics/gynecology	70.8 %
Pathology	50.3 %
Pediatrics	65.1 %
Psychiatry	50.0 %
Surgery (general)	23.8 %

Will women's increasing presence in medicine (and the increasing number of part-time physicians) reduce the quality of care? Not according to many patients, who report that they prefer women physicians, who tend to spend more time during office visits on counseling[23] and prevention[ix] than their male counterparts.

Organizations of women physicians are pushing to make medicine more family-friendly. The Association of Women Surgeons has issued the following maternity leave guidelines for hospitals: "A period of not less than six weeks maternity leave [with full pay and benefits] should be provided based on the needs of the expectant

---

[ix] Remarkably, in one study of 200 children ages 8 through 13, 80 percent of girls and an almost equal number of boys expressed a preference for a female doctor when visiting a pediatric emergency room to receive "stitches." See: Waseem, M. and Ryan, M. (2005) "Doctor or 'doctora': Do patients care?" *Pediatric Emergency Care* 8, pp. 515–517.

surgeon, separate from vacation time. Accrued vacation time and sick leave may be added to this period."

Six weeks isn't eighteen months, but it's a start. Will hospitals go for this? If they want to attract the best doctors, they may have to. Antonia Marr, in her late thirties, heads the surgical unit at a major teaching hospital on the West Coast. "When I took over the unit, I was working like crazy," she said. "I was really dedicated to my patients. It was a dream come true. After about a year of this, the chair of my department sat me down for a meeting. 'You have a husband and a young child,' he said. 'You're not spending enough time at home. You're going to burn out, and I don't want that to happen. You're doing a great job, and we want to keep you here for a long time. What do you need?' I was shocked. I told him that I needed to hire another surgeon and two full-time secretaries. He said, 'Fine. Consider it done.'"

Antonia says that although her department chair's focus on family is atypical, the field of medicine is changing. Alpha physicians will enter a very different environment than she did when she finished medical school.

⁓

Medicine is not the only field that women are changing. In the same month, January 2006, that Ellen Johnson-Sirleaf was inaugurated as Liberia's president, another woman, Michelle Bachelet, was elected as Chile's president, a first for that country.

Lydia Polgreen and Larry Rother, reporting for the *New York Times*, contrasted the "feminine virtues" of Bachelet and Johnson-

Sirleaf to Margaret "the Iron Lady" Thatcher and Golda Meir, the "strong women" of previous generations. They quoted Rosaline McCarthy, leader of the Women's Forum in Sierra Leone, who said: "To see the first female president [Johnson-Sirleaf] elected from a war-torn country shows people are now beginning to see what men have wrought in this region. It is the minds of men that make war. Women are the architects of peace." On the campaign trail, Johnson-Sirleaf was referred to as "Ma Ellen," and she compared Liberia to a sick child in need of a loving mother's tender care.[24]

Another woman took the reins of power in the fall of 2005—Angela Merkel was sworn in as the first woman Chancellor of Germany. And, while Nancy Pelosi has been chosen as the first female Speaker of the House, Senator Hillary Clinton is running for the Democratic nomination in the 2008 presidential election. Soon enough our own first in command might be a woman. These firsts for women are hard to ignore. They signal the growing influence that women are having on the fields of law and government. Clinton, a lawyer by training, and Pelosi, who has a long history in Congress, are helping to pave the way for the increasing number of women who are entering these fields.[x]

In the U.S. today, three out of every ten lawyers are women, ten times as many as in the early 1960s, and women comprise nearly half

[x] The Democratic Party is taking the initiative in recruiting women candidates, at least for the most competitive races in the House of Representatives. Besides Nancy Pelosi, one of the most visible of these is Major L. Tammy Duckworth, an army helicopter pilot who lost both legs during combat in Iraq. The Democrats' strategy is based on voter dissatisfaction. "In an environment where people are disgusted with politics in general, who represents clean and change?" asks Rahm Emanuel of Illinois, chairman of the Democratic Congressional Campaign Committee. "Women." See: The Democratic Party has taken the initiative in recruiting women candidates. Toner, R. "Women Wage Key Campaigns for Democrats." *New York Times*, Friday, March 24, 2006, A1, A16.

of current law school enrollments.[25] Projections for the future suggest that women will slowly but steadily outnumber men in law school graduating classes, reaching 60 percent by 2050.[xi]

Figure 7-3

LAW SCHOOL GRADUATES—PERCENT FEMALE, PROJECTED TO 2050

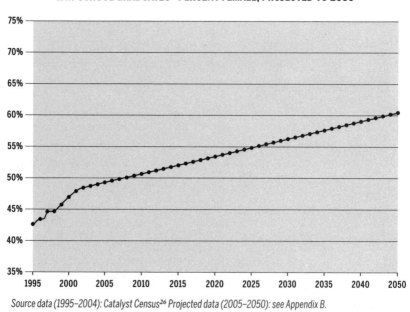

Source data (1995–2004): Catalyst Census[26] Projected data (2005–2050): see Appendix B.

Women, however, tend to work in less prestigious and lucrative law subspecialties and tend to advance more slowly than their male counterparts. Consider the following:

➤ According to a study by the National Association for Law Placement,[27] women were only 17 percent of large law-firm partners in 2005. Firms attributed the low percentage to a "pipeline"

[xi] See Appendix B for projection methodology.

Dan Kindlon, PhD

issue, reasoning that the number will increase as more females enter the profession. This, however, does not seem to be a reasonable explanation. In 1994, 42.6 percent of law school graduates were women. Thus, by 2005, approximately 40 percent of partners in large firms should be women. But this is not the case.

➤ The American Bar Association Commission on Women found that men earn salaries that are 20 percent higher than women, and a man is twice as likely to obtain a partnership than a woman with similar qualifications.[28]

➤ Women from the class of 2002 were slightly less likely to enter private practice and more likely to accept positions in government or public interest organizations or as judicial clerks. Women are twice as likely as men to take public interest jobs, although these jobs represent less than 10 percent of legal employment opportunities.[29]

Rosie Silver, who served as a deputy attorney for the state attorney general's office in Massachusetts, said that she thinks that there will be increasing numbers of both women lawyers and judges, but not at the highest levels of government or in the most lucrative jobs in private practice.

"I think the larger law firms are pretty open to women," she said. "But working in these firms is really soul-shrinking. Most of the work you do involves one corporation suing another corporation. It doesn't matter who wins. People work incredibly long hours to justify extraordinarily high fees. Associates are paid a salary, but the firms charge clients by billable hours, so cases are over-lawyered. An immense amount of time and money is spent on pretrial discovery motions and appeals on motions. The pretrial procedures can go on and on and on. When I was in the Attorney General's office, I hired a lot of women who had gone into law hoping to do something that they believed in. They took very large pay cuts to come work in the public sector. I don't know if I'm talking bullshit, but my sense is that the lower levels of the profession will continue to be open to women, but not the higher levels."

Liza Janoff, who graduated from law school in 1990 and now runs a public defender's office in Colorado, says that her University of Colorado Law School class was more than 50 percent female, but that her area of criminal defense is still mostly male. "Clients go to men for criminal defense because they think a male attorney will be tougher," she said. "There are two exceptions. The first are sex crimes. The defendant figures that the jury will think that if this guy is being defended by an attractive woman, there is no way he's guilty. Second, women defendants go to women [to represent them]. We're seeing a surge of women defendants these days from cases involving methamphetamine. Women in their thirties and forties are picking up several felonies in a matter of months because of the drug."

Janoff says that she has experienced absolutely no sexism in the courts: "Judges have seen women appear before them in numbers for the last 25 years. They're totally used to it." She sees no difference between her generation of female attorneys and the young women who are entering law today—except, perhaps, that the younger women are more casual. "Men have to wear a jacket and tie to court. But you can get away with more as a woman. I sometimes go into court with a skirt and sweater. But I've been shocked at how dressed down some of these younger women are. One of them had that kind of short, stylish haircut, you know, dyed platinum blond

Dan Kindlon, PhD

on top with dark underneath, and she wore a jean jacket into court! I kid you not."

~

The legal profession—especially the bigger, high-status law firms—has been much slower in hiring part-time workers than the medical profession. The National Association for Law Placement determined from a survey of law firms that the number of attorneys working on a part-time basis increased from 2.9 percent in 1999 to only 4.1 percent in 2003. Although nearly all of the firms surveyed said that they have a policy of allowing part-time opportunities on a case-by-case basis, the small number of lawyers actually doing part-time work would seem to indicate that the policy is more theory than reality.

In an interview with *The Reporter,* Diane Yu, chair of the American Bar Association's Commission on Women in the Profession, said that part-time workers aren't taken seriously at law firms, and anyone asking for a reduced work schedule is ruining any chance she would have of making partner.[30]

Adam, a partner at a New York City law firm, said that in big-city practices like his, entering classes of new lawyers are about 50-50 men and women. The attrition rate for women, however, is significantly higher than for men. "By year seven or eight," he said, "there are maybe only 10 percent of women left over. They mostly leave to have kids. There is a retention price for the firm—you have all these talented women, and they're leaving. So, this isn't just altruism—you invest so much in training that even if you can keep someone for one extra year it is a big advantage."

Adam admits that children are not the only reason women defect from firms like his. "There is still a big macho culture at a lot of firms," he said. "Everybody complains about all the work, but it's also a badge of honor. In some cases, these environments aren't all that friendly to women anyway—it can be kind of like a big fraternity house."

Adam says that in his firm and others there has been some movement toward non-equity counsels and even non-equity partnerships, and the firm has a flex-time program that is a partnership track. "We are trying to convince ourselves that it will work," he said. "Last year, we had a woman who made partner who had been on flex-time for two or three years. That was huge, really big. We've had other women who have gone to flex-time after making partner. I think the real breakthrough will come when it isn't just women who want flex-time."

The overall impression that Adam and other lawyers gave us was that flex-time was becoming a pressing issue at big firms. Talented women were going into law, but the profession was unable to keep most of them, unlike medicine. The attrition of women out of law was costing big firms substantial sums, and they were grappling with how to deal with this issue. By the time today's teenaged girls graduate law school, we expect the field to have changed at least somewhat and become more woman-friendly.[31]

Judgeships are an area of law where women are clearly making their presence felt. Since 1981, when the first female U.S. Supreme Court justice, Sandra Day O'Connor, was appointed to the bench by President Ronald Reagan, the number of women judges has risen sharply. Currently there are 225 women who are sitting federal judges, 29 of whom are chief judges, each about 18 percent of the total.[32]

Just as women doctors tend to be more aware of "women's health" issues than male doctors, there is evidence that women judges may be more sympathetic to women's legal issues than their male counterparts. Gender composition of the bench affected federal appellate court outcomes in Title VII sexual harassment and sex discrimination cases in 1999, 2000, and 2001. Female judges decided for plaintiffs more often than male judges. Moreover, male judges on panels with female judges decided for plaintiffs more than twice as often as those on all-male panels.[33]

This does not mean that female judges are soft on crime. Women do not dispense a gentler form of justice than men. Three studies found that offenders sentenced by female judges were significantly more likely to be sent to prison than comparable offenders sentenced by male judges. Female judges in Pennsylvania imposed longer sentences than their male colleagues, and black female judges in Detroit imposed substantially longer sentences on offenders convicted of sexual assault than black male judges did.[34]

It is clear that women can be as tough as men when they need to be. The psychology of hybrid alpha girls is decisive and "rule-based" as well as empathetic and nurturing. They will have as much determination, charisma, and self-confidence as any man.

We have all known women who project authority and moral clarity and instill courage. Still, the association between the words "leader" and "man" persists in most people's minds.[35] Americans today would prefer, by a two-to-one margin, to work for a man rather than for a woman.[36] Since the 1980s, however, this gap has shrunk. Twenty-five years ago only 7 percent of us preferred to work under a woman, while 63 percent felt that a man would make the best boss (30 percent didn't care one way or another).

Although the general public still thinks men should lead and women should follow, some business leaders are beginning to challenge that assumption.

→ Popular books on business, such as *The Female Advantage: Women's Ways of Leadership* and *Why the Best Man for the Job Is a Woman* suggest that "what business needs now is exactly what women are able to provide."[37] They argue that women corporate leaders "blend feminine qualities of leadership with classic male traits." Women have shown that they "can play with the 'big boys' and beat them at their own game."[38]

→ Margaret Heffernan, a former CEO of eCommerce giant CMGI analyzes the current business environment and writes in the tech-business periodical *Fast Track* that "women are building a parallel business universe. It's one in which companies work differently." Moreover she believes that because of their more honest approach to their work and personal lives, "the future of business depends on women."[39]

→ A cover story in *Business Week* magazine titled the "New Gender Gap" says that "Men could become losers in a global economy that values mental power over might."[40]

More women are rising into leadership roles at all levels in the business world, including elite executive positions. In 1972, women occupied only 18 percent of managerial and administrative positions in the U.S. By 2002, that figure had increased to 46 percent.[41]

In Fortune 500 companies, both the percentage of women among all corporate officers (15.7 percent) and CEOs (1.4 percent) are at all-time highs,[42] although the CEO figure especially shows us how far women have to go to attain real parity with men in the business world. Projected out to the time when the oldest of the alpha girls in our sample will be approaching retirement age, women's presence on major corporate boards—although steadily rising—will still not be at the level mandated by the Norwegian parliament for 2008 (see Figure 7-4).

Nonetheless, one of the main reasons that businesswomen are on the rise is that their traditionally feminine qualities are more suited to the "new" business climate of today. The twenty-first-century corporation has become a kinder, gentler place to work. Management

Figure 7-4

FORTUNE 500 BOARD SEATS—PERCENT FEMALE, PROJECTED TO 2050

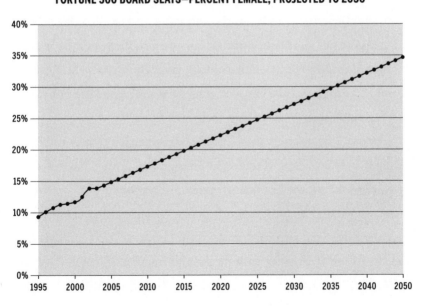

gurus emphasize that the "my way or the highway" style of management and top-down hierarchical systems are obsolete.

Progressive business leaders today are using a "transformational" rather than "transactional" style to run their companies. The transactional style rewarded employees with salary bonuses or perks when they met desired goals and punished or corrected them when they failed to meet objectives. The transformational approach focuses on building a *team,* whose members can act on their own initiative to creatively solve problems. The team approach is less hierarchical than the traditional business model and does not depend on a system of individual punishments and rewards.

A look at the management styles of some of the top women executives in the U.S. suggests that they have adopted this transformational management style. Orit Gadiesh is one of *Forbes* top 100 most powerful women. As chairman of the board of Bain & Company, a business consulting firm, *Forbes* reports that she has been successful because "rather than pursuing conformity among her employees or issuing orders, she tries to guide colleagues and to encourage them to experiment." Gadiesh says that her management style "serves to unify a global organization like ours in an environment where everything is changing. It builds a level of trust so that we are not just a collection of people each doing their own thing." [43]

Cynthia Harriss is unabashed about showing her nurturing, feminine side as president of retail clothing giant Gap Inc. "Gap is very inclusive and it's not just about women, it's about people. . . . We've got policies that make it easy for people to have an opportunity to live their lives and still contribute to the company."[44] When the Girl Scouts of the USA went looking for a new CEO in late 2003, they chose Kathy Cloniger because of her "warm and inclusive management style, her skill at partnering and her deep commitment to diversity."[45]

The effectiveness of the inclusive leadership style may have to do with the fact that women are perceived as better than men at forming and maintaining relationships, says Sally Helgesen, author of *The Female Advantage,* applying Carol Gilligan's arguments of boys-as-separate and girls-as-connected to corporate leadership.

"Male children," writes Helgesen, "learn to put winning ahead of personal relationships or growth, to feel comfortable with rules, boundaries, and procedures . . . Females learn to value cooperation and relationships; to disdain complex rules and authoritarian structures and to disregard abstract notions like the quest for victory if they threaten harmony in the group as a whole."[46]

Do all women business leaders have a transformational rather than transactional style of leadership? And is the transformational style really more effective in the marketplace? Alice Eagly and Linda Carli found that women managers tend to be slightly more transformational than their male counterparts, and the transformational style tended to be a bit more effective than the transactional style, although that wasn't true in all managerial contexts.[47]

For some companies, it may important that women are *perceived* to be better managers than men, because the public thinks of them as less greedy than men and more likely to be honest and fair. Americans don't trust corporations to play by the rules. In a recent Roper poll, 72 percent of Americans said that corporate corruption was widespread; only 2 percent rated chief executives as "very trustworthy."[48]

The public's confidence has been battered by the recent scandals of Enron, Tyco, and Adelphia and disgust over Halliburton's cozy relationship with the Bush administration. The public is also fed up with the reports of the huge salaries, bonuses, and golden parachutes that have been given to business executives.[xii] Phillip Purcell, for example, received $113 million dollars to *leave* Morgan Stanley.

Some institutions hire women for leadership positions to make a statement about the nature of their organization. A woman executive signals that the organization is modern, progressive, and innovative. In some cases, hiring a woman for a top management position demonstrates that an institution has changed. When MIT hired its first female president, the move was heralded as having "great symbolic importance at a school that has publicly examined its own history of bias against women and still struggles to recruit female faculty members in the sciences and engineering."[49]

As a group, people tend to trust women more than men—with good reason! Men commit far more crimes than women[50] and consume more alcohol and drugs. Even among relatively conservative, Red State Americans, almost half believe the country would be better governed overall if more women were in political office and that women would be especially beneficial in areas such as health care reform and environmental protection.[51.]

Our survey supports the idea that women are more worthy of our trust than men. In our sample, there were some interesting differences between girls and boys on our indicators of moral and ethical

---

[xii]Today, American CEOs earn 185 times what the typical U.S. worker makes, up from a 26:1 ratio in 1965. Source: Sylvia Allegretto, Jared Bernstein and Lawrence Mishel, *The State of Working America 2004/2005*. Ithaca, NY: Cornell University Press (2005).

Dan Kindlon, PhD

behavior. There were also notable differences between alpha and non–alpha girls.

One of the biggest differences between boys and girls in our sample was how bad they feel when they lie. Girls feel worse than boys and alpha girls feel worst of all. This is true for all children in grades six through twelve. But it was especially pronounced when we restricted our analysis to students in grades nine through twelve (see Figure 7-5). This last analysis is important because it is more predictive of adult behavior.[52]

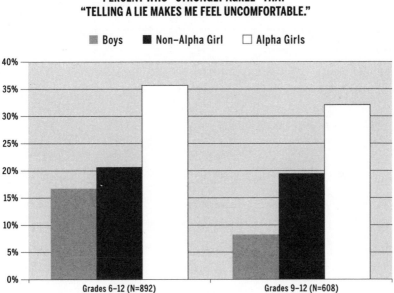

Figure 7-5

**PERCENT WHO "STRONGLY AGREE" THAT
"TELLING A LIE MAKES ME FEEL UNCOMFORTABLE."**

The other side of the lying question may even be more relevant, that is, the group of adolescents who say that lying *doesn't* make them feel uncomfortable. As Figure 7-6 on page 208 shows, there are almost no alpha girls in this category. Antisocial personality disorder—a category of persons who, in earlier terminology, would have been referred to psychopaths or sociopaths—is characterized by a lack of guilt or remorse after wrongdoing.[53] A marvelous book of case studies of psychopaths, *The Mask of Sanity* by Hervey Cleckley,[54] included many successful businessmen. Indeed, the most direct route to fattening the "bottom line" may be the ruthless ability to cut ethical and legal corners, bilk unwary consumers, or mercilessly destroy a competitor.

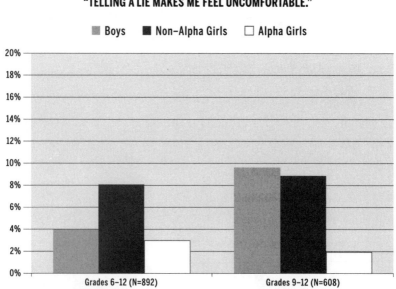

Figure 7-6

PERCENT WHO "STRONGLY DISAGREE" THAT "TELLING A LIE MAKES ME FEEL UNCOMFORTABLE."

Parents should strive assiduously to give children a set of principles to live by, and children should feel bad when they fail to live up to these principles. Not so bad that they are incapacitated or massively depressed. But bad enough so that they will work harder to avoid that feeling the next time around.

Dan Kindlon, PhD

We know that we have done our job as parents if our children uphold these principles even if they know they wouldn't be caught if they didn't. That is clearly the case with alpha girls: they are far more likely than boys or non–alpha girls to have an internal set of controls on their behavior.[55]

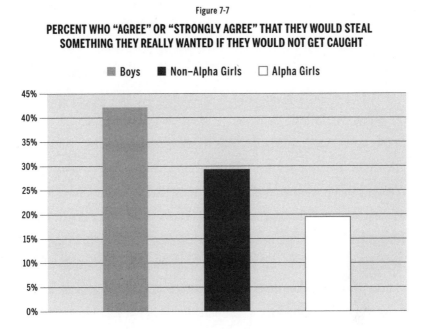

Figure 7-7

PERCENT WHO "AGREE" OR "STRONGLY AGREE" THAT THEY WOULD STEAL SOMETHING THEY REALLY WANTED IF THEY WOULD NOT GET CAUGHT

Psychopaths or near-psychopaths have trouble internalizing these principles. They are physiologically under-reactive to discipline or punishment. Our alpha girls, on the other hand, were prime examples of children who readily absorb these lessons. The alphas were, for the most part, temperamentally more sensitive than the norm.

It should hearten employers who want to create gender equality that the evidence points to the conclusion that women in management make companies more profitable, even among the Fortune 500. A 2004 study by Catalyst, an organization that works to advance women in business, looked at a representative sample of Fortune 500 companies between 1996 and 2000 and ranked them on their level of "gender diversity."[56] These firms had, on average, 10 percent women in top management. Some companies had no women at all in top management; others had enough women big shots to satisfy the Swedes—close to 40 percent. (Companies with gender diversity percentages no higher than 5 percent included: Bank of America, ExxonMobil, Northwest Airlines, Proctor & Gamble, Goodyear, Motorola, and the Disney Company. The most women-heavy companies, those that averaged just over 20 percent women in top management, included: American Express, Coca Cola, Enron, Halliburton, McDonalds, Phillip Morris, Merck, Mattel, and U.S. Air.)

Catalyst reported that the companies with the most female top executives outperformed those with the fewest. Women-friendly companies had a 32 percent higher return to investors than companies with fewer women in top spots. The study does, however, have a major flaw: correlation is not causation. Although there is a link between how much money a company made between 1996 and 2000 and the number of women in top management, it is not necessarily the case that having more women bosses actually had anything to do with the higher earnings.

Women are more likely to be found in certain kinds of industries: health care, utilities, consumer goods, and pharmaceuticals. They were less likely to work for companies in aerospace, defense, energy, and information technology. The late 1990s were a boom period for pharmaceuticals and a bust for the energy and the defense industry. Give the Catalyst researchers credit. They looked into this possible flaw, corrected for it in their statistical analysis, and found that the more women-heavy companies still made more money for their shareholders.

The most straightforward way to test this hypothesis is to look at a given industry and see if the relationship between the percentage of female execs and higher earnings still emerges. It does. Take consumer discretionary products—items such as soft drinks, toys, and computers. The companies with the greatest number of women at the top returned a whopping 70 percent more money to their shareholders than those with the fewest women on their management teams.

There was one notable exception. Information technology companies that had the most *men* in management far outperformed those with the most women at the top. Nonetheless, the weight of the evidence is in businesswomen's favor, and it is hard for anyone interested in making money to ignore Catalyst's conclusion: "Giving women a seat at the decision making table is smart business."

At least one Wall Street investor agrees, according to *New York Times* OP-ED columnist John Tierney. In a column titled "What Women Want," Tierney discusses the Catalyst study along with other research that suggests, compared to women, men are overconfident and far too competitive for their own good. Tierney writes, "You can argue that this difference is due to social influences, although I suspect it's largely innate, a byproduct of evolution and testosterone. Whatever the cause, it helps explain why men set up the traditional corporate ladder as one continual winner-take-all competition—and why that structure no longer makes sense."

Tierney backs up his conclusion with an anecdote: "A friend of mine, a businessman who buys companies, told me one of the first things he looks at is the gender of the boss. 'The companies run by women are much more likely to survive,' he said. 'The typical guy who starts a company is a competitive, charismatic leader—he's always the firm's top salesman—but if he leaves he takes his loyal followers with him and the company goes downhill. Women CEOs know how to hire good salespeople and create a healthy culture within the company Plus they don't spend 20 percent of their time in strip clubs.'"[57]

Alphas may forego the corporate world and start their own businesses, which is already a trend among women. As one bright young alpha said: "If I don't fit into GE or Ford or IBM that's not my problem. That's their problem." According to the Center for Women's Business Research (CWBR), women are starting businesses at twice the rate of men, many using their corporate experience as a training program.[58] If corporations can't adapt—if they can't provide an ethical, collegial, egalitarian work environment—it's their loss.

This generation of alpha girls may be our best hope for stopping corruption in business and politics. Their intellect, drive, and leadership skills, combined with their strong ethical sense, will, one can hope, help institutions move from Machiavellian tactics to ways of operating in the world that are more honest and humane.

In whatever profession—business, politics, medicine, or law—that alphas choose to ply their talents, they will doubtless leave their mark. They are entering a work world in which there is an accelerating movement toward parity and opportunity for women. As a group, they realize the scope of this trend, and they intend to exploit it.

CHAPTER EIGHT

ALPHAS IN LOVE

"I want to be able to support my kids. I don't want to be dependent.
I want control over my life."

—Seki, age 16

As ambitious as alphas are as a group, many of them realized that they'll be faced with tough choices if they want to get married or have kids.

Women of past generations have often had to compromise their personal ambitions to fulfill more traditional domestic roles. But our sense was that if members of the alpha generation choose to stop working when they have kids it will be a *choice*, not a necessity that has been forced upon them. The workplace is already morphing to accommodate women, and the alphas will continue to force changes that reflect what we will see are their family-centric values and their desire for challenging work.

As we've seen, alpha girls are more achievement-oriented and highly motivated to become experts in their fields than non–alpha girls. More of them want to be successful at their jobs. As it turns out, they are also more motivated to be "successful" on the home front. Alpha girls are nearly unanimous in agreeing that having a good marriage and family someday is extremely important to them. It is more important to them than their non-alpha counterparts, for whom job prospects are not as good[1] (see Figure 8-1).[i]

Figure 8-1

PERCENT WHO "AGREE" OR "STRONGLY AGREE"
THAT IT IS IMPORTANT FOR THEM TO SOMEDAY HAVE...

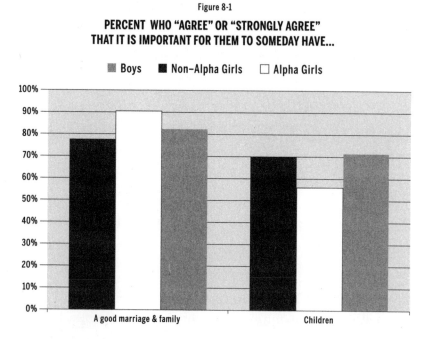

Will the alphas be able to "have it all"—the rich family life they say they want and the dynamic careers they say are important to them? Do they think that they can have it both ways because they're young and naive? Many of their older sisters have found that the juggling act between career and family just doesn't work.

[i] Difference between alpha girls and both boys and non–alpha girls is statistically significant at $p < .05$ in multivariable analysis adjusting for socioeconomic status, grade in school, race/ethnicity, and stay-at-home mom.

Dan Kindlon, PhD

Shannon, a 35-year-old medical researcher, bears the primary workweek childcare burden for her 2-year-old daughter. Her husband, an attorney, often works 12-hour days. The couple is thinking about having another baby, but Shannon is torn: She has only three months of maternity leave.

"I don't want to give up my job," Shannon said. "But how will I be able to leave a new baby? Society doesn't make it easy. 'Having it all' is a farce. For most of my friends there is no balance—either they put their kids in daycare and work full-time jobs or they give up their own aspirations to stay home full-time."

The alphas were aware of this dilemma. Courtney, a ninth grader at a competitive private school in California, is a straight-A student, speaks French, and plays varsity tennis. Her father, a venture capitalist, has a doctorate in economics from MIT. Her mom, an MBA from Stanford, moved up the corporate ladder to become the chief financial officer of a mid-sized technology company. "But then she quit when she had kids," Courtney said.

Courtney (like many other alphas her age) is already is thinking about a career. "I want a job where I'm happy AND make lots of money, maybe in venture capitalism like my dad," she said. "But I want to have kids when I'm older—after I've had a career. I want to stay home and focus on them. That's what my mom did and it was really good."

Helen, a junior at the top of her class in a large public school in Portland, Oregon, says her parents were relatively young when she was growing up, but she doesn't plan on following in their footsteps. "I am definitely going to get married," she said. "Sometimes I think about my ideal wedding. I have a fantasy about my dress—a romanticized idea. But I don't want to get married until I'm in my forties."

Helen said she plans to be the "dominant one" in her marriage, modeling herself on her mom, who is an insurance executive, rather than her father, who is a computer programmer. "I'm not going to get bogged down with a man," Helen said. "I want to accomplish a lot. I have great dreams. I'd like to be an astronaut. I'm really opinionated. I don't want to have to defer to anyone. My mom wears the pants in the family. She's outspoken and everyone bows down to her. Yet she's totally feminine."

Recent trends show that alpha girls like Helen and Courtney won't be alone if they decide to delay having children in order to establish a career and gain financial independence. Over the last 10 years, the percentage of births to mothers over 30 has been steadily growing, while the number of babies born to women in their early twenties has fallen (see Figure 8-2).

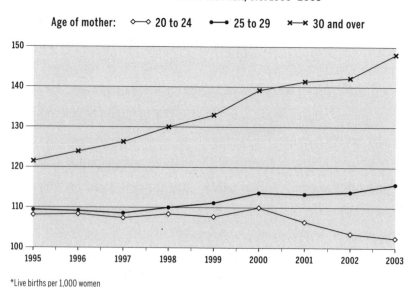

Figure 8-2

BIRTH RATES* BY AGE OF MOTHER, U.S. 1995–2003

Age of mother: ◇—◇ 20 to 24   ●—● 25 to 29   ✕—✕ 30 and over

*Live births per 1,000 women

Dan Kindlon, PhD

A number of the alphas we interviewed, especially those who come from more disadvantaged homes, want to make sure they are successful enough in their careers to be able to provide for their children by themselves, without having to rely on their partners. For these girls "having it all" doesn't necessarily include being with a man.

Seki is a stellar student and vice president of her sophomore class. Her father is an African American computer technician; her mother, who is Japanese, owns a cleaning service. Seki wants to be the first in her family to go to college. "I want to be a kid surgeon," she said. "I want to be able to support my kids. I don't want to be dependent. I want control over my life."

That impulse wasn't confined to alphas from the lower end of the socioeconomic spectrum. We would have thought that alpha girls who came from broken homes might place a high value on independence.[ii] But even girls who came from marriages that were intact had strong feelings about self-sufficiency.[2]

Becky, the alpha who wants to be a movie producer, said: "I don't want to live in the suburbs. I want to travel. I don't want to settle down. Money is important. I want to have a job where I don't want to have to depend on a husband. My husband's career would have to fit with my career. I want to know that if anything happened to him or our marriage that I'd be okay. I want to be able to support my child by myself."

Seki and Becky are good examples of the new alpha girl psychology. As they deal with identity issues of adolescence, they are follow-

[ii] 76 percent of alpha girls from intact families indicated that they expected to get married vs. 55 percent of alpha girls from non-intact families. Chi-square = 10.4 (df = 4); p < .05.

ing a route that has traditionally been associated with boys. These girls are forming an identity based on what *they* want, not based on the needs of the collective web of their most important relationships. There is also a theme of connectedness in their stories, however. They want connection with a child, perhaps in order to reproduce the symbiotic bliss of their own early maternal connections. In this part of their approach to life, as elsewhere, alpha girls are hybrids.

Not all alphas wanted to wait until their late thirties or early forties to have kids. Some said they wanted to become moms in their late twenties or early thirties. They cited studies that had shown that it was harder for women to become pregnant as they aged and that the risk of health problems for both mother and child increased as women got older. They also wanted to be younger rather than older parents, both so that they had more energy for their kids and so they would be able to better relate to them—there wouldn't be as large a generation gap.

Courtney was one of a number of alpha girls who envisioned working part-time or stopping work when she had kids. These alphas thought it was healthier for kids to have a stay-at-home mom. They also didn't want to dilute their experience of motherhood—they wanted to give themselves to it completely. One summed up the feelings of many: "I don't want to miss my child's first step."

Regardless of whether they were going to work or not work, cut back or "opt out," almost all the alphas we interviewed wanted a family. In this, they are typical of their generation. A 2002 study commissioned by the American Business Collaboration (ABC)—a consortium of eight major corporations including ExxonMobil, General Electric, and IBM—clearly showed that young people of both sexes in the workforce are more family-centric than their parents were.[3]

Dan Kindlon, PhD

The ABC study surveyed a random sample of workers in four age groups, which they designated as Gen-Y (18–22 yrs.), Gen-X (22–37), Baby Boomers (38–57), and Matures (58 and older). The researchers also looked at similar survey material from 1977 to compare, for example, how Boomers felt about their careers when they were the age of the current Gen-Ys.

Some of the study's major findings are relevant to the alpha future:

→ Younger workers not only say that they want to spend more time with their families—they do, especially working fathers. About 50 percent of both Gen-X and Gen-Y workers say that they put family before work, compared to only 41 percent of Baby Boomers. Gen-X dads spend about an hour more per day with their children than dads did in 1977 (see Figure 8-3 on page 220)[iii]

→ Workers who put families on a par with or above work are mentally healthier, have greater satisfaction with their lives, and higher levels of job satisfaction than those who say that work comes first.

→ Younger workers want to work fewer hours and are less likely than workers in previous generation to want more job responsibilities. This is especially true for younger, college-educated workers, precisely the candidates that corporations view as most likely to move into higher levels of management when they are older.

[iii] There weren't yet enough Gen-Y dads to analyze whether they were more involved fathers, although the preliminary findings suggest that they may end up being even more involved than their Gen-X counterparts.

➤ Married men spend about 42 minutes more per day doing household chores than married men 25 years ago. Married women do about 42 fewer minutes of housework than their counterparts in 1977 (see Figure 8-3, opposite)

➤ One gender stereotype still holds true, however: Among younger college-educated workers, men are more likely (52 percent) than women (36 percent) to have career advancement ambitions.

The ABC study concluded that although much has been written about the "Opt-Out Revolution," defined as employed women leaving the workforce when they have very young children, the real revolution in the younger portion of today's workforce has to do with a downtrend in career ambition. Large numbers of men and women are working hard, but they don't want the trade-offs they would have to make by advancing into jobs with more responsibility.

"There are many possible reasons why Gen-X and Gen-Y employees might be more family- or dual-centric than Boomers," the study's authors write. "These generations are more likely to know first hand what it's like to have had a working mother. They also know what it's like to have seen their parents or other adults put everything into work only to lose their jobs as wave after wave of downsizing hit the economy during their growing-up years. In fact . . . we found that 42 percent of all U.S. employees worked for companies (including large, mid-sized, and small companies) that had downsized over the past year. They have seen the notion of a job-for-life replaced by the notion of 'employment at will,' where employers are less loyal to employees whom they see as 'free agents' responsible for their own 'employability.' Furthermore, today's younger employees have seen

Dan Kindlon, PhD

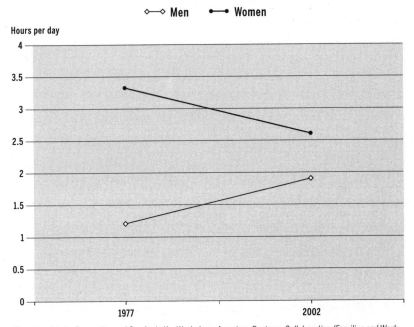

Figure 8-3

**WEEKDAY HOURS SPENT DOING HOUSEHOLD CHORES—
A COMPARISON OF MARRIED EMPLOYEES: 1977 AND 2002**

◇—◇ Men   ●—● Women

Hours per day

Based on data in: Generation and Gender in the Workplace. American Business Collaboration/Families and Work Institute.

work become more and more demanding as the 24/7 global economy has taken hold. Finally, they have been shaped by September 11, 2001, which has caused many people to step back and ask themselves what is truly important in their lives . . . Women tend to be more future-oriented than men, thinking about the potentially negative future consequences of taking a job with greater responsibility . . . Women have broader concerns about the way in which more demanding jobs might disrupt not only their immediate personal and family lives but also other primary social relationships with friends and extended family that they highly value. Employers might think about providing ways for women—and men—to step

Alphas in Love

on and off the fast track and about re-defining the fast track all together."

⧜

Even with changes in the workplace, some alphas said they would happily trade in their career ambitions for motherhood. This is an anathema to the feminists in their mother's generation.

"Many Women at Elite Colleges Set Career Path to Motherhood,"[4] was the headline of a September 2005 article by *New York Times* reporter Louise Story. The article quoted Cynthia Liu, a Yale freshman with all of her alpha girl credentials in place (1,510 SAT, 4.0 GPA, accomplished athlete, musician, and orator) who plans to go to law school but become a stay-at-home mom when she has children. "My mother always told me you can't be the best career woman and the best mother at the same time," said Liu. "You always have to choose one over the other."

According to Story, about 60 percent of girls at Yale agree with Liu—to some extent, anyway. Eighty-five of the 138 girls returning questionnaires to Ms. Story (out of 220 mailed to a random sample of female undergraduates) indicated that "when they had children, they planned to cut back on work or stop working entirely. About half of those women said they planned to work part-time, and about half wanted to stop work for at least a few years."

Not exactly a mass exodus from the workforce, but enough of a problem to make Marlyn McGrath Lewis, director of undergraduate admissions at Harvard, wonder about whether society should expect more from alphas. "When we work so hard to open academics and other opportunities for women, what kind of return do we expect to get for that?" Lewis asked. She went on to note that many of the women at elite colleges like Harvard, women who are being groomed to be society's leaders, may not even have to work. "They are likely to marry men who will make enough money to give them a real choice about whether to be full-time mothers, unlike those women who must work out of economic necessity."

The ease with which some alphas may be willing to give up the careers and independence that feminists fought so hard to make possible for them is a new phenomenon. Alphas have embraced the family-centric values of their generation, and that is part of what distinguishes them from both their mothers and from women who are slightly older than they are.

Sara, 32, is a proto-alpha, an example of what we've come to think of as the link between today's teenagers and the attitudes of the alphas' feminist mothers and, in some cases, grandmothers. Sara, whose father is one of the country's leading hand surgeons, is a surgical resident at a Boston hospital. She did her undergraduate work at Harvard and won a gold medal in crew in the 1998 World Championships as a member of the U.S. Women's National Rowing Team.

Sara and her two sisters were groomed for alpha status. "My parents wouldn't allow dolls in the house," Sara said. "We didn't have toys period. We had Legos, blocks, and books. They wanted to make sure that we had careers—that we would never be dependent on a man for financial support. I think they had friends who had gotten screwed when their husbands divorced them, and they wanted to make damn sure that it would never happen to us.

"My dad would always try to involve us in things he did. On Saturday mornings, we would always make rounds with him. When he entered a patient's room, people treated him like a celebrity. 'The doctor's here!' they'd say, almost gasping. 'That's my dad!' I thought. I wanted to be like him."

Sara had to decide exactly how much she wanted to be like her father when she applied for residencies. "I was trying to decide between surgery and another field, maybe pediatrics or pathology, something with a reasonable residency where you're not always on call. My father had a conniption. He wanted me to be a surgeon. Lots of women say that they want to be surgeons but then bail because they can't take it. I didn't want to be a 'bailer.' And when my boyfriend came to visit me he couldn't believe that I was working so much . . . and I was only a medical student! 'This is just the beginning,' I told him. 'I'm not sure that I want to be a part of that,' he said. 'I'm coming here to be with you, not to watch you work.'"

It was a hard choice, but Sara decided on surgery. "I have to be here at 4:30 every morning," she said. "Can you believe it? It isn't as bad as it used to be. We're required to go home after a certain number of hours. Although its part total chaos and part a total pain in the ass, surgery is just sooo exciting. I mean look at what I'm doing for a living!"

Sara tells me about the "cool" laparoscopic procedures that she's been doing. "Everything is done through these cameras. You just hold the thing up and tease it off the liver, and you put these little clamps on the duct and another one on the artery, and you just kind of burn it off and, whoosh, you're outta there. As much as this is a hectic life, I would so much rather have a full life that I'm trying to back off from."

Sara split with her boyfriend, but she's found someone new who, so far, isn't bothered by her ambition and drive. "He was a Navy

SEAL for seven years," she said. "But he's got the softest side you've ever seen. He's so well prepared to let me do my thing. He came here for a month when I was in the middle of my hardest rotation. I didn't have a day off for weeks. And he was fine with it."

Sara won't be through with her full surgery residency until she is 38 or 39. There are no guarantees that she'll be able to strike a satisfactory work-life balance—loving husband, kids, stellar career. But the fact that she made the decision that felt right for her and didn't compromise because she felt constrained by someone else bodes well for the teenage alpha girls who are years away from these tough choices.

Sara said that men and women generally want different things from marriage, or, more precisely, are willing to accept different conditions. "There are a lot of women who are willing to marry a man that they won't see for the next five years during a residency and put up with it. I can almost guarantee you that a man will not tolerate that in a wife."

This is part of the conundrum that women have faced in the last decades as they've tried to balance the competing needs of marriage and work. In the traditional arithmetic of marriage, men put their own needs above those of their spouse. In broad strokes, men were selfish, women selfless. Women served. They were pliable, flexible, and sympathetic. They were the warm, supportive center from which their husbands drew sustenance and strength to go out and conquer the world.

Sara, of course, will be a very different kind of wife. But she doesn't want a man who will fill the traditionally feminine role and mold his life around her long hours, unpredictable schedule, and the primacy of her career. "I'm not sure that I want to be with a man who is willing to put up with that," she said. "I know a woman surgeon—a real up-and-comer—who came back to work a day and a half after her child was born. She's married to a golf pro at a country club. He's exactly what men want in a wife. He can make his own schedule. But everybody asks: Why is that great lady married to this loser guy—somebody who is nowhere near as accomplished as she is. Well, I'll tell you why: No great guy is going to marry her because no great guy would put up with it."

I see Sara's perception of marriage as traditional in some ways—she doesn't want a man who is subordinate to her. She knows that relationships where women are more powerful than the men they are with tend not to work. She has an unspoken suspicion that in an unbalanced relationship where she is dominant, her partner's pride would be wounded. Sara is also worried that she will be dissatisfied with a man who doesn't match her high level of accomplishment. She is quick to say that her current ex-Navy SEAL boyfriend wakes at four each morning, before she does, to work at his fledgling construction business. He matches her intensity and drive.

Sara is a transitional figure between the alphas and their mothers. The sense we got from alpha girls is that they are, as a group, much more fluid in the way that they view traditional approaches to dominance and subordination in relationships. Sara is psychologically closer in many ways to Judy, the feminist we met in Chapter One, than she is to teenage alpha girls. Judy said that women of her generation were vigilant about any union with a man that led to dependence. "I wince when I hear that a woman has taken her husband's name in marriage," Judy said. "Doesn't she know about chattel?"

Sara was surprised that she was even considering marriage. "I can't believe that I'm thinking about getting married," she said. "It never occurred to me before. I mean there were two guys that I went out with and both of them wanted to get married. I laughed at them. Oh my God, no way!"

Underneath the disdain for marriage that some talented women express is an unstated fear that, as Sara put it, no *great* guy would have them. The younger generation of alpha girls, however, is less cowed by the prospect that their talents are in any way a liability. If a man or boy finds them threatening, they reason, it's *his* problem, not theirs.

Some of our alpha girls did say that boys seemed threatened by them. Roxanne, a brilliant African American alpha, is president of her senior class at an exclusive prep school in Savannah and belongs to Interfaith, a community group linked to the NAACP. Roxanne said she wanted to marry after college but before law school, hopefully to someone who is as focused as she on a career. "It would be kind of weird if he wasn't," she said, adding, "I want one, possibly two kids."

Roxanne said she was taken aback at a recent Interfaith meeting. "All these guys came up to me and were, like, 'Guys don't like you 'cause you're intimidating. You're too strong-willed and people want a girlfriend whose going to be, like, 'Oh, hi,'" Roxanne chirped, doing a dead-on impression of a ditzy "girly-girl." This experience hasn't changed Roxanne's strong personality.[iv] "I'm not like that," she said. "I can't do that."

~~~~~

[iv] As a matter of record, none of her teachers nor anyone in our research group experienced Roxanne's personality as grating or intimidating.

Some alphas haven't been able to find boys who are smart enough to interest them. Ariana, a senior at a Virginia prep school, was one of two students who had received "The Jefferson Award," the school's highest honor, which is given to students with a Jeffersonian range of talents.[v] 2005 was the first year in the school's history in which two kids in the same class received the award. The other recipient was Ariana's girlfriend.

"We've been going out for more than a year," Ariana said. "I approached her. She looks more stereotypically 'whatever' than I do—really short hair, always wears pants. She was caught by surprise."

I asked Ariana if she and her girlfriend had a formal "coming out."

"We never officially came out," she replied. "But we started letting ourselves be seen together in an affectionate way."

"Do you plan to go to the same college or at least try to keep seeing each other?"

"We plan to stay together. You never know what will happen, but it's unique being with her because she and I are on the same level. Boys I've gone out with have been jealous. They were always comparing themselves to me. She's in most of my classes. We're taking Arabic as an independent study. We sit together in AP History. We're in the same math class. It's nice."

Nearly a year after I interviewed Ariana, I re-contacted her by e-mail. She was at Yale. I asked her whether she was still seeing her

[v] Jefferson's genius was celebrated by President Kennedy at a White House dinner for Nobel Prize winners in which he said, "I think this is the most extraordinary collection of talent, of human knowledge, that has ever been gathered together at the White House—with the possible exception of when Thomas Jefferson dined here alone."

Dan Kindlon, PhD

girlfriend. I also asked her to comment on whether she thought her intelligence intimidated prospective mates.

Ariana responded that she was still with her girlfriend, who is in a joint program at Brown University and the Rhode Island School of Design. "Our relationship is very strong, so right now I'm really not considering my 'marriage prospects' other than how they relate to gay marriage. It is easier to be an intelligent woman here, and most women at Yale only date either other Ivy League people or past acquaintances. When people go to parties in Boston or New York, a lot of times they lie about where they go to school so that people will further pursue their interest in them. The men at Yale as a whole are not fazed by intelligent women. It has been really nice, even in just friendly terms."

Ariana and her girlfriend are part of a trend. The alpha generation's wide array of choices includes a new freedom in how they express their sexuality, and their sexual awakening is occurring during a period in which sex between women is no longer taboo. In 2005, the largest federal study of the nation's sexual practices found that 11 percent of women ages 18 to 44 reported having had at least one homosexual experience, almost three times as many as in a similar survey conducted in 1992.[5] Nearly three million women in the U.S. had had sex with a woman during the last 12 months, but only half of these had sex *only* with women during that period. When we asked our adolescent survey group about their sexual orientation, the prevalence of "non-straights" was high. Five percent of the girls labeled themselves as lesbian or bisexual.[6]

Some girls, including Ariana, have political or social reasons for becoming lesbians or bisexuals. Their bisexual identity is not a combination of attractions to women and to men but an attraction to people regardless of their gender. Sexuality is an assertion of the determined egalitarianism of the alpha generation. It is yet another emancipatory proclamation.

Sexuality is part of the expression of the new generation's global identity. They are connected to each other around the world through e-mail and cell phones. They are breaking down the traditional borders between people, and that includes sexual borders.

We shouldn't completely equate idealism and tolerance with the new sexuality. Crossing traditional gender or sexual boundaries gets attention and signals to a society that is increasingly being divided into actors and audience that you are on the cutting edge. Androgyny is hip, cutting edge, the new form of cool.

Emma, a Vassar senior who wants to go into publishing, says her sexual experiences are typical of many of her more intellectually and artistically inclined peers. "I've never 'dated' a woman," she said. "But my relationship with my closest female friend in high school was sort of like dating."

Emma refused to specify her sexuality. "I don't believe in being straight, gay, or bi," Emma said. "Everyone is in ambiguous, weird relationships. I have a back and forth physical relationship with a guy. Sometimes he's gay. Sometimes he's not. Gay, shmay! Who knows? Vassar has a vibrant gay population. They are not singularly motivated by sex. They are emotionally complex men. This type of guy is artistically oriented. There are a fair number of women here who are gay until graduated. The campus lesbians are now getting married to guys."

Emma referred to a growing phenomenon.[7] Since the 1980s, large numbers of college girls have been either "coming out" as lesbians or defining themselves as not exclusively heterosexual. Even though the increase in girl-girl sexual contact seemed to be increasing, it has been difficult for researchers to determine both how widespread it is and why it has been occurring. To further complicate matters, many of these girls do not remain lesbians after they graduate. They are known as LUGs (lesbian until graduation) or hasbians.

The LUG phenomenon now appears to be moving into high school. Dora, an outspoken St. Bridget's junior with a 3.5 GPA who is into rock climbing and riflery, refused, like Emma, to label herself as straight, gay, or bisexual. Dora's "look" was masculine: short dark hair, cargo pants, boots, and a gray T-shirt.

"What about this phenomenon of 'lesbian until graduation?'" I asked her.

"You mean four-year queers? One reason that you see so many lesbian relationships here is that everyone is sexually 'angsty' and there are no boys around. It's like, you might not be gay, but you're gay enough."

The LUG phenomenon may occur because some girls want sex, intimacy, and commitment in the same relationship, while boys are not as interested in commitment, or lack the emotional maturity to cultivate an intimate relationship. As girls age, however, the pool of males who are willing or able to have a committed relationship grows, and some lesbians become hasbians and begin dating men.

Ariana Diamond, a psychologist at the University of Utah, followed 80 non-heterosexual women between 18 and 25 who lived in New York State in the late 1990s for five years, in order to determine if their self-identified sexuality changed during that time. She found that over a quarter of these women relinquished their lesbian or bisexual identities. Half reclaimed heterosexual identities and half gave up all identity labels.[8]

Women's sexuality is more flexible than men's, partially as a result of socialization. Sexual intimacy among women can be an outgrowth of socially acceptable emotional intimacy; this may give women greater freedom than men to explore their affectionate feelings for each other. A greater stigma attaches to homosexual activity among men. We were told by several alphas at St. Bridget's that the school is "lesbian-friendly." But Dora says that boys are homophobic and she'd be "terrified to be gay at a boy's school."

Sympathetic portrayals of lesbians in prime-time media has given girls the message that it's okay to experiment with their sexual identity, a model for their mirror neurons to copy and reproduce at a later time. Prime-time lesbian relationships began to appear as the older girls we studied were moving toward adolescence. The first lesbian kiss on prime-time television was in 1991 on the series *L.A. Law*. Ellen DeGeneres came out on her show in 1997. *Buffy the Vampire Slayer* featured a lesbian relationship that lasted through the 2000–2002 seasons. *The L Word*, which follows a group of gay and straight friends, is a signature series for Showtime.

The alpha girls are not a homogeneous group. While about half feel that there is nothing wrong with two women having sex (about the same percentage as non-alphas) and another 20 percent thinks that it is only "a little wrong," about one in four alphas thinks that it is "extremely wrong."

By no means are all alphas experimenting sexually. About three-fourths of both alpha and non–alpha girls were virgins when they took our survey. Around another 10 percent in both groups were virgins but had had oral sex. A sizeable percentage of them weren't

Dan Kindlon, PhD

interested in sex—they say they're too busy! Others don't want the emotional entanglement, which they feel would divert them from their studies and extracurricular activities.

Natasha, the African American alpha at CATCH, said: "I'm a virgin. I have no plans for having sex. Thirteen- and fourteen-year-old girls here are having sex. But I don't relate to it. It's only for pleasure."

Becky told us: "I don't have a boyfriend. I don't have time. I barely have time for a social life."

Natasha and Becky are at one end of the spectrum. Dora said there are plenty of girls at the spectrum's other end: "When St. Bridget's co-sponsors a dance with one of the boys boarding schools, all the boys have an agenda—they just want to get some." She quickly adds, "But so do the girls."

St. Bridget's girls are not unique. High school girls today are a little more likely to be sexually active than high school boys.[9] Some girls, even middle schoolers, are far more promiscuous than our alpha sample. A couple of girls we interviewed said that sensational media accounts of young girls having oral sex with multiple partners, while rare, does occur.

One 17-year-old alpha told us: "Middle school girls having oral sex with many boys at once is definitely happening and it's starting younger and younger. It's atrocious and sad—a direct result of media exposure, peer pressure, bullying. If a girl has been in a relationship, maybe by grade eleven it would be okay to do it with her long-term boyfriend, provided it is a well-thought-out decision and something she actually wanted to do. Otherwise, it results in loss of self-respect for the girl and continued expectations on the part of boys."

Another alpha was more succinct. She said, simply, "These girls are becoming sex toys."

⌒⌒⌒

Alphas will not only have a choice about how to express their sexuality, but also whether they want to co-parent. Some alphas may choose to be part of the trend of single-parenting that is catching on among educated women. While no one tracks the number of women who actively choose single motherhood, their ranks, while still small, seem to be rapidly growing. Census data for 2004 lists 150,000 women with college degrees with children under 18 who have never

Figure 8-4

**WORKDAY HOURS SPENT CARING FOR AND DOING THINGS WITH CHILDREN–
A COMPARISON OF MARRIED EMPLOYEES: 1977 AND 2002**

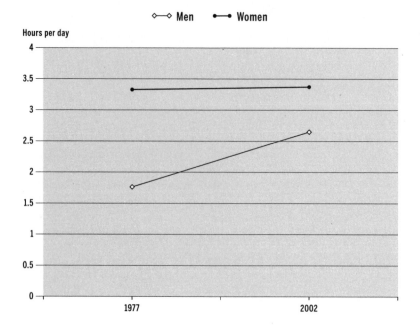

Dan Kindlon, PhD

been married and are the only adult in their household. Their number has tripled since 1990. Family sociologists say women in that group are likely to be single by choice, not chance.[10]

A record 1.5 million babies were born to unmarried women in the U.S. last year, 24 percent of these to teens. Overall, 35.7 percent of all births were to unmarried mothers[vi] (see Figure 8-5).[11]

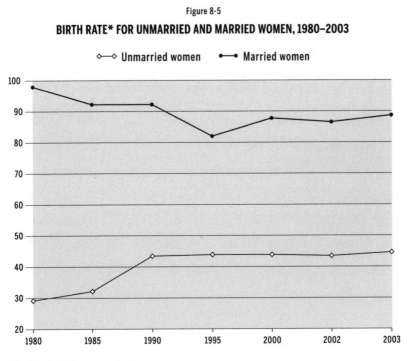

Figure 8-5

BIRTH RATE* FOR UNMARRIED AND MARRIED WOMEN, 1980–2003

◇—◇ Unmarried women　　●—● Married women

*Live births per 1,000 women ages 15–44

The California Cryobank, the largest sperm bank in the country, sent 9,600 vials of sperm to single women in 2005.[12] "Women who order sperm are engaged in a kind of agency that is new and is

---

[vi] These trends were essentially the same for all racial/ethnic groups. Overall, there was a 1.1 percent increase in births to unmarried women. For whites, the rate of increase was 0.9; for blacks, 0.7, and for Hispanics, 1.4.

gaining momentum," said Rosanna Hertz, a sociologist at Wellesley College who is working on a book titled *When Baby Makes Two*. "It's different from women who adopt, who are not breaking sexual norms." Once the norm is broken, however, the rest is easy. Buying sperm over the Internet is a lot like online dating and is almost as simple to order as a book from Amazon.com.

A percentage of women are also choosing to conceive with no intention of having the father around for the pregnancy, birth, or the child's life. This is an interesting reversal: historically, far fewer women with high income and a college education have had children out of wedlock than those with less money and education.

Professional women in their fifties regret not having had a child far more than not having married, said Sylvia Ann Hewlett, an economist whose 2002 book *Creating a Life: Professional Women and the Quest for Children* found that more than a third of women with high-status jobs were childless at 40. Alpha girls have taken note of the problems of older women who have thrown themselves into careers only to find themselves lonely and unfulfilled as they age.

The trends toward single motherhood, lesbian relationships, and greater financial independence for women can be construed as being "anti-family." But these trends have only come about because too many women were paying too high a price to maintain the institution of marriage as it has traditionally played itself out. This generation's girls will accelerate these trends and continue to find new ways to take control of their lives.

Dan Kindlon, PhD

American society has invested heavily in alpha girls. We have poured enormous amounts of social, cultural, and economic capital into their development. Their formative years were an era of economic prosperity and domestic tranquility. Even the shock waves generated by the September 11 attacks and the ensuing U.S. military action did little to restrict the flow of our collective attention to their welfare. They are our best and brightest.

Some alphas will work because they have to; others because they want to. Some will be single moms; some will end up in lesbian relationships and give birth to or adopt kids who will have two mothers. Some will wait to establish careers before they marry. Others will take the plunge and marry young.

Many alphas will couple up with capable men who will earn enough money to take care of them and their children. These alphas may be tempted to opt out, letting their male partners earn the money and be the couple's representative in the professional or business world. These women will be tempted to devote themselves to raising children and enjoy the pleasures that money can buy. But I hope they won't succumb to that temptation. I hope their partners will encourage them to fully engage in the world and to keep exercising and developing their dazzling intelligence and talent. My hope is that these girls will feel some responsibility to devote themselves to the greater good.

Men owe it to themselves to be part of the alpha girl future. When men share the joys and burdens of child care, children can absorb the best of both parents. The alphas have benefited enormously by drawing on the strengths of both their mothers and fathers. It's a crucial part of why they are so impressive.

Alpha girls have the potential to change the world. They are capable of becoming the leaders of the future. They will show us what women look like who are truly emancipated. They embody the best in the American character, and I think that they will be a beacon to the rest of the world. I hope that they further expand the freedoms that their mothers and grandmothers fought so hard for. Of this I have no doubt—these remarkable girls, when they come of age, will be an inspiration for people everywhere.

APPENDIX A–
INTERVIEW AND SURVEY METHODS[i]

The two primary research components for *Alpha Girls* were the Adolescent Life Survey and the Alpha Girl Interviews.

ADOLESCENT LIFE SURVEY

The Adolescent Life Survey (ALS) is a standard short-answer/multiple-choice questionnaire that students completed anonymously, either online or on paper. We designed the ALS to provide a quantitative description of several dimensions of adolescent life, focusing on relationships with parents, self-esteem, mental health, substance use, sexual activity, participation in school activities, and attitudes and aspirations towards career and family. We wanted to use the

[i] The author wishes to gratefully acknowledge the work of Amy Sapp in the design of the ALS and in the preparation of this appendix.

survey results to characterize alpha girls, especially as they were distinguished from boys and "non-alpha" girls.

The following dimensions were included on the ALS:

A. Demographic characteristics (e.g. age, grade in school, race/ethnicity; family size, parental occupations and educational attainment)

B. Relationship with parents (items designed for ALS; CDS-II, 2004)

C. Attitudes toward marriage, family, and career (Herzog, 1982, and Fiorentine, 1988)

D. Career aspirations (NELS, 1988; Albion, 2002)

E. Other future aspirations (Institute of Behavioral Science, 1990)

F. Social relationships (Flewelling et al, 1993; Weinberger and Schwartz, 1990; Vaux, 1988)

G. Attitudes towards delinquency (IBS, Denver Youth Survey)

H. Gender identity (Boldizar, 1991, and Bem, 1974)

I. Sexual identity and behaviors (YRBSS, 2004)

J. Academic achievement (NELS, 1988)

K. Involvement in extracurricular activities (NELS, 1988)

L. Political views (Herbert, 1994; General Social Survey, 2000)

M. Locus of control (Nowicki and Strickland, 1973)

N. Media exposure; Religiosity (ELS, 2002)

O. Behavior problems/anxiety (Achenbach & Rescorla, 2001)

P. Self-esteem (Rosenberg, 1965)

Q. Substance abuse (YRBSS, 2004)

R. Eating disorders (YRBSS, 2004)

S. Common fears (designed for ALS)

We pilot-tested the survey in a convenience sample of 37 middle school and high school students in Boston and refined our measures according to feedback from those data.

STUDY PARTICIPANTS
Schools

The survey was administered to students in grades six through twelve from 16 schools in nine U.S. states and one Canadian province. These states were dispersed geographically in the Northeast, South, Midwest, and Far West. Although the sample of schools is based on convenience, it attempts to represent different types of schools (e.g. 3 religious, 13 secular; 3 urban, 13 rural/suburban) serving a range of students. The table below contains a description of the number of boys and girls by selected school characteristics.

As the table below clearly shows, the school sample is weighted toward independent schools. Obtaining permission to do research at public schools was much more difficult than at independent schools due to legal constraints mandated by the No Child Left Behind law or other logistic obstacles.

Six schools (N=414), including almost all students in grades six through eight, opted to administer an edited version of the ALS that did not contain questions about sexual activity.

School Type	Number	Sample composition		Total
		Male	Female	
Public	6	72	130	202
All girls (independent)	3	0	380	380
All boys (independent)	1	118	0	118
Coed (independent)	6	38	190	228
Total	16	228	700	928

Sample Characteristics

A total of 928 students (700 girls and 228 boys) completed the survey. The tables below give a descriptive breakdown by race/ethnicity, socioeconomic status (SES), and grade level. SES was measured using the father's education or, if that was unavailable, by the socioeconomic level of the school the student was attending. (e.g. affluent prep school = high SES; disadvantaged urban school = low SES).

Race

Race/Ethnicity	Boys	Girls	Total
White	151	483	634
Black	32	74	106
Hispanic	14	27	41
Asian	20	65	85
Other/No answer	11	51	61

Grade in School

Grade	Boys	Girls	Total
6	75	22	97
7	60	48	108
8	7	78	85
9	40	163	203
10	9	116	125
11	14	103	117
12	23	170	193

Socioeconomic status (Father's education level)	Boys	Girls	Total
1 (graduate degree)	122	451	573
2 (completed college)	48	123	171
3 (some college)	17	38	55
4 (high school or below)	41	88	129

Appendix A—Interview and Survey Methods

Within each school, administrators were asked to select a random sample of students to complete the survey during the school day. A random selection of students, for example, could be those in a non-tracked class, such as health/wellness, in which all students in a specific grade have an equal probability of enrollment.

ALPHA GIRL INTERVIEWS

The goal of the alpha girl interviews was to obtain qualitative "ethnographic" information to supplement the data collected from the Adolescent Life Survey. Although we had a semi-structured interview that roughly followed the survey questions to use as a guide, these interviews were meant to be free-form, to allow the girls to tell us about their lives in their own words.

The middle and high schools from which the alpha girls were drawn were primarily from the convenience sample used for the ALS survey. Three additional schools allowed us access to alpha girls for interviews, but refused to participate in the survey.

The interview sample consisted of 113 girls, 32 in grades six through eight, 81 in grades nine through twelve. They came from 15 different schools in eight states and one Canadian province. Like the survey participants, the interview sample was weighted towards independent (N=80) rather than public schools (N=32). Fifty-seven girls attended coed schools, the remainder, single sex. About one-third of the alpha girl interviewees attended schools with a religious (Christian or Jewish) focus. Approximately 15 percent of the interview sample was nonwhite, the majority of these African American.

School administrators were asked to choose one or two girls from each grade who met our alpha criteria—talented, high-achieving leaders. All interviewees and their parents (if students were younger than 18 years old) completed a release form. Girls were almost always interviewed singly in a quiet room at their school, although, on occasion, we chose to interview in groups of two or three. Most of the interviews were digitally recorded. Dr. Kindlon was present, either alone or with one of the other two interviewers (one male, one female) at two-thirds of the interviews and listened to all other recorded interviews.

In addition to our school sample, we interviewed and recorded approximately 40 young alpha women, most of whom were either in college or graduate school. These were chosen by convenience, although all had clear "alpha" credentials.

APPENDIX B–
PROJECTION METHODOLOGIES[i]

Statistical projection, sometimes known as forecasting, is an attempt to predict future trends based on information about what has influenced these trends in the past. In this book, we were primarily interested in predicting trends for women's participation in higher education and selected occupations. All projections are based on underlying assumptions, and these assumptions determine forecasts to a large extent. As in any type of forecast (e.g. weather), accuracy tends to decline over time. It is easier to predict what will happen next year than it is to predict what will happen in 20 years. In our analyses, the trends forecast for the first 5 to 15 years (i.e. 2005–2020) are based on demographic, social, and economic changes projected by the U.S. Census Bureau and U.S. Bureau of Labor.

[i] The author gratefully acknowledges the invaluable collaboration of Amy Sapp in conducting the forecasting analyses and in the preparation of this appendix.

For each projection, we created an influence diagram, outlining the factors we expected to have a significant impact on the outcome. We analyzed these diagrams using Monte Carlo simulation, a Markov modeling technique that uses the description of the provided factors as well as the defined calculations and influences to calculate one possible outcome. The results are a statistically accurate representation of the range and likelihood of all possible outcomes. Deterministic and probabilistic sensitivity analyses were used to examine the potential impact of parameter assumptions and to determine which factors will significantly impact the outcomes in the future. Using this information, we used simulation models to project data into the future, applying smoothers as relevant. Single exponential smoothers were used when historical data have a basically horizontal pattern and double exponential smoothing were used when data were expected to change linearly with time.

Our projections, as with any forecast of the future, cannot account for possible rare or unexpected occurrences, such as infectious diseases and environmental catastrophes. Moreover, the farther apart observations are spaced in time, the more likely it is that there are changes in the underlying social, political, and economic structure during the time gaps. As a result, the underlying processes for annual models (as opposed to models that use observations collected on a weekly or monthly basis) tend to be less stable from one observation to the next. Therefore, caution should be used in interpreting the projections. Statistical modeling was conducted with SAS statistical software, version 9.1 (SAS Institute), TreeAge software 5.1 (TreeAge Software, Inc.), Stata 8.0 (Stata Corporation), and SMLTree (Microsoft Excel add-on).

PART A. ACADEMIC DEGREES CONFERRED

Projections of associate's, bachelor's, master's, doctorate, and first professional degrees took into account the influence of forecasted changes in cohort age structure,[1] post-secondary graduates by sex, race/ethnicity, educational level,[2] institution type,[3] per capita income, and unemployment rate. (Per capita income represents ability to pay tuition,[4] and age-specific unemployment rate acts as a proxy for opportunity costs faced by students.[5])

Degree data used for each academic projection model:

- Bachelor's degrees: Full-time undergraduate enrollment in four-year institutions (lagged two years).[6]
- Master's degrees: Full-time master's degree program enrolment.[3]
- Doctorate degrees: The number of doctorate degrees is a linear function of graduate enrollment lagged one year and the unemployment rate.[7]
- First professional's degrees: Full-time first professional enrollment (lagged one year) and part-time enrollment (lagged two years).[8]
- Medical school graduates (MDs): Medical school enrollment (lagged two years).[9]
- Law school graduates (JDs): Law school enrollment (lagged two years).[3,10]

PART B. BACHELOR'S DEGREE HOLDERS IN THE U.S. POPULATION

We estimated the percent of U.S. women and men aged 25 and over who would have bachelor's degrees in the future by applying our projections of earned bachelor's degrees to projections of the U.S. resident population. Specifically, we summed the projected number of bachelor's degrees into five-year intervals and divided these estimates by the U.S. Census Bureau's projections of the U.S. resident population by sex and age group in five-year intervals.[11]

PART C. WIVES WHO EARN MORE THAN THEIR HUSBANDS

Projection models of wives who earn more than their husbands accounted for historical trends in married-couple earnings ratios,[12] marriage rate, age at first marriage,[13] and income by sex, age, and degree level.[14, 15] These projections also accounted for forecasted estimates of percent women in the labor force,[16] U.S. resident female-to-male population ratio by age,[2] and changes in postsecondary degrees conferred by sex and level (see Part A of this appendix). To account for our assumption that the data will change linearly with time, we applied double exponential smoothing.

$$Y = aX_1^{b_1}X_2^{b_2}$$

PART D. PHYSICIANS IN THE U.S. POPULATION

Projections models of the number of physicians in the U.S. population accounted for forecasted changes in the number of male and female medical school graduates (see "Medical School Graduates" on page 247), changes in the percent of international physicians who will practice in the U.S. (including U.S. and non–U.S. medical school graduates), and forecasted demands for physicians in the U.S. To account for our assumption that the data will change linearly with time, we applied double exponential smoothing.

PART E. FORTUNE 500 BOARD SEATS– PERCENT FEMALE

Projections of Fortune 500 board seats occupied by women accounted for historical trends of female Fortune 500 board members,[17] forecasted estimates of the female labor force,[18] business tax structures,[19] and projections of female MBA recipients[20] (see "First Professional Degrees" on page 247). To account for our assumption that the data will change linearly with time, we applied double exponential smoothing.

REFERENCES

Achenbach, T. M. and Rescorla, L. A. (2001). "Chapter 1: Features of ASEBA School-Age Forms." *Manual for the ASEBA School-Age Forms & Profiles.* Burlington, VT: University of Vermont, Research Center for Children, Youth, & Families; pp. 1–23.

Albion, Majella J. and Fogarty, Gerard J. (2002). "Factors Influencing Career Decision Making in Adolescents and Adults." *Journal of Career Assessment* 10: 91–126.

Bem, S. L. (1974). "The measurement of psychological androgyny." *Journal of Consulting and Clinical Psychology*, 42, pp. 155–62.

Boldizar, J. P. (1991). "Assessing sex typing and androgyny in children: The children's sex role inventory." *Developmental Psychology*, 27, pp. 505-515.

ELS, 2002. Education Longitudinal Study, 2002. National Center for Education Statistics. Student Questionnaire Base Year: 10th Grade. Available at: http://nces.ed.gov/surveys/els2002/questionnaires.asp. Accessed 10/10/04.

Fiorentine, R. (1988). "Increasing similarity in the values and life plans of male and female college students? Evidence and implications." *Sex Roles*, 18, 143–58.

Flewelling, R. L.; Paschall, M. J.; and Ringwalt, C. L. (1993). Social consciousness scale from SAGE Baseline Survey. Research Triangle Park, NC: Research Triangle Institute. (Unpublished)

General Social Survey, 2000. David, J. A.; Smith, T. W.; and Marsden, P. V. National Opinion Research Center. University of Chicago. Online source: http://webapp.icpsr.umich.edu/GSS.

Herzog, A. R. and Bachman, J. G. (1982). "Sex role attitudes among high school seniors: Views about work and family roles." *Institute for Social Research Report No. 9014*. (Ann Arbor: University of Michigan)

Institute of Behavioral Science. Achievement Motivation Scale, Youth Interview Schedule: Denver Youth Survey. Boulder: University of Colorado, 1990 (Unpublished). Available at: www.cdc.gov/ncipc/pub-res/pdf/sec2.pdf. Accessed 10/10/04.

Slaney, R. B. (1988a). "The assessment of career decision making." In W. B. Walsh and S. H. Osipow (Eds.), *Career decision making* (pp. 33-76). Hillsdale, NJ: Lawrence Erlbaum Associates.

NELS, 1988. National Education Longitudinal Study of 1988. Second Follow-up. Student Questionnaire. Prepared by: U.S. Department of Education, National Center for Education Statistics and National Opinion Research Center (NORC), University of Chicago.

NHIS, 2004. National Health Interview Survey Questionnaire, Adult Sample. Document Version Date: 03-May-04. Centers for Disease Control and Prevention. National Center for Health Statistics. Available at: www.cdc. gov/nchs/about/major/nhis/quest_data_related_1997_forward.htm. Accessed 10/10/04.

Nowicki, S., Jr. and Strickland, B. R. (1973). "A locus of control scale for children." *Journal of Consulting and Clinical Psychology*, 40, pp. 148–54.

Rosenberg, M. (1965). *Society and the Adolescent Self-Image*. Princeton, NJ: Princeton University Press.

Vaux, A. (1988). *Social Support: Theory, Research, and Intervention*. New York, NY: Praeger.

Weinberger, D. A. and Schwartz, G. E. (1990). "Restraint inventory from distress and restraint as superordinate dimensions of adjustment; a typological perspective." *Journal of Personality* 58(2): pp. 381-417.

YRBS, 2004. State and Local Youth Risk Behavior Survey. Centers for Disease Control & Prevention. National Center for Chronic Disease Prevention and Health Promotion. Available at: www.cdc.gov/HealthyYouth/yrbs/index. htm. Accessed 10/10/04.

ENDNOTES

Introduction

[1] In addition to the works already named, see also: *In a Different Voice* by Carol Gilligan, *Queen Bees and Wannabees* by Rosalind Wiseman, and *Odd Girl Out* by Rachel Simmons; furthermore, the Harvard Graduate School of Education continues to offer a course entitled "Rethinking Girls:" education in which the students read books such as *Reviving Ophelia*, *In a Different Voice*, and *Failing at Fairness: How America's Schools Cheat Girls*.

[2] See Appendix A for details of the interview methodology.

[3] The alpha girls in this book should be distinguished from the designation used by Rosalind Wiseman in her widely read *Queen Bees and Wannabees*. Wiseman grouped girls as alphas, betas, and gammas. Her alphas were cliquely, cheerleader-type, in-crowd girls. They are mean. Our alphas are, for the most part, positively assertive, appealingly confident leaders.

[4] See Appendix A for details of the survey methodology.

Chapter One

[1] Information on the National High School Mock Trial Championship can be found at. www.nationalmocktrial.org.

[2] Source: U.S. Department of Education, National Center for Education Statistics (2005). *Postsecondary Institutions in the United States: Fall 2003 and Degrees and Other Awards Conferred: 2002-03* (NCES 2005-154).

[3] Source: NCES—Digest of Ed. Statistics; see also Table 2-7 in Costello et al. (2004) SOURCE: U.S. Department of Education, National Center for

Education Statistics, Higher Education General Information Survey (HEGIS), "Degrees and Other Formal Awards Conferred" surveys, and Integrated Postsecondary Education Data System (IPEDS), "Completions" surveys. (This table was prepared September 2002.) N.B. 2001 data were not available for MD and Law.

[4] www.congress.org/congressorg/directory/demographics.tt?catid=gend& chamber=house; Center for American Women and Politics, www.cawp. rutgers.edu/Facts/Officeholders/cong-current.html; Amer, Mildred L. CRS Report for Congress. "Membership of the 109th Congress: A Profile." Order Code RS22007. Updated October 25, 2005. www. senate.gov/reference/resources/pdf/RS22007.pdf.

[5] Source: Costello et al. (2003) Table 8-3.

[6] Source: Center for American Women in Politics, Women in State Legislatures Fact Sheet, 2005. www.cawp.rutgers.edu/Facts/Officeholders/stleg.pdf

[7] Twenge, J. M. (2001) "Changes in women's assertiveness in response to status and roles: A cross-temporal meta-analysis 1931–1993." *Journal of Personality and Social Psychology* 81, pp. 133–45.

[8] According to the U.S. Census Bureau: The amount women age 15 and older, who worked full-time, year-round, earned for every $1 their male counterparts earned in 2004. This amount is up from 76 cents for every dollar in 2003. Online source: www.census.gov/Press-release/www/ releases/archives/income_wealth/005647.html.

[9] See www.usatoday.com/money/companies/management/2003-12-03-womendirectors_x.htm). In 2005, nine Fortune 500 companies, and 19 Fortune 1000 companies are run by women (Source: The 2005 Fortune 500. Women CEOs. *Fortune 500* magazine, 2005). In Canada in 2004, women held 14.4 percent of corporate officer positions in the FP500 (Source: 2004 Catalyst Census of Women Corporate Officers and Top Earners of Canada, 4/27/2005).

[10] 71 percent of mothers with children under 18 work outside the home. (Source: U.S. Department of Labor, Bureau of Labor Statistics. *Women in the Labor Force: A Databook*. May 2005. www.bls.gov/cps/wlf-databook2005.htm)

[11] See also Gentile, D. A. and Walsh, D. A. (2002, January 28). "A normative study of family media habits." *Applied Developmental Psychology* 23, pp. 157–78. The report does note that girls spend less time watching TV and playing video games than boys, but more time on the phone.

[12] Wartella, E., Caplovitz, A.G., and Lee, J. (2004) "From Baby Einstein to Leapfrog, from Doom to The Sims, from Instant Messaging to Internet chat rooms: Public interest in the role of interactive media in children's lives" *Social Policy Report* 18, pp. 3–16. Washington, D.C.: Society for Research on Child Development.

TIME SPENT ON THE INTERNET FOR FUN (NOT SCHOOL)			
	Non–Alpha Girls (%)	Alpha Girls (%)	Boys (%)
Less than 1 hour	33.53	43.31	39.72
1-2 hours	32.36	32.28	34.58
3-4 hours	20.93	15.75	18.22
5-6 hours	7.95	5.51	4.21
7 or more hours	5.23	3.15	3.27

Significant difference between alpha and non–alpha girls in multiple regression model analysis controlling for socioeconomic status, grade in school, and race/ethnicity: (Ð= .2434, SE= .1127, p= .0312).

[14] McCall, R. B.; Parke, R. D.; and Kavanough, R. D. (1977) "Imitation of live and televised models by children one to three years of age." *Monographs of the Society of Research in Child Development* 42, (5, serial No. 173): pp. 1–93.

[15] See Giacomo Rizzolatti, G. and Arbib, M. A. (1998) "Language within our grasp." *Trends in Neuroscience* 21, pp. 188–94. For an excellent non-technical discussion of these neurons, see Blakeslee, S. "Cells that read minds." *New York Times*, Science Desk, Tuesday, January 10, 2006, D1, D4.

[16] *Children Now: Fall Colors: Prime Time Diversity Report* 2001–2002.

[17] The shift toward gender parity on television is supported by empirical data. A recent study conducted by "Children Now" found that among the most popular TV shows for teen girls, a similar proportion of male and female characters rely on themselves to achieve their goals and solve their own problems. (*Children Now. Fall Colors 2003–04: Prime Time Diversity Report*. Printed May 2004.) In 2005, adult male and female characters on prime-time television were almost equally likely to be portrayed as professionals. Thirty percent of male characters and 28 percent of female characters held high-status jobs, such as business executive, physician, attorney, judge, journalist, or politician. The most common occupation for a female character on prime time was attorney (9 percent). An additional 9 percent were portrayed as business professionals, and 5 percent were physicians. As we will see in Chapter Seven, these are three of the most popular projected career choices for the alpha girls in our sample.

[18] For more on this see *Action Chicks: New Images of Tough Women in Popular Culture*, Palgrave Macmillan, 2004.

[19] See for example the discussion of this phenomenon in: Garbarino, J. (March 2006) *See Jane Hit.*

[20] Buckingham, D. and Bragg, S. "Young people, media, and personal relationships." Independent Television Commission, British Broadcasting System. November 2003. www.bbc.co.uk/guidelines/editorialguide-lines/assets/research/youngpeople.pdf.

[21] Becker, A. E. (1995) *Body, Self, and Society: The View from Fiji*. Philadelphia: University of Pennsylvania Press.

[22] Ms. Musings, Blog of *Ms.* magazine. www.msmusings.net/archives/2005/08/what_is_most_un.html. Posted August 19, 2005. Accessed September 7, 2005.

[23] 2004 Fourth Quarter complaints report, *Advertising Standards Canada*—Gender Portrayal Guidelines—www.adstandards.com/en/standards/report.asp

[24] Bavidge, J. (2004) "Chosen Ones: Reading the contemporary teen heroine." In G. Davis & K. Dickinson (eds.) *Teen TV: Genre, Consumption, Identity* (pp. 41–53). London: British Film Institute.

[25] Guttmacher Institute report, February 2004. "Facts in Brief: Contraceptive Use."

Chapter Two

[1] Significant results* comparing alpha girls' and non–alpha girls' responses to father-daughter relationship items:

	β Coef.	SE	p
Quality of relationship with father (Composite variable of 17 father variables)	3.0941	0.9421	0.0011
How would you describe your relationship with your father?	0.2858	0.1163	0.0143
My father can tell when I'm upset.	0.1906	0.1078	0.0775
I can count on my father when I need to get something off my chest.	0.3068	0.1105	0.0057
My father helps me talk about my difficulties.	0.4063	0.1065	0.0002
I tell my father about my problems and troubles.	0.5749	0.2143	0.0080
My father respects my feelings.	0.1921	0.0985	0.0515
I get upset a lot more than my father knows.	-0.3578	0.1100	0.0012
My father doesn't understand what I am going through these days.	-0.2934	0.1164	0.0120

*From multiple regression analysis adjusting for socioeconomic status, grade in school, and race/ethnicity. Alpha girls are the reference group (= 1).

FEMALE SURVEY PARTICIPANTS' RESPONSES TO FATHER-DAUGHTER RELATIONSHIP ITEMS:				
	Always true or Often true		Never true or Not often true	
	Non–Alpha Girls	Alpha Girls	Non–Alpha Girls	Alpha Girls
My father can tell when I'm upset.	29.2%	37.9%	24.6%	19.4%
I can count on my father when I need to get something off my chest.	18.8%	19.0%	33.3%	25.0%
My father helps me talk about my difficulties.	47.9%	55.7%	48.8%	34.7%
I tell my father about my problems and troubles.	21.4%	38.5%	52.4%	32.3%
My father respects my feelings.	75.4%	83.9%	8.5%	4.8%

[3] See Harvey Araton, "Sports of the Times: Proud Fathers Cheer the Women's Sports Movement," *New York Times*, July 17, 2003.

[4] In NCAA Division I athletics, the number of women participating has increased by 150 percent since 1981-1982. Source: http://nces.ed.gov/pubs2005/2005016.pdf.

[5] Significant difference between alpha and non–alpha girls in multiple regression model adjusting for confounders: socioeconomic status, grade in school, and race/ethnicity ($N = 619$, $\beta = -1.0161$, $SE = .3763$, $p = .0071$). No significant difference between alpha girls and boys in multiple regression model adjusting for confounders: socioeconomic status, grade in school, and race/ethnicity ($N = 328$, $\beta = -0.1837$, $SE = .5487$, $p = .7381$).

[6] Significant difference between alpha and non–alpha girls in multiple regression model adjusting for confounders: socioeconomic status, grade in school, and race/ethnicity ($\beta = -0.3944$, $SE = .1108$, $p = .0023$). No significant difference between alpha girls and boys in multiple regression model adjusting for confounders: socioeconomic status, grade in school, and race/ethnicity ($\beta = -0.0556$, $SE = .1339$, $p = .678$).

[7] "I often discuss my future occupational plans with my father."

	Non–Alpha Girls	Alpha Girls
Strongly agree/Agree	68.38%	76.86%
Neutral	21.08%	15.70%
Strongly disagree/Disagree	10.54%	7.44%

Alphas are significantly more likely to discuss their career plans with their fathers, as indicated by multiple regression analysis adjusting for socioeconomic status, grade in school, and race/ethnicity ($\beta = 0.2127$, $SE = 0.1004$, $p = 0.0345$).

"I value my father's opinions about my future occupational plans."

	Non–Alpha Girls	Alpha Girls
Strongly agree/Agree	23.72%	31.66%
Neutral	58.39%	59.17%
Strongly disagree/Disagree	17.89%	9.17%

Alphas are significantly more likely to value their fathers' opinions about future occupational plans, as indicated by multiple regression analysis adjusting for socioeconomic status, grade in school, and race/ethnicity (β= 0.2587, SE= 0.0880, p= 0.0034).

[8] "Are you closer to your father or mother?"

	Non–Alpha Girls	Alpha Girls
Closer to mother	30.0%	24.0%
A little closer to mother	41.7%	39.2%
Equally close to both	18.6%	31.2%
A little closer to father	4.6%	4.0%
Closer to father	5.0%	1.6%

No significant difference between alpha girls and non–alpha girls in multivariable analysis after adjusting for socioeconomic status, grade in school, and race/ethnicity

[9] See page 93 in Parke, R. (1996) *Fatherhood*, Cambridge, MA: Harvard University Press. He reports that in the U.S., Britain, India, Brazil, and other countries, three to four times as many men express a wish for a son as opposed to a daughter.

[10] See, for example, Steinberg, L. (1987) "Recent research on the family at adolescence: The extent and nature of sex differences." *Journal of Youth and Adolescence* 16, pp. 191–97. The exact quote from page 196 of the article is worth reproducing here, if only for the beauty of its language: "Taken together, these and other recent studies…suggest that the father-daughter relationship at adolescence is an outlier: It is distinguished from the other three parent-child dyads by its affective blandness and low level of interaction."

[11] Chaplin, T. M.; Cole, P. M.; and Zahn-Waxler, C. (2005) "Parental socialization of emotion expression gender differences and relations to child adjustment." *Emotion* 5, pp. 80–88. N.B. Although this study was published in 2005, the research on which it is based on data collected in 1988.

[12] Langlois, J. H. and Downs, A. C. (1980) "Mothers, fathers and peers as socialization agents of sex-typed play behavior in young children." *Child Development* 51, pp. 1217–47.

[13] Nancy Hass, "Hey Dads, Thanks for the Love and Support (and the Credit Card)." *New York Times* Style Desk, Sunday, June 16, 2002.

[14] See biographies . . . footnote on Marie Curie

[15] See pages 98–100 in Kindlon, D. and Thompson, M. (1999) *Raising Cain: Protecting the Emotional Life of Boys*. New York: Ballantine, for a trenchant, lucid, and entertaining discussion. See also Fleming, L. M. and Tobin, D. J. (2005). "Popular Child-Rearing Books: Where Is Daddy?" *Psychology of Men and Masculinity* 6, pp. 18–24, in which the authors find that in a random sample of 23 recent parenting books, "Of the 56,379 paragraphs contained in these books, 2,363 (4.2 percent) referred to fathers' roles. Fathers' roles were predominately ancillary to mothers' and often portrayed as voluntary and negotiable."

[16] Other than the Lamb and Parke books, some of the important research articles that discuss the salutary effects of father involvement are: Amato, P. R. and Rivera, F. (1999).

"Paternal involvement and children's behavior problems," *Journal of Marriage and the Family* 61, pp. 375–84; Flouri, E. and Buchanan, E. (2004) "Early father's and mother's involvement and child's later educational outcomes," *British Journal of Educational Psychology* 74, pp. 141–53; Kenny, M. E. and Gallagher, L. A. (2002) "Instrumental and social/relational correlates of perceived maternal and paternal attachment in adolescence," *Journal of Adolescence* 25, pp. 203-219; Koestner, R.; Franz, C.; and Weinberger, J. (1990) "The family origins of empathic concern: A 26-year longitudinal study," *Journal of Personality and Social Psychology* 58, pp. 709-717; Harris, K.; Furstenberg, F. F.; and Marmer, J. K. (1998) "Paternal involvement with adolescents in intact families: The influence of fathers over the life course," *Demography* 35, pp. 201-216; Yogman, M.; Kindlon, D; and Earls, F. (1995) "Father involvement and cognitive/behavioral outcomes of preterm infants," *Journal of the American Academy of Child and Adolescent Psychiatry* 34, pp. 58–66.

[17] See Meaney, M. J.; Aitken, D. H.; van Berkel, C.; Bhatnagar, S.; and Sapolsky, R. M. (1988) "Effect of neonatal handling on age-related impairments associated with the hippocampus," *Science* 239, pp. 766–68.

[18] Henning, M. (1977) *The Managerial Woman*. New York: Anchor Doubleday.

[19] Non–alpha girls were more likely to say that they were more like their mothers than their fathers in multiple logistic regression model adjusting for confounders: socioeconomic status, grade in school, and race/ethnicity (OR= 1.62, 95 percent CI= 1.05 to 2.51).

[20] Mustanski, B. S.; Viken, R. J.; Kaprio, J.; Pulkkinen, L.; and Rose, R. (2004) "Genetic and environmental influences on pubertal development: Longitudinal data from Finnish twins at ages 11 and 14," *Developmental Psychology* 40, pp. 1188–98.

[21] See Ellis, B. J. (1999) "Quality of early family relationships and individual differences in the timing of pubertal maturation in girls: A longitudinal test of an evolutionary model," *Journal of Personality and Social Psychology* 77, pp. 387-401. The explanation for this phenomenon is that very young girls notice at some fundamental biochemical level whether men are important assets to child rearing. If her father is present and involved, her body will delay the onset of puberty until she is older and thus more able to have an involved father for her offspring. If her father is not involved, her biochemistry, shaped by eons of evolution, reasons that she might as well get started bearing children as soon as possible. It is also important to note that most research indicates that later menarche is healthier for girls then early menarche—"early maturing girls are at greater risk later in life for breast cancer and unhealthy weight gain, have higher rates of teenage pregnancy, are more likely to have low-birthweight babies, and tend to show more disturbances in body image, to report more emotional problems such as depression and anxiety, and to engage in more problem behaviors such as alcohol consumption and sexual promiscuity" (from the abstract).

[22] A 3-point increase in father-daughter relationship quality score is associated with a 1-year increase in age of first period among girls in the survey sample after adjusting for confounders: BMI, race/ethnicity, and socioeconomic status (β= 3.02, SE= 1.30, p=.03, Model R2= .40).

Chapter Three

[1] See for example: Jean Baker Miller's *Toward a New Psychology of Women*, second edition. Beacon Press, Boston, 1974. In a section of her book titled "Ego Development," Miller says that "[f]or women, as we have seen, the very structuring of the relationship to other people is basically different than it is for men." See also Carol Gilligan, "In a Different Voice" (1982), page 8: "Since masculinity is defined through separation while femininity is defined through attachment, male gender identity is threatened by intimacy while female gender identity is threatened by separation."

[2] Gilligan, C, (1985) "In a Different Voice: Women's Conceptions of Self and Morality." In H. Eisenstein and A. Jardine, (eds.) *The Future of Difference.* New Brunswick, NJ: Rutgers University Press.

[3] Freud's account of his treatment of Dora, one of his most famous hysterical patients, was seized upon by feminists as an indication of how male psychology was so wrongheaded when it came to understanding women. Dora first saw Freud when she was 18 years old because she was depressed and suicidal. In addition she had fainting spells, aphonia (loss of voice), and bouts of choking. The fainting, aphonia, and choking were diagnosed as hysterical in that they had no known physical origin (e.g. there was nothing wrong with Dora's vocal cords). Her symptoms had begun when she was 14 years old after an attempted seduction,

which included a forced, "passionate" kiss by an older, married, close family friend, "Mr. K." Mr. K. continued his unwelcome advances on several other occasions. Dora was disgusted by Mr. K. Who could blame her? Freud did. Freud's take on the case was that rather than be disgusted by Mr. K's advances Dora should give in to the sexual pleasure that would "naturally" arise from Mr. K's advances. If she stopped repressing her sexual feelings, Freud felt that the hysterical symptoms would vanish.

[4] Gilligan, C. (1982) *In a Different Voice: Psychological Theory and Women's Development.* Cambridge, MA: Harvard University Press. For a review of Gilligan's views on moral development, see Sarah Jaffee and Janet S. Hyde's article, "Gender differences in moral orientation: A meta-analysis," *Psychological Bulletin* 126, pp. 703-726 (2000).

[5] See the case of Little Hans, Freud, S. (1909), "Analysis of a phobia in a five-year-old boy," *Standard Edition* 10, pp. 1–149. A good summary of Freud's ideas on fathers can be found in Etchegoyen, A. (2002) "Psycho-analytic ideas about fathers." In J. Trowell and A. Etchegoyen (eds.) *The Importance of Fathers: A Psychoanalytic Re-evaluation.* New York: Taylor and Francis Inc.

[6] Chodorow, N. (1978) *The Reproduction of Mothering.* Berkeley: University of California Press.

[7] Quotes found on pages 53 and 57 in Chodorow, N. (1978). *The Reproduction of Mothering.* Berkeley: University of California Press.

[8] See page x in the preface to the second edition for some of Chodorow's comments on her psychoanalytic orientation.

[9] See Jean Baker Miller's *Toward a New Psychology of Women,* second edition. Beacon Press, Boston, 1974. Note that Chodorow's *Reproduction of Mothering* was first published *after* Miller's *Toward a New Psychology of Women,* but Miller had drawn on earlier scholarly work by Chodorow (and others) for her book. Even though the two writers independently arrived at some of their ideas about connectedness, for the sake of our narrative I am simplifying their intellectual debts to one another. Another reason that I present Chodorow's ideas before Miller's is that they are more of a direct reaction against Freud.

[10] Quote found on pages 73–74 in *Toward a New Psychology of Women,* second edition. Beacon Press, Boston.

[11] Quote found on page 41 of *Toward a New Psychology of Women,* second edition. Beacon Press, Boston.

[12] For a discussion of evolutionary psychology as it relates to gender differences in behavior, see, for example, Wood, W. and Eagly, A. H. (2002) "A cross-cultural analysis of the behavior of women and men: Implications for the origins of sex differences," *Psychological Bulletin* 128, pp. 699–727.

[13] See Lansford, J. E. and Parker, J. G. (1999) "Children's interactions in triads: behavioral profiles and effects of gender and patterns of friend-

ships among members," *Developmental Psychology* 35, pp. 80-93. See also chapter 2 in Maccoby, E., *The Two Sexes: Growing Up Apart, Coming Together.* Cambridge, MA: Harvard University Press (1998).

[14] Cole, D. and La Voie, J. C. (1985) "Fantasy play and related cognitive development in 2-to-6-year olds," *Developmental Psychology* 21, pp. 233–40.

[15] See page 2 in Maccoby, E., *The Two Sexes: Growing Up Apart, Coming Together.* Cambridge, MA: Harvard University Press (1998).

[16] See *Year-By-Year Chronology Of The Secretarial Profession* by Marjorie Gottlieb Wolfe. Syosset, New York. Available at: www.crazycolour.com/os/secretary_01.shtml.

[17] See, for example the discussion of social structural theory in Eagly, A. H. and Wood, W. (1999) "The origins of sex differences in human behavior: Evolved dispositions versus social roles," *American Psychologist* 54, pp. 408–23. See also Martin, C. L.; Ruble, D. N.; and Szkrybalo, J. (2002) "Cognitive theories of early gender development," *Psychological Bulletin* 128, pp. 903–33.

[18] Erikson, E. *Identity, Youth, and Crisis.* New York: Norton (1968).

[19] See, for example, Lucas, M. (1997) "Identity development, career development, and psychological separation from parents: Similarities and differences between men and women," *Journal of Counseling Psychology* 44, pp. 123–32. See also Bartle-Haring, S. (1997) "The relationships among parent-adolescent differentiation, sex role orientation, and identity development in late adolescence and early adulthood," *Journal of Adolescence* 20, pp. 553–65.

[20] See, for example Bartle-Haring, S. (1997) "The relationships among parent-adolescent differentiation, sex role orientation, and identity development in late adolescence and early adulthood," *Journal of Adolescence* 20, pp. 553–65. See also discussion in Wichstrøm, L. (1999) "The emergence of gender difference in depressed mood during adolescence and the role of intensified gender socialization," *Developmental Psychology* 35, pp. 232–45.

[21] From the Introduction to *School Girls: Young Women, Self-Esteem, and the Confidence Gap*, by Peggy Orenstein. New York: Anchor Books (1994).

[22] American Association of University Women (1991) "Shortchanging Girls, Shortchanging America: Executive Summary." Washington, D. C.: American Association of University Women. The quoted material is from page 5 of that report.

[23] Although the AAUW researchers measured several aspects of self-esteem (e.g. academic confidence, social acceptance), the finding that the authors of the report said was most central to the self-esteem drop for girls was based on a global measure or self-esteem index. This index was simply the average rating a teenager gave to the following questionnaire items:

1)I like the way I look; 2) I like most things about myself; 3) I'm happy the way I am; 4) Sometimes I don't like myself that much; and 5) I wish I were somebody else. The results for this self-esteem composite index showed an even more dramatic drop in self-esteem for girls beginning in middle school as seen below:

SELF-ESTEEM INDEX

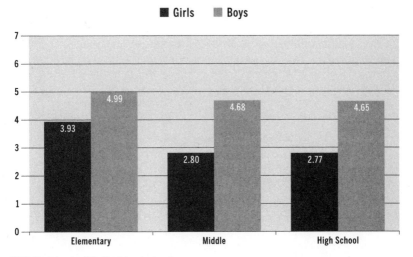

AAUW. Shortchanging Girls, Shortchanging America

[24] See for example: Wichstrøm, L. (1999) "The emergence of gender difference in depressed mood during adolescence and the role of intensified gender socialization," *Developmental Psychology* 35, pp. 232–45. From the article (citations omitted): "Poor self-esteem, that is, self-devaluation, is considered to be intimately associated with depression and low self-worth has on a theoretical basis been suggested as a proximal mediator of stressors and the diatheses in depression has been substantiated by recent research. The crucial role of self-esteem is underscored by the fact that it has been found to be one of the very few factors that are specific to depressive disorders. Moreover, when self-esteem has been accounted for, the gender difference in depressed mood is substantially reduced."

[25] Quote is found on page 5 of the AAUW executive summary report.

[26] For a discussion see, for example, pages 29–30 of Basow, S. A. and Rubin, L. R. (1999) "Gender Influences on Adolescent Development." In N. G. Johnson, M. C. Roberts, and J. Worrell, *Beyond Appearances: A New Look at Adolescent Girls* (pps. 25–52), Washington, D.C.: American Psychological Association. The original citation concerning gender intensification can be found in Hill, J. P. and Lynch, M. E. (1983) "The

intensification of gender-related role expectations during early adolescence." In J. Brooks-Gunn and A. C. Petersen (eds.) *Girls at Puberty: Biological and Psychological Perspectives*. New York: Plenum (pp. 201-230).

[27] Quote from page 83 of Jean Baker Miller's *Toward a New Psychology of Women*, second edition.

[28] For a description of the physical changes accompanying puberty see: Marshall, W. A. and Tanner, J. M. (1970) "Variations in pattern of pubertal changes among girls," *Archives of Diseases in Childhood* 45, pp. 13–23.

[29] See for example: Wichstrøm, L. (1999), "The emergence of gender difference in depressed mood during adolescence and the role of intensified gender socialization," *Developmental Psychology* 35, pp. 232–45. Further, physical attractiveness has repeatedly been found to correlate negatively with depressed mood. Several studies have provided the important evidence that the gender difference in depressed mood is substantially reduced when the difference in body dissatisfaction is accounted for.

Chapter Four

[1] The chart shows level of self-esteem between grades six and twelve for boys, alpha girls, and non–alpha girls adjusted for SES, race/ethnicity, school. All differences between alphas and boys are not statistically significant, although alpha girls had significantly higher self-esteem than non–alpha girls in grade nine, eleven, and twelve.

SELF-ESTEEM

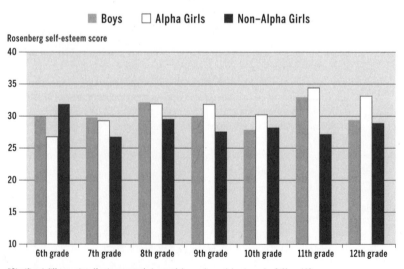

*Significant difference in self-esteem score between alphas and non-alphas in grades 9, 11, and 12.
No significant differences between alphas and boys.

[2] *Method note: The difference between our findings and the AAUW's is also partially due to how self-esteem was measured. The AAUW relied primarily on very globalized measures such as their index based on the average rating of 5 items:* 1)I like the way I look; 2) I like most things about myself; 3) I'm happy the way I am; 4) Sometimes I don't like myself that much; and 5) I wish I were somebody else. In our study we used the 10-item scale from the Rosenberg Self-Esteem Scale (Rosenberg, Morris. 1989. *Society and the Adolescent Self-Image,* revised edition. Middletown, CT: Wesleyan University Press), which is more of the "industry standard." (See Kling, K. C.; Hyde, J. S.; Showers, C. J.; and Buswell, B. N. (1999) "Gender Differences in Self-Esteem: A Meta-Analysis," *Psychological Bulletin* 125, pp. 470-500.) Even when we used a measure more similar to that used by the AAUW, one item—"On the whole I am satisfied with myself"—we did not find any sex differences in self-esteem. See chart below.

RESPONSE TO: "ON THE WHOLE, I AM SATISFIED WITH MYSELF."

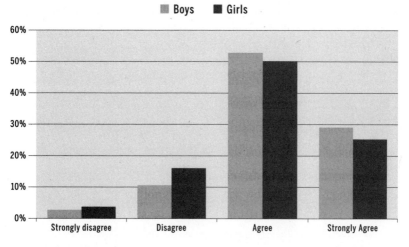

No significant differences between boys and girls.

[3] Kling, K. C.; Hyde, J. S.; Showers, C. J.; and Buswell, B. N. (1999), "Gender Differences in Self-Esteem: A Meta-Analysis," *Psychological Bulletin* 125, pp. 470-500. The overall effect size in this meta-analysis was .21, a small difference favoring males. A relevant passage from that article referring to the difference between these findings and the AAUW study: the relevant section from their article is: "Given these points of comparison, it is probable that the AAUW effect size is inflated. Whether this inflation is due to the particular items used to assess self-esteem, the questions surrounding the self-esteem items, or

random sampling error is a question that is beyond the scope of the current investigation."

[4] For a discussion of measured changes in women's assertiveness, see Twenge, J. M. (2001) "Changes in women's assertiveness in response to status and roles: A cross-temporal meta-analysis 1931-1993," *Journal of Personality and Social Psychology* 81, pp. 133–45. A relevant section of that article states: "The results indicate that sex differences in assertiveness decreased significantly during the contemporary period (1968-1993) . . . the average d [a statistic used in meta-analysis] in 1968 was .40 (a moderate male advantage), whereas in 1993, it was -.07, indicating a slight female advantage. Thus although women used to score considerably lower than men on measures of assertiveness, they now score the same or slightly higher.

[5] Low self-esteem, based on the average of the 10-item Rosenberg scale, was operationalized as a score approximately 1 standard deviation (sd) below the sample mean (mean = 30.4; sd = 5.1). There were 148 students in this group (16.9 percent of the sample).

Effect	Odds ratio	95% confidence interval
SES 1 (lowest)	.37	.19 to .72*
SES 2	.44	.21 to .92*
SES 3	.69	.30 to 1.58
SES 4 (highest)	reference	—
Sex (boy = 0; girl = 1)	.62	.36 to 1.04
Grade level (1 = 6th–8th; 2 = 9th–12th)	.95	.59 to 1.54
Race (0 = White; 1 = Nonwhite)	1.06	.64 to 1.74

*Statistically significant difference comapred to the reference (highest SES) group after adjusting for nonwhite race-ethnicity, sex, and grade in school.

[6] "Boys Academic Slide Calls for Increased Attention," *USA Today*, December 21, 2003; Price, H. (2004) "More than 75 percent of 2004 Washington County valedictorians are female," *Observer-Reporter*: Washington; Vaishnav, A. "Lopsided at the top: Girls outnumber boys among valedictorians," *Boston Globe*, B1, B6, June 6, 2004.

[7] Kindlon, D. *Tough Times, Strong Children*. New York: Miramax\Hyperion (2003).

[8] McCarthy, M. *The Group*. New York: Harvest (1954\1989). Quote is found on pages 227–228.

[9] The link for the WCW Web site is: www.wcwonline.org.

[10] American Association of University Women Educational Foundation/ Wellesley College Center for Research on Women, *How Schools Shortchange Girls—The AAUW Report*. New York: Marlowe and Company (1992).

[11] For a discussion of the new rules for Title IX see http://feministing.com/archives/001127.html.

[12] See AEI Web site at www.AEI.com.

[13] See Rhoads, S. *Taking Sex Differences Seriously*. AEI (2004); and Grigsby, C. and Cobb, N. *The Politically Incorrect Wife: God's Plan for Marriage Still Works Today*. Sisters, Oregon: Multnomah (2003).

[14] See page 105 in Arnold, K. D. *Lives of Promise: What Becomes of High School Valedictorians*. San Francisco: Jossey-Bass (1994).

[15] Steinem, G. *Revolution from Within: A Book of Self-Esteem*. Boston: Little, Brown (1992).

[16] Arnold, K. D. *Lives of Promise: What Becomes of High School Valedictorians*. San Francisco: Jossey-Bass (1994).This quote can be found on page 130.

[17] Other researchers have arrived at a similar conclusion. A 1991 study of adolescent self-esteem that showed boys having higher self-esteem than girls concluded that: We are unsure whether this finding reflects true gender differences in self-esteem or a response bias, because boys tend to be more self-congratulatory than girls in their responses to self-report measures (Maher & Nicholls, 1980), whereas girls may be more modest in their self-reports. Robert Josephs and his colleagues at the University of Michigan and the University of Texas at Austin saw a similar phenomenon—"false uniqueness" among college men. They asked a group of undergraduates with high self-esteem (based on their answers to questionnaires) to rate their uniqueness in 4 ability domains—social, athletic, academic, and creative). The men (more than the women with high self-esteem) judged that fewer individuals would be as good as them in that ability.

[18] See for example Gottesman, E. *The Presentation of Self*. New York: Doubleday (1956).

[19] Gottesman, E. *The Presentation of Self*. New York: Doubleday (1956).

[20] See Kindlon, D. *Tough Times, Strong Children*. New York: Miramax\ Hyperion (2003).

[21] Anxiety, worry, and self-esteem: masculine- vs. non-masculine-identified girls

	Gender Role Identity:	
SURVEY RESPONSE TO:	Girls in bottom quartile (least masculine-identified)	Girls in top quartile (most masculine-identified)
"I am too fearful or anxious."*		
Not true	46.5%	64.6%
Somewhat or sometimes true	36.9%	20.8%
Very true or often true	16.6%	14.6%
"I worry a lot."*		
Not true	34.4%	50.0%
Somewhat or sometimes true	41.3%	33.3%
Very true or often true	24.3%	16.7%
Self-esteem*		
Average Rosenberg self-esteem score	29.7	32.5

*Significant difference between masculine-identified vs. non-masculine-identified girls in multiple logistic regression models adjusting for: socioeconomic status, grade in school, and race/ethnicity.

[22] Substance Use and Sex: Masculine- vs. non-masculine-identified girls

	Gender Role Identity:	
	Girls in bottom quartile (least masculine-identified)	Girls in top quartile (most masculine-identified)
Substance use		
Smoked cigarettes in past 30 days^	10.1%	13.7%
Drank alcohol in past 30 days^	35.6%	36.1%
Used marijuana in past 30 days^	11.1%	11.0%
Sex		
Ever had oral sex^	27.8%	29.1%
Ever had sexual intercourse^	22.3%	27.8%
3 or more oral sex partners^	12.0%	15.6%
3 or more sexual intercourse partners^	6.3%	11.9%

^No significant difference between masculine- vs. non-masculine-identified girls in multiple regression analysis adjusting for socioeconomic status, grade in school, and race/ethnicity.

23

Protective Buffers among Non–Alpha and Alpha Girls	Non–Alpha Girls	Alpha Girls
Grade Point Average over 3.8 (based on 4.0 scale)	35.2%	82.3%
Ever won an academic honor	13.9%	15.6%
Sports involvement score (averaged sum of involvement in all sports)	13.6	14.7
Sports are a "very important" part of life	26.7%	44.4%
Have caring friends to talk with about feelings	91.3%	92.3%
Have friends who can give good advice	87.5%	86.3%
Have friends who help with practical problems, like homework	92.7%	85.8%
Can count on father when "I need to get something off my chest"	18.8%	29.0%
Can count on mother when "I need to get something off my chest"	37.2%	43.2%

[24] See my discussion of religion as a coping mechanism in chapter 5 of *Tough Times, Strong Children*.

[25] In our own work, we have empirically demonstrated with both adolescents (Harter et al., 1996) and adults (Harter, Waters, Pettitt, Whitesell, Kofkin, and Jordan, 1997) that those who acknowledge high levels of false self-behavior also report a constellation of reactions that includes depressed affect, hopelessness, and low global self-worth. We have also found global self-worth to be related to level of voice (Johnson, 1995).

[26] The 3 indicators used to assess anxiety and depression were: 1) Low self-esteem, based on the 10-item Rosenberg scale (rated from 1–4) and operationalized to be a score approximately 1 sd below the mean (sample mean = 30.4; sd = 5.1). This included approximately 17 percent of the sample (score less than or equal to 25, n = 148); 2) Anxiety, based on the mean score of 5 items—fearful/anxious, nervous/tense, self-conscious, worries a lot, feel too guilty scored on a 3-point scale (sample mean = 1.7, sd = .54) and operationalized as a score greater than or equal to 2.25). This identified 17 percent of the sample as high anxious (n = 141); 3) Depression, identified as both high anxious and low self-esteem as defined above (n = 50; 6 percent of the sample). Results for "depression" appear on page 270.

Effect Groups	Odds ratio	95% confidence interval
SES 1 (highest)	.33	.12 to .93*
SES 2	.50	.16 to 1.6
SES 3	.65	.17 to 2.4
SES 4 (lowest)	reference	—
Female	.37	.14 to 1.01
Male	reference	—
Grade 9–12	.94	.43 to 2.1
Grade 6–8	reference	—
Nonwhite race/ethnicity	1.5	.64 to 3.4
White race/ethnicity	reference	—

*Statistically significant difference when compared to reference group after adjusting for sex, grade level, and non-white race/ethnicity.

[27] See Sumuru Erkut, (2001) *Inside Women's Power: Learning from Leaders, CRW Special Report No. 28.* Center for Research on Women, Wellesley College.

Chapter Five

[1] Jo Handelsman, Nancy Cantor, Molly Carnes, Denice Denton, Eve Fine, Barbara Grosz, Virginia Hinshaw, Cora Marrett, Sue Rosser, Donna Shalala, and Jennifer Sheridan. "More Women in Science," *Science* 19 August 2005: pp. 1190-1191. *Note:* Data on PhDs and faculty come from the same "Top 50" departments for each discipline; departments are ranked by NSF according to research expenditures in that discipline. Top 50 departments detailed at D. J. Nelson, "Nelson diversity surveys" (*Diversity in Science.* Norman, OK, 2004). PhD data are from 2001 to 2003, NSF survey of earned doctorates/doctorate records file, Web-CASPAR; faculty data are for 2002 except Astronomy (2004) and Chemistry (2003) from D. J. Nelson, "Nelson diversity surveys" (*Diversity in Science.* Norman, OK, 2004).

[2] Summers, Lawrence H. Remarks at NBER Conference on Diversifying the Science & Engineering Workforce. Cambridge, Massachusetts, January 14, 2005. Available at www.president.harvard.edu/speeches/2005/nber.html.

[3] Bombardieri, Marcella. "Summers' remarks on women draw fire." *Boston Globe,* January 17, 2005.

[4] Dobbs, Michael. "Harvard Chief's Comments on Women Assailed." *Washington Post*, January 19, 2005. Page A02.

[5] Committee for the Equality of Women at Harvard Reports, 2002, 2003. Available online at http://world.std.com/~cewh/index.html. O'Rourke, Meghan. "Don't Let Larry Summers Off the Hook Yet." MSN online newsjournal, Slate.com. Posted Friday, January 28, 2005. Available online at www.slate.com/id/2112799.

[6] Naitonal Organization for Women. "NOW Calls for Resignation of Harvard University's President." Press release January 20, 2005. Available online at www.now.org/press/01-05/01-20-Harvard.html. See also Bombardieri, Marcella. "Harvard women's group rips Summers." *Boston Globe*, January 19, 2005.

[7] These quotes are taken from the letter that was e-mailed to all Harvard faculty (including me) titled: "Letter to the Faculty Regarding NBER Remarks," February 17, 2005.

[8] Finder, Alan. "Harvard Will Spend $50 Million to Make Faculty More Diverse." *New York Times*, May 17, 2005.

[9] Fausto-Sterling, A. *Sexing the Body*. New York: Basic Books (2000). Quote is taken from page 118.

[10] These conclusions come primarily from Halpern, D. F. *Sex Differences in Cognitive Abilities*, third edition. Mahwah, NJ: Lawrence Erlbaum (2000).

[11] www.mathgym.com.au/history/pythagoras/pythgeom.htm. For more on the relations between spatial abilities and mathematical thinking, see Spelke (2005), "Sex Differences in Intrinsic Aptitude for Math and Science: A Critical Review," *American Psychologist* 60, pp. 950–58 . See also: Dehaene, S.; Spelke, E.; Pinel, P.; Stanescu, R.; and Tsivkin, S. (1999), "Sources of mathematical thinking: Behavioral and brain-imaging evidence," *Science* 284, pp. 970–74.

[12] Spelke, E. (2005) "Sex Differences in Intrinsic Aptitude for Math and Science: A Critical Review," *American Psychologist* 60, 950–58.

[13] American Psychiatric Association. *Diagnostic and Statistical Manual of Mental Disorders*, fourth edition. Washington, D.C.: American Psychiatric Association (1994).

[14] Connellan, J.; Baron-Cohen, S.; Wheelwright, S.; Bataki, A.; and Ahluwalia, J. (2000) "Sex differences in human neonatal social perception," *Infant Behavior and Development* 23, pp. 113–18.

[15] Personal communication, Elizabeth Spelke, PhD, November 3, 2005. Spelke believes that in order to really answer the question about sex differences in spatial abilities, rather than focus on the one finding that shows a consistent sex difference (mental rotation) and basing all of your conclusions on that, one should start at the bottom, ask yourself what kinds of spatial abilities are there, find ways to assess all of them, and then compare the performance of boys and girls. Spelke has done that and the results are consistent: neither sex has a big edge when it comes to working with spatial concepts. Boys do a little better at some tests, girls on others, and on others there are no differences. Girls do a little better on some of the most difficult spatial problems; boys do a little better on others. Spelke has tested men and women, boys and girls, Americans and indigenous Amazonians. She has presented her findings to academic groups, but at the time of this writing, they are unpublished.

[16] See U.S. Department of Education, National Center for Educational Statistics, *The High School Transcript Study*. See also Conlin, M. "The New Gender Gap," *Business Week*, May 26, 2003. Cover story, no. 3834, p. 74; Dwyer, C. A. and Johnson, L. M. "Grades, Accomplishments, and Correlates," In *Gender and Fair Assessment*. (Warren W. Willgham and Nancy S. Cole, eds.) Educational Testing Service, 1997. pp. 127–56.

[17] Will, G. "Harvard hysterics," *The Washington Post*, Thursday, January 27, 2005; Page A19.

[18] The AEI Web site can be accessed at www.aei.org.

[19] Herrnstein, R. and Murray, C. *The Bell Curve: Intelligence and Class Structure in American Life*. New York: Free Press (1994).

[20] See for example Stephen Jay Gould's November 28, 1994, *New Yorker* article, "Curveball."

[21] Murray, C. "Sex Ed at Harvard," *New York Tmes* Op-Ed, January 23, 2005.

[22] Between 1998 and 2004, American Enterprise Institute for Public Policy Research has received $1,385,000 from ExxonMobil. Sources: Exxon-Mobil 1998 grants list, ExxonMobil Foundation 2000 IRS 990, ExxonMobil 2001 Annual Report, ExxonMobil 2002 Annual Report, ExxonMobil 2003, Corporate Giving Report, Exxon Giving Report 2004. Other corporate supporters have included: Phillip Morris/Kraft Foundation (Source: Legacy Tobacco Documents Library. University of California, San Francisco. Bates Number 2065244019.), General Electric Foundation, Amoco, Ford Motor Company Fund, General Motors Foundation, Eastman Kodak Foundation, Metropolitan Life Foundation, Proctor & Gamble Fund, Shell Companies Foundation, Chrysler Corporation, Charles Stewart Mott Foundation, General Mills Foundation, Pillsbury Company Foundation, Prudential Foundation, American Express Foundation, AT&T Foundation, Corning Glass Works Foundation, Morgan Guarantee Trust, Smith-Richardson Foundation, Alcoa Foundation, and PPG Industries. (Sources: People for the American Way: American Enterprise Institute. Available online at: www.pfaw.org/pfaw/general/default.aspx?oid=4456. MediaTransparency.org: Foundation Grants: American Enterprise Institute. Available online at: www.mediatransparency.org/search_results/info_on_any_recipient.php?recipientID=19.)

In addition to Murray, other conservative AIE scholars have included Lynne Cheney, wife of Vice President Dick Cheney; Newt Gingrich, former Speaker of the House; Christina Hoff Sommers, anti-feminist crusader; David Frum, presidential speechwriter for President Bush; and Robert Bork, failed Supreme Court nominee. Most of AEI's Board of Directors are CEOs of major companies, including ExxonMobil, Motorola, American Express, State Farm Insurance, and Dow Chemicals. Kenneth Lay, former Enron CEO, sat on the board of trustees. So did Vice President Dick Cheney.

23 For a fuller account of Murray's view, see Murray, C. "The inequality taboo," *Commentary* magazine, September 1, 2005. A relevant passage from that article: "One such premise is that the distribution of innate abilities and propensities is the same across different groups. The statistical tests for uncovering job discrimination assume that men are not innately different from women, blacks from whites, older people from younger people, homosexuals from heterosexuals, Latinos from Anglos, in ways that can legitimately affect employment decisions."

24 Quote from: Bates, J. (2002), "Equal, but different." ConservativeTruth. org: The Antidote to the Liberal Media Bias. Online source: www. conservativetruth.org/article.php?id=127.

25 Bosman, J. "WPP executive resigns over remarks about women," *New York Times*, Friday, October 21, 2005, Business Day C1, C5.

26 Allen, Elizabeth. "Ex-broker awarded $2.2 million; Panel support S. A. woman's claims against Merrill Lynch." *San Antonio Express-News* (Texas), Business Section, 1E.

27 See Halpern, D. F. *Sex Differences in Cognitive Abilities*, third edition. Mahwah, NJ: Lawrence Erlbaum (2000), especially pp. 16–17.

28 A cogent discussion of these issues can be found in Rutter, M. and O'Connor, T. G. (2004) "Are there biological programming effects for psychological development?: Findings from a study of Romanian adoptees," *Developmental Psychology* 40, pp. 81–94.

29 For a discussion of critical periods in development see Kuhl, P. K. et al. (1997) "Cross-language analysis of phonetic units in language addressed to infants," *Science* 277, pp. 684–86. See also Rutter, M. and O'Connor, T. G. (2004) "Are there biological programming effects for psychological development?: Findings from a study of Romanian adoptees," *Developmental Psychology* 40, pp. 81–94.

30 Hart, B. and Risley, T. R. *Meaningful Differences in the Everyday Experience of Young American Children*. Baltimore: Paul H. Brookes (1995).

31 According to CDC National Center for Health Statistics, NHANES 1999–2002: Average height for a U.S. male ages 20–74: 5 feet, 9.4 inches. Average height for a U.S. female: 5 feet, 4 inches. Thus, the average woman is taller than about 6.5 percent of men. (93.5 percent of men are taller than a woman of average height.) The average man is taller than about 97.7 percent of women. (2.3 percent of women are taller than a man of average height.)

32 Hyde, J.S. (2005) "The gender similarities hypothesis," *American Psychologist* 60, pp. 581–92.

33 These findings come primarily from Halpern, D. F. *Sex Differences in Cognitive Abilities*, third edition. Mahwah, NJ: Lawrence Erlbaum (2000), especially beginning on p. 88.

[34] (Halpern). However, even before this intentional sex neutrality was introduced, measures of intelligence showed trivial or no sex differences (Terman, 1916, cited in Loechlin, 2000). Standardized intelligence tests do not show appreciable sex differences (Loechlin, 2002). Small sex differences exist (the effect size is less than 0.10), but group differences of this size are considered negligible (Cohen, 1988). In addition, the negligible sex differences favor males on one of the most popular tests of intelligent—the Wechsler Scales—and females one the other—the Stanford Binet.

[35] Educational Testing Services. Data available online at: www.colleg-eboard.com/about/news_info/sat.

[36] ACT, Inc. "Average National ACT Score Unchanged in 2005." National data release, August 17, 2005. Available online at www.act.org/news/releases/2005/8-17-05.html.

[37] The ACT has a much smaller gender gap in math scores (0.2 points on the 36-point composite score), and the National Assessment of Educational Progress (NAEP) standardized tests found no gender difference on math scores in a large sample of U.S. twelfth graders.

[38] Liu, J.; Feigenbaum, M.; and Dorans, N. J. "Invariance of the Linkings of the Revised 2005 SAT Reasoning Test to the SAT I: Reasoning Test Across Gender Groups." College Board Research Report No. 2005–6. Available online at www.ets.org/Media/Research/pdf/RR-05-17.pdf.

[39] Tarvis, C. *The Mismeasure of Woman*. New York: Simon and Schuster (1992). In Monastersky, R. (2005) "Separating Science from stereotype," (editorial) *Nature Neuroscience* 8, p. 253.

[40] Willingham, W. W. and Cole, N. S. (1997). *Gender and Fair Assessment*. Mahwah, NJ: Lawrence Erlbaum. Gallagher, A.; Levin, J. Y.; and Cahalan, C. (2002) "Cognitive patterns of gender differences on mathematics admissions tests." ETS Research Report 02-19.

Gallagher, A. M. and Kaufman, J. C. *Gender Differences in Mathematics*. NY: Cambridge University Press (2005). Chipman, S. F. "Research on the women and mathematics issue: A personal casehistory." In A. M. Gallagher and J. C. Kaufman (eds.), *Gender Differences in Mathematics*. NY: Cambridge University Press (2005).

[41] Gallagher & Kaufman, 2005; Willingham & Cole, 1997; *Nature Neuroscience*, 2005.

[42] Programme for International Assessment, 2000 data. Organisation for economic co-operation and development. Available online at: http://pisaweb.acer.edu.au/oecd/oecd_pisa_data.html.

[43] Programme for International Student Assessment, 2003 data. Organisation for economic co-operation and development. Available online at: http://pisaweb.acer.edu.au/oecd_2003/oecd_pisa_data.html.

[44] Organization for Economic Cooperation and Development (OECD), Program for International Student Assessment (PISA), 2003, Learning

for Tomorrow's World, 2003, and Problem Solving for Tomorrow's World, 2003; U.S. Department of Education, National Center for Education Statistics, PISA, 2003, International Outcomes of Learning in Mathematics Literacy and Problem Solving, 2003. Table 399. Average reading literacy, mathematics literacy, science literacy, and problem-solving scores of 15-year-olds, by sex and country: 2003. (This table was prepared March, 2005.)

[45] BBC News. "Women are cleverer than men, says MP." December 8, 2004. Available online at: http://news.bbc.co.uk/go/pr/fr/-/1/hi/education/4079653.stm.

[46] Byrnes, J.; Hong, L.; and Xing, S. (1997) "Gender differences on the math subtest of the Scholastic Aptitude Test may be culture-specific," *Educational Studies in Mathematics* 34, pp. 49–66.

[47] Monastersky, R. "Primed for numbers," *Chronicle of Higher Education.* March 4, 2005.

[48] Gur, R. et al. (1995) "Sex differences in regional cerebral glucose metabolism during a resting state," *Science* 267, pp. 528–31.

[49] The original article, based on a sample of 9 men and 5 women, is: deLacoste-Utamsing, C. and Holloway, R. L. (1982) "Sexual dimorphism in the human corpus callosum," *Science* 216, pp. 1431–32.

For a discussion of the corpus callosum controversy see: Halpern, D. F. *Sex Differences in Cognitive Abilities*, third edition. Mahwah, NJ: Lawrence Erlbaum (2000), pages 118-200, and Fausto-Sterling, A. *Sexing the Body: Gender Politics and the Construction of Sexuality*. New York: Basic Books (2000), Chapter 5: "Sex on the Brain: The Corpus Callosum, Lateralization, and Cognitive Abilities."

[50] See for example: Gur, R. C., et al. (2002) "Sex differences in temporolimbic and frontal brain volumes of healthy adults," *Cerebral Cortex* 12, pp. 998–1003. In her article, Witelson reports that the average correlation between brain size and IQ in these studies is .4, with a range of 0 to .6.

[51] Goldin, C. and Rouse, C. (2000). "Orchestrating Impartiality: The Impact of 'Blind' Auditions on Female Musicians," *American Economic Review* 90, pp. 715–741.

[52] Hyde, J. S. (2005) "The gender similarities hypothesis," *American Psychologist* 60, pp. 581–92.

[53] Hyde, J. S. (2005) "The gender similarities hypothesis," *American Psychologist* 60, pp. 581–92.

[54] Terman, L. M. and Miles, C. C. *Sex and Personality: Studies in Masculinity and Femininity.* New York: McGraw-Hill (1936).

[55] This figure is taken from an ESPN/Chilton from 1999 for females age 12 or older. www.sportspoll.com/index.asp. In addition, The Gallup organization reports that 51 percent of American women describe themselves as pro football fans and 39 percent as college football fans.

Jones, J. M. "Six in 10 Americans Are Pro Football Fans," Gallup News Service: February 4, 2005.

Chapter Six

[1] Lonsdorf, E. V.; Eberly, L. E.; and Pusey, A. E. (2004) "Sex differences in learning in chimpanzees," *Nature* 428, pp. 715–716.

[2] Dillon, S. "For one student, a college career becomes a career." *New York Times*, Thursday, November 10, 2005, A1, A22.

[3] See Table 247, Digest of Educational Statistics, 2003, Washington, D.C.: U.S. Department of Education. Online source: http://nces.ed.gov/ programs/digest/d04/tables/dt04_247.asp.

[4] U. S. Department of Education, National Center for Education Statistics, Earned Degrees Conferred, 1869–70 through 1964–65; Projections of Education Statistics to 2014; Higher Education General Information Survey (HEGIS), "Degrees and Other Formal Awards Conferred" surveys, 1965–66 through 1985–86; and 1986–87 through 2002–03 Integrated Postsecondary Education Data System, "Completions Survey" (IPEDS-C:87-99), and Fall 2000 through Fall 2003.

[5] Source: U.S. Dept. of Education, NCES: Integrated Postsecondary Education Data System (IPEDS), "Completions Survey," various years; and Earned Degrees Conferred Model. (See reference tables 26 through 30.)

[6] U.S. Department of Education, National Center for Education Statistics, Higher Education General Information Survey (HEGIS), "Degrees and Other Formal Awards Conferred" surveys 1976–77 through 1984–85, and Integrated Postsecondary Education Data System (IPEDS), "Completions" surveys, 1986–87 through 1998–99, and Fall 2000 through Fall 2002 surveys. (This table was prepared August 2003.)

[7] Hesketh, T.; Lu, L.; and Xing, Z. W. (1997) "Health in China: The one child family policy: the good, the bad, and the ugly," *British Medical Journal* 314, p. 1685. Many couples will choose to have a second child only if their first child is a girl.

[8] See Hesketh, T.; Lu, L.; and Xing, Z. W. (2005) "The Effect of China's One-Child Family Policy after 25 Years," *New England Journal of Medicine* 353, pp. 1171–76. The one-child policy is not instituted in the same way across groups. For example, families in most rural areas are allowed to have a second child after an interval of 5 years. See also: Jones, S. *Y: The Descent of Men*. Boston: Houghton Mifflin (2003).

[9] U.S. Department of Education, National Center for Education Statistics. (2002). The Condition of Education 2002 (NCES 2002–025), table 25-3 and previously unpublished tabulations for 2002–03 (December 2004). Data from U.S. Department of Commerce, Bureau of the Census, Current Population Survey (CPS), March Supplement, 1971–2003.

[10] U.S. Census Bureau. Current Population Survey 2003, Annual Demo-

graphic Supplements. Table F-22. Married-Couple Families with Wives' Earnings Greater Than Husbands' Earnings: 1981 to 2003.

[11] Source: Annual Demographic Survey, a Joint Project Between the Bureau of Labor Statistics and the Bureau of the Census, 2004.

[12] Meade, L. K. "Baby makes three for partners in blue," *Boston Globe*, Thursday, January 5, 2006, W2, W3.

[13] See "Hopping aboard the daddy track," *Business Week* magazine, November 8, 2004.

[14] See Heritage Foundation Web site: www.heritage.org.

[15] Nock, S. L. (1995) "Commitment and Dependency in Marriage," *Journal of Marriage and the Family* 57, pp. 503–514.

[16] Nock, S. L. (2000) "Marriage in Men's Lives," "Time and Gender in Marriage," *Virginia Law Review* 86, no. 8, pp. 1971–87.

[17] Waite and Gallagher. *The Case for Marriage*. New York: Broadway Books (2000).

[18] Durkheim E. *Suicide*, New York: Free Press (1951).

[19] Shaw, K. (1987), "The quit propensity of married men," *Journal of Labor Economics* 5, no. 4, pp. 533–60.

[20] Kostiuk, P. and Follman, D. A. (1989), "Learning Curves, Personal Characteristics, and Job Performance," *Journal of Labor Economics* 7, no. 2, pp. 129–46.

[21] Cohen S.; Tyrrell, D. A. J.; and Smith, A. P. (1991), "Psychological stress and susceptibility to the common cold," *New England Journal of Medicine* 325, pp. 606–612.

[22] Smith, J. C.; Mercy, J. A.; and Conn, J. M. (1988), "Marital Status and the Risk of Suicide," *American Journal of Public Health* 78, pp. 78–80.

[23] Willitts, M.; Benzeval, M.; and Stansfeld, S. (2004), "Partnership history and mental health over time," *Journal of Epidemiol. Community Health* 58, pp. 53–58.

[24] Norris, Michelle. "Laura Bush: Putting boys in the spotlight," *All Things Considered*, National Public Radio, February, 9, 2005. Online source: www.npr.org/templates/story/story.php?storyId=4492617.

[25] BBC News, Wednesday, 8 December, 2004, 16:13 GMT. "Women cleverer than men, says MP." Online source: http://news.bbc.co.uk/1/hi/education/4079653.stm.

[26] Kindlon, D. and Thompson, M. *Raising Cain: Protecting the Emotional Lives of Boys*. New York: Ballantine (1999).

[27] Pleck, J. F., et al. (1993), "Masculinity ideology: Its effect of adolescent males' heterosexual relationships." *Journal of Social Issues* 49, pp. 11–29.

[28] See Children Now. *Boys to Men: Entertainment Media Messages About Masculinity*. Oakland, CA: Children Now (September 1999).

[29] L. Rowell Huesmann, Jessica Moise-Titus, Cheryl-Lynn Podolski, and Leonard D. Eron of the University of Michigan, "Longitudinal

Relations Between Children's Exposure to TV Violence and Their Aggressive and Violent Behavior in Young Adulthood: 1977–1992," *Developmental Psychology* vol. 39, no. 2.

[30] See chapter 2 in Bainbridge, D. *The X in Sex: How the X Chromosome Controls Our Lives.* Cambridge, MA: Harvard University Press (2003). The Y chromosome appears to have an in-built back-up by virture of its palindromic structure. See Skaletsky H., et al. (2003), "The male-specific region of the human Y chromosome is a mosaic of discrete sequence classes," *Nature* 423, no. 6942, pp. 825–37.

[31] For an informative, scholarly, yet readable account of sex chromosomes, see: Bainbridge, D. *The X in Sex: How the X Chromosome Controls Our Lives.* Cambridge, MA: Harvard University Press (2003) and Jones, S. *Y: The Descent of Men.* Boston: Houghton Mifflin (2003).

[32] *American Psychiatric Association Diagnostic and Statistical Manual of Mental Disorders*, Fourth Edition. Washington, D. C.: American Psychiatry Association.

[33] Rutter, M., et al. (2004), "Sex Differences in Developmental Reading Disability: New Findings From 4 Epidemiological Studies," *Journal of the American Medical Association* 291, pp. 2007–2012. *American Psychiatric Association Diagnostic and Statistical Manual of Mental Disorders*, Fourth Edition. Washington, D. C.: American Psychiatry Association.

[34] Edelson, S. M. *Fragile X Syndrome.* Salem, Oregon: Center for the Study of Autism. Online source: www.autism.org/fragilex.html.

[35] Zechner, U., et al. (2001) "A high density of X-linked genes for general cognitive ability: a run-away process shaping human evolution?" *Trends in Genetics* 17, pp. 697–710.

[36] Check, E. (2005) "The X factor," *Nature* 474, pp. 266–67.

[37] It is, naturally, a bit more complicated. The action of sex hormones play a part, as does the inactivation, or especially, non-inactivation of one of the X chromosomes in each non-germ cell. See Arnold, A. P., et al. (2004), "Minireview: Sex chromosomes and brain sexual differentiation," *Endocrinology* 145, pp. 1057–62. See also: Kuehn, B. (2005), "Mysteries of the X chromosome revealed: Silent X not always mute," *Journal of the American Medical Association* 293, pp. 1961–62.

[38] National Center for Health Statistics, "Estimated life expectancy at birth in years by race and sex, Table 12." Volume 52, no. 14, February 18, 2004. Available at: www.cdc.gov/nchs/data/dvs/nvsr52_14t12.pdf.

[39] Dyer, O. (2005) "Disparities in health widen between rich and poor in England," *British Medical Journal* 331, p. 7514

[40] Tsuchiyaa, A. and Williams A. (2005) "A 'fair innings' between the sexes: are men being treated inequitably?" *Social Science and Medicine* 60, pp. 277–86.

[41] U. S. Census Bureau (2004); Statistical Abstracts of the United States, 2003 (U. S. Government Printing Office, Washington, D. C.) For

reasons for this decline see: Norberg, K. (2004), "Partnership status and the human sex ratio at birth" (manuscript submitted for publication). See also the discussion in Fukuda, M.; Fukuda, K.; Shimizu, T.; and Møller, H. (1998) "Decline in sex ratio at birth after Kobe earthquake," *Human Reproduction* 13, pp. 2321–22.

[42] Catalano, R. A. and Bruckner, T. (2005), "Economic antecedents of the Swedish sex ratio," *Social Science and Medicine* 60, pp. 537–43.

[43] Catalano, R. A. (2003) "Sex ratios in the two Germanys: a test of the economic stress hypothesis," *Human Reproduction* 18, no. 9, pp. 1972–75.

[44] Fukuda, M.; Fukuda, K.; Shimizu, T.; and Møller, H. (1998), "Decline in sex ratio at birth after Kobe earthquake," *Human Reproduction* 13, pp. 2321–22.

[45] Mackenzie, C. A.; Lockridge, A.; and Keith, M. (2005) "Declining sex ratio in a first nation community," *Environmental Health Perspectives* 113, pp. 1295-98.

[46] Crenson, M. (2005) "Canadian Chippewa birth ratio badly out of whack," The Associated Press, December 18, 2005. online source: www. azstarnet.com/allheadlines/107461.

[47] Much of the information for this section comes from Colborn, T.; Dumanoski, D.; and Myers, J. P. *Our Stolen Future: Are We Threatening Our Fertility, Intelligence, and Survival? A Scientific Detective Story.* New York: Plume (1997). In addition I consulted with two biologists familiar with Colborn's work: Drs. Steven Orzack and Bill Stubblefield from the Fresh Pond Research Institute in Cambridge, MA.

[48] Gray, L. E. Jr., et al. (2001), "Effects of environmental antiandrogens on reproductive development in experimental animals," *Human Reproduction Update* 7, pp. 248–64. See also from Colborn, T.; Dumanoski, D.; and Myers, J. P. *Our Stolen Future: Are We Threatening Our Fertility, Intelligence, and Survival? A Scientific Detective Story.* New York: Plume (1997).

[49] Blount, B. C.; Silva, M. J.; Caudill, S. P.; Needham, L. L.; Pirkle, J. L.; Sampson, E. J.; Lucier, G. W.; Jackson, R. J.; and Brock, J. W. (2000) "Levels of seven urinary phthalate metabolites in a human reference population," *Environmental Health Perspectives* 108, no. 10, pp. 979–82.

[50] See page 22 in Bainbridge, D. *The X in Sex: How the X Chromosome Controls Our Lives.* Cambridge, MA: Harvard University Press (2003).

[51] Carlsen, E.; Giwercman, A.; Keiding, N.; and Skakkebæk, N. E. (1992) "Evidence for decreasing quality of semen during past 50 years," *British Medical Journal* 305, pp. 609–613. Carlsen's results were initially criticized, but according to Pajarinen, J. (1997), "Incidence of disorders of spermatogenesis in middle aged Finnish men, 1981-91: two necropsy series," *British Medical Journal* 314, 13, this observation has subsequently been corroborated by several reports additionally suggesting that a similar deterioration may have taken place in the morphology and

motility of sperm. This same study indicates that decreased sperm quality or quantity has significant geographical variation.

[52] de Kretser, D.M. (1996) "Declining sperm counts: Environmental chemicals may be to blame," *British Medical Journal* 312, pp. 457–58.

[53] See for example: LaRossa, R. *The Modernization of Fatherhood: A Social and Political History.* Chicago: University of Chicago Press (1997).

Chapter Seven

[1] Kindlon, D. *Too Much of a Good Thing: Raising Children of Character in an Indulgent Age.* New York: Miramax Books (2001).

[2] As the table below shows, alpha girls are more likely than non-alphas to say that being successful in their future career is "extremely important."

RESPONSE	Not Important or A Little Important			Extremely Important		
Survey Question	Boys	Alpha Girls	Non–Alpha Girls	Boys	Alpha Girls	Non–Alpha Girls
How important is having a job that is interesting to you?	1.0%	0.7%	0.9%	57.5%	75.4%	61.7%
How important is having a job in which you help people?	6.6%	2.1%	5.3%	19.6%	48.4%	28.0%
For you, how important is finding a job in which you can work from home?	85.6%	91.4%	92.7%	1.3%	3.9%	1.7%
For you, how important is finding a job in which you can set your own work hours?	49.3%	45.5%	53.9%	12.7%	18.2%	11.1%
For you, how important is having a job in which you will make a lot of money?	10.1%	17.2%	16.0%	47.6%	34.1%	36.0%
How important is it for you to be successful in your future career?	1.5%	2.4%	2.0%	59.0%	66.9%	54.6%
How important is it for you to become an expert in your future occupational field?	5.5%	5.0%	6.9%	50.8%	52.1%	42.2%

³ Terman's studies of genius are the longest running study of a group of human beings and are described in a series of 5 volumes beginning with Terman, L. M. *Genetic Studies of Genius I: Mental and Physical Traits of a Thousand Gifted Children*. Stanford University: Stanford University Press (1925) and ending with Terman, L. M. and Oden, M. H. *Genetic Studies of Genius V: The Gifted Group at Mid-Life: Thirty-Five Years' Follow-Up of the Superior Child*. Stanford University: Stanford University Press (1959). For a more complete description of this study see: Sears, R. R. "The Terman gifted children study." In S. A. Mednick, M. Hanway, and K. M. Finello (eds.) *Handbook of longitudinal Research Volume 1: Birth and Childhood Cohorts*. New York: Praeger (1984).

⁴ Terman, L. M. and Oden, M. H. *Genetic Studies of Genius IV: The Gifted Child Grows Up: Twenty-Five Years' Follow-Up of a Superior Group*. Stanford University: Stanford University Press (1947).

⁵ The material for this section on Barbara Kerr and the Cold War girl geniuses is taken from Kerr, B. *Smart Girls: A New Psychology of Girls, Women, and Giftedness* (revised edition). Dayton, OH: Ohio University Press (1995).

⁶ These figures are taken from the National Center for Educational Statistics. The figures for medicine and law are, respectively 8.4 percent and 5.4 percent in 1970 compared to 23.4 percent and 30.2 percent in 1980.

⁷ Arnold, K. D. *Lives of Promise: What Becomes of High School Valedictorians*. San Francisco: Jossey-Bass (1994).

⁸ Arnold, K. D. *Lives of Promise: What Becomes of High School Valedictorians*. San Francisco: Jossey-Bass (1994), page 115.

⁹ For more on the WEF, visit their Web site: www.weforum.org.

¹⁰ See the full report for details: Lopez-Claros, A. and Saadia Zahidi, S. *Women's Empowerment: Measuring the Global Gender Gap*. Geneva, Switzerland: World Economic Forum (2005).

¹¹ The data on which this index is based comes from several sources, including the United Nations, World Bank, and the World Health Organization.

¹² Bernstein, R. "Men chafe as Norway ushers women into the boardroom," *New York Times*, Thursday, January 12, 2006, International Desk, A3.

¹³ Taken from "Jämt och ständigt," Government Communication to Parliament on the Government's Gender Equality Policy. Skr. 2002/03:140. June 2003 as quoted in SCB, Women and Men in Sweden. Facts and Figures 2004. Online source: www.scb.se/statistik/LE/LE0201/2004A01/LE0201_2004A01_BR_X10ST0402.pdf.

¹⁴ The Clearinghouse on International Developments in Child, Youth and Family Policies at Columbia University Table 1 Maternity, Paternity, and Parental Leaves in the OECD Countries 1998–2002. Online source: www.childpolicyintl.org/issuebrief/issuebrief5table1.pdf.

[15] Eligible employees are those who have worked at the company for a minimum of 1,250 hours during the previous 12 months. U.S. Department of Labor Online source: www.dol.gov/esa/regs/statutes/whd/fmla.htm#SEC_101_DEFINITIONS.

[16] Laura Bush CNN interview with Zain Verjee, January 13, 2006. Online source: www.cnn.com/2006/POLITICS/01/13/laura.bush.

[17] Source: Physician Characteristics and Distribution in the U.S. 2005 Edition and prior editions. American Medical Association.

[18] Source: NCES–Digest of Ed. Statistics (2004).

[19] American Association of Medical Colleges, Data Warehouse. Applicants, Accepted Applicants, and Matriculants by Gender, 1992–2005.

[20] See Jennifer Steinhauer. "For women in medicine, a road to compromise, not perks," New York Times, Monday, March 1, 1999, Metropolitan desk.

[21] Dale, N. and Grayson, M. (2003) "Trends in Career Choice by U.S. Medical School Graduates," 290, no. 9, pp. 1179–82.

[22] Source: Journal of the American Medical Association, September 1, 2004, vol. 292, no. 9, pp. 1099–1101.

[23] Kotulak, R. "Increase in women doctors changing the face of medicine," Chicago Tribune, January 12, 2005, News Desk. Baskett, T. F. (2002) "What women want: don't call us clients, and we prefer female doctors," Journal of Obstetrics and Gynaecology Canada 7, pp. 572–74.

[24] Polgreen, L. and Rohter, L. "Where political clout demands a maternal touch." New York Times, Sunday, January 22, 2006, International Desk.

[25] Sources: Bureau of Labor Statistics, "Employed persons by detailed occupation, sex, race, and Hispanic or Latino ethnicity" 2004; American Bar Association, Fall 2004 Enrollment Statistics. www.abanet.org/legaled/statistics/stats.html

[26] "Women CEOs," Fortune, April 14, 2003. Catalyst Census of Women Corporate Officers and Top Earners, 2002. Catalyst Census of Women Board Directors, 2003.

[27] National Association for Law Placement (NALP) Associate Salary Survey www.nalp.org/content/index.php?pid=302.

[28] ABA Commission on Women study, The Unfinished Agenda: A Report on the Status of Women in the Legal Profession. www.abanet.org/ftp/pub/women/unfinishedagenda.pdf.

[29] American Bar Foundation Lawyer Statistical Report. For more information see www.abfn.org/images/reslawwin05.pdf.

[30] Chang, A. and Wolff, S. R. "Number of lawyers working part time grows, but slowly," The Reporter, November 22, 2004. Online source: www.sachnoff.com/media/media_detail.aspx?type=354&archive=yes&id=732.

[31] For a similar discussion of these issues see: O'Brien, T. L. "Why Do So Few Women Reach the Top of Big Law Firms?" New York Times, March 19, 2006.

[32] History of the Federal Judiciary. www.fjc.gov. Web site of the Federal Judicial Center, Washington, D. C.

[33] Peresie, Jennifer L. (2005), "Female Judges Matter: Gender and Collegial Decision making in the Federal Appellate Courts," *The Yale Law Journal* 114, no. 7.

[34] Spohn, Cassia C. *How Do Judges Decide?* Sage Publications, Inc. (2002), page 117.

[35] For an excellent review of recent research on gender and leadership, see Eagly, A. E. and Carli, L. L. (2003) "The female leadership advantage: An evaluation of the evidence," *The Leadership Quarterly* 14.

[36] Simmons, W. W. (2001) "When it comes to choosing a boss, Americans still prefer men." Retrieved August 18, 2001 from The Gallup Poll News Service Web site, www.gallup.com/poll/releases/pr010111.asp.

[37] Quote from page 39 in Helgesen, S. *The Female Advantage: Women's Ways of Leadership*. New York: Doubleday (1990).

[38] Quotes from pages 2 and 6 in: Book, E. W. *Why the Best Man for the Job is a Woman*. New York: Harper Business (2000).

[39] Heffernan, M. (2002) "The female CEO," *Fast Track* 61, p. 58.

[40] Conlin, M. "The New Gender Gap: From kindergarten to grad school, boys are becoming the second sex," *Business Week*, May 23, 2003. Online source: www.businessweek.com/magazine/content/03_21/b3834001_mz001.htm.

[41] U.S. Bureau of Labor Statistics, 1982, 2002 U.S. Bureau of Labor Statistics, *Labor force statistics derived from the current population survey: A databook* (Vol. 1: Bulletin 2096), U.S. Department of Labor, Washington, D.C., 1982 and U.S. Bureau of Labor Statistics (2002).

[42] See: Black, J. "The women of tech," *Business Week*, May 29, 2003. www.businessweek.com/technology/tc_special/03women.htm and 2002 Catalyst release: "Catalyst census marks gains in numbers of women corporate officers in America's largest 500 companies." Retrieved February 20, 2003 from www.catalystwomen.org/press_room/press_releases/2002_cote.htm. These studies are discussed in Eagly, A. E. and Carli, L. L. (2003) "The female leadership advantage: An evaluation of the evidence," *The Leadership Quarterly* 14.

[43] Quotes are from pages 26–27 of Book, E. W. *Why the Best Man for the Job is a Woman*. New York: Harper Business (2000). For more on Orit Gadiesh see "Consulting in the right direction," *Economist* 377, October 22, 2005, p. 72. See also MacDonald, E. and Schoenberger, C. R. "The 100 most powerful women," *Forbes*, July 28, 2005. Gadiesh is #95 on the Forbes list.

[44] Porrazzo, K. A. "The case of corporate life," *OC Metro*, July 21, 2005, Business\News, page 36.

[45] From GSUSA Web site: www.girlscouts.org/for_adults/leader_
magazine/2003_winter/kathy_cloninger.asp.

[46] Quote is from page 38 of Helgesen, S. *The Female Advantage: Women's
Ways of Leadership*. New York: Doubleday (1990).

[47] Eagly, A. E. and Carli, L. L. (2003), "The female leadership advantage:
An evaluation of the evidence," *The Leadership Quarterly* 14.

[48] See for example: Nussbaum, B. "Can you trust anyone anymore?"
Business Week Online, January 28, 2002, www.businessweek.com/
magazine/content/02_04/b3767701.htm and Deutsch, C. "Take your
best shot: New surveys show that big business has a P.R. problem," *New
York Times*, Friday, December 9, 2005, Business Day, C1, C14.

[49] Bombardieri, M. "MIT set to pick its first female president," *Boston
Globe*, August 26, 2004, A26.

[50] "Men account for around 75 percent of all criminal arrests—Table 42,
U.S. Department of Justice, Federal Bureau of Investigation, Uniform
Crime Reports, Crime in the United States, 2004, Washington, D.C.
Online source: www.fbi.gov/ucr/cius_04/persons_arrested/table_
38-43.html.

[51] University of Arkansas, Survey Research Center poll of 767 Arkansas
residents 18 years or older. 44 percent of respondents said women would
do a better job, 15 percent worse, and 33 percent no difference. For
reforming health care, 47 percent thought women would do better, 4
percent worse, and for environmental protection, the figure were 31
percent better; 6 percent worse. Online source: ftp://ftp.irss.unc.edu//
pub/search_results/POLL..19Jan2006.15.31.14.txt.

[52] It is a truism in the social sciences that the shorter the time period over
which one is trying to make a prediction, the more accurate the
prediction is likely to be. Thus, for example, senior year high school
GPA is more predictive of college GPA than GPA from eighth grade;
attitudes toward drug use measured at age 14 are more predictive of
drug use in college than attitudes towards drug use measured in third
grade.

[53] *American Psychiatric Association Diagnostic and Statistical manual of Mental
Disorders*, Fourth Edition. Washington, D. C.: American Psychiatric
Association.

[54] Cleckley, H. *The Mask of Sanity*-fourth edition. New York: C. V. Mosby
(1964).

[55]

	Non–Alpha girls	Alpha Girls	Boys
Locus of Control- Average Score*	8.44	9.45	7.86

*Adjusted scores.
Significant difference between alpha- and non-alpha girls in multiple regression adjusted for s: socioeconomic status, grade in school, and race/ethnicity. B= -0.9992, SE=.2367, p<.0001.
Significant difference between boys and alpha girls in multiple regression adjusted for socioeconomic status, grade in school, and race/ethnicity. B= 0.7925, SE=.1933, p<.0001.

[56] Catalyst. *The Bottom Line: Connecting Corporate Performance and Gender Diversity*. New York: Catalyst (2004).

[57] Tierney, J. "What Women Want," *New York Times*, May 24, 2005, Op-Ed.

[58] Center for Women's Business Research. National Trends for Women-owned Businesses, 2004. www.womensbusinessresearch.org/national-numbers.html.

Chapter Eight

[1] Complete results for family-related survey items is given in the table below:

SURVEY QUESTION:	Strongly Disagree or Disagree			Strongly Agree or Agree		
	Boys	Alpha Girls	Non–Alpha Girls	Boys	Alpha Girls	Non–Alpha Girls
I am likely to get married in the long run.	19%	15%	14%	65%	73%	68%
I expect that I will be a home-maker or stay-at-home parent someday.	62%	48%	49%	22%	29%	24%
Working mothers can have relationships with their children that are just as warm and secure as mothers who do not work.	19%	7%	11%	65%	83 %	77%
Working fathers can have rela-tionships with their children that are just as warm and secure as fathers who do not work.	14%	13%	24%	66%	74%	72%
A preschool child is likely to suffer if both parents work full-time.	14%	31%	32%	61%	49%	44%
Having a good marriage and family is extremely important to me.	6%	4%	9%	82%	91%	78%
I want to work full time while also raising children.	7%	20%	23%	58%	42%	39%
*#For me, having children someday is...	5%	7%	11%	72%	85%	70%

*Statistically significant difference between boys and alpha girls in multivariable analysis adjusting for socioeconomic status, grade in school, race/ethnicity, and stay-at-home mom.
#Statistically significant difference between alpha girls and non-alpha girls in multivariable analysis adjusting for socioeconomic status, grade in school, race/ethnicity, and stay-at-home mom.

2 One indicator of this is that there was no statistically significant difference between the percentage of alpha girls from intact families and the percentage of alpha girls from non-intact families on the stated desire to work full time while raising kids.

3 Family and Work Institute (2004). Generation and Gender in the Workplace, American Business Collaboration.

4 Story, L. (2005) "Many women at elite colleges set career path to motherhood," *New York Times*, September 20, 2005, National Desk. For more information on the study's methodology, see Story, L. (2005) Web Edition Only: "Background: Reporting on the Aspirations of Young Women," *New York Times*, September 23, 2005, National Desk.

5 Mosher, W. D.; Chandra, A.; and Jones, J. (2005) "Sexual Behavior and Selected Health Measures: Men and Women 15–44 Years of Age, United States, 2002," Advance Data from *Vital and Health Statistics*, Number 362; September 15, 2005, National Center for Health Statistics.

6 In our full sample, 95 percent of boys and 94 percent of girls identified themselves as straight. 1.2 percent of boys identified as gay and .5 percent of girls as lesbians; 2.4 percent of boys and 4.36 percent of girls identified as bisexual; 1.2 percent boys and 1.34 percent of girls identified as other. For our other category we gave kids a write-in option. A few identified themselves as "queer," a way people have started referring to themselves when they don't want to categorize their sexual behavior. There was no significant difference in the reported sexual orientation of alpha and non–alpha girls. These figures are given for comparison purposes only. Several schools in the survey sample did not permit us to ask about sexual orientation or behavior.

7 Rust, P. C. (2000) "Review of statistical findings about behavior, feelings, and identity." In P. C. Rust (ed.) *Bisexuality in the United States: A Social Science Reader*. New York: Columbia University Press, pp. 129–84.

8 Diamond, L. M. (2003) "Was it a phase? Young women's relinquishment of lesbian/bisexual identities over a 5-year period," *Journal of Personality and Social Psychology* 84, pp. 352–64.

9 CDC—2003 YRBSs shows that by the time they are in 12th grade girls more likely to have had sexual intercourse than boys. Online source: www.cdc.gov/mmwr/PDF/SS/SS5302.pdf. MMWR May 21, 2004 vol. 53. Accessed May 19, 2006.

10 See: Schmid, R. E. "More unmarried women but fewer teens giving birth," *Boston Globe*, Saturday, October 29, 2005, A3.

11 Hamilton, B. E.; Ventura, S. J.; Martin, J. A.; and Sutton, P. D. "Preliminary births for 2004." *Health E-Stats*. Hyattsville, MD: National Center for Health Statistics. Released October 28, 2005.

12 Egan, J. "Wanted: A Few Good Sperm," *New York Times*, March 19, 2006.

Appendix B

[1] U.S. Census Bureau, Population Projections Branch. "Interim Projections by Age, Sex, Race, and Hispanic Origin. Middle series." Release date: May 11, 2004. (The Census Bureau bases these projections on the 2000 census and middle series assumptions for the fertility rate, internal migration, net immigration, and mortality rate.)

[2] U.S. Department of Education, National Center for Education Statistics, Integrated Postsecondary Education Data System, "Fall Enrollment Survey" (IPEDS-EF), various years; Enrollment in Degree-Granting Institutions Model.

[3] Projections of post-secondary enrollment: We assume that enrollment in institutions of higher education is a linear function of the projected population by age and sex (see above) and also: disposable income per capita (a), consumer price index (b), and educational expenditures (c).

(a) Disposable income per capita: U.S. Department of Labor. Bureau of Labor Statistics. Disposable income per capita. Various releases; and Global Insight, Inc., "U.S. Quarterly Model: February 2004 Long-Term-Projections." October 2004.

(b) Consumer Price Index: U.S. Department of Labor. Bureau of Labor Statistics. Cosumer Price Index. Various releases; and Global Insight, Inc., "U.S. Quarterly Model: February 2004 Long-Term-Projections." October 2004.

(c) U.S. Department of Education, National Center for Education Statistics, Common Core of Data (CCD), "National Public Education Financial Survey," 1988–89 through 2002–03; Revenue Receipts From State Sources Model, 1971–72 through 2001–02; and Global Insight, Inc., "U.S. Quarterly Model: February 2004 Long-Term-Projections." October 2004. (Projections of educational expenditures by degree-granting instructions to 2014, which take into account the various revenue measures of state and local governments.)

[4] National Center for Education Statistics. "Projections of Education Statistics to 2013." Appendix A, Projection Methodology, 2004.

[5] National Center for Education Statistics. "Projections of Education Statistics to 2013." Appendix A, Projection Methodology, 2004.

[6] U.S. Department of Education, National Center for Education Statistics, *Earned Degrees Conferred*, 1869–70 through 1964–65; *Projections of Education Statistics to 2014*; Higher Education General Information Survey (HEGIS), "Degrees and Other Formal Awards Conferred" surveys, 1965–66 through 1985–86; and 1986–87 through 2002–03 Integrated Postsecondary Education Data System, "Completions Survey" (IPEDS-C:87-99), and Fall 2000 through Fall 2003.

[7] U. S. Department of Labor. Bureau of Labor Statistics. "Labor Force Participation to 2050."

[8] U.S. Department of Education, National Center for Education Statistics, Earned Degrees Conferred, 1869–70 through 1964–65; Projections of Education Statistics to 2014; Higher Education General Information Survey (HEGIS), "Degrees and Other Formal Awards Conferred" surveys, 1965–66 through 1985–86; and 1986–87 through 2002–03 Integrated Postsecondary Education Data System, "Completions Survey" (IPEDS-C:87-99), and Fall 2000 through Fall 2003.

[9] American Association of Medical Colleges, Data Warehouse. Applicants, Accepted Applicants, and Matriculants by Gender, 1992–2005.

[10] American Bar Association. JD degrees awarded by sex, 1984–2004.

[11] U.S. Department of Commerce, Census Bureau, U. S. Census of Population, 1960, volume 1, part 1; Current Population Reports, Series P-20 and unpublished tabulations; and 1960 Census Monograph, *Education of the American Population* by John K. Folger and Charles B. Nam. March 2005.

[12] U.S. Census Bureau. Current Population Survey 2003, Annual Demographic Supplements. Table F-22. Married-Couple Families with Wives' Earnings Greater Than Husbands' Earnings: 1981 to 2003.

[13] 2003 Current Population Surveys' (CPS) Annual Social and Economic Supplement (ASEC). The ASEC supplement to the CPS is conducted in February, March, and April at about 100,000 addresses nationwide. For further information on the source of the data and accuracy of the estimates, including standard errors and confidence intervals, see Appendix G of www.census.gov/apsd/techdoc/cps/cpsmar03.pdf.

[14] U.S. Bureau of Labor Statistics. "Education & Training Pays." December 7, 2005.

[15] "Projecting the U.S. gender wage gap 2000–2040," *Atlantic Economic Journal*, December 1, 2003.

[16] U.S. Department of Labor. Bureau of Labor Statistics. "Labor Force Participation to 2050."

[17] Catalyst. Census of Women Board Directors, 2005. Online source: www.catalyst.org/knowledge/titles/title.php?page=cen_WBD03.

[18] U.S. Department of Labor. Bureau of Labor Statistics. "Labor Force Participation to 2050."

[19] Business taxes are indirect business taxes and tax accruals per capita. Source: U.S. Department of Education, National Center for Education Statistics, Common Core of Data (CCD), "National Public Education Financial Survey," 1988–89 through 2002–03; Revenue Receipts From State Sources Model, 1971–72 through 2001–02; and Global Insight, Inc., "U.S. Quarterly Model: February 2004 Long-Term Projections." (This table was prepared October 2004.)

[20] U.S. Department of Education, National Center for Education Statistics, *Earned Degrees Conferred*, 1955–56 through 1963–64; Higher Education

General Information Survey (HEGIS), "Degrees and Other Formal Awards Conferred" surveys, 1965–66 through 1985–86; and 1986–87 through 2002–03 Integrated Postsecondary Education Data System, "Completions Survey" (IPEDS-C:87-99), and Fall 2000 through Fall 2003. (This table was prepared April 2005.)

INDEX

Boldface page references indicate graphs and charts. <u>Underscored</u> references indicate boxed text.

inherent or intrinsic ability and, 114, 123,
126, 129, 141
in intelligence, 140–41
learning, 141–43
lying, 207–8, **207, 208**
marriage goals, 225
math ability, 120–25, 134–35, **134**, 137
math SAT scores, 134–35, **134**
memory, 120
mental rotation, 120–21
money, interest in, 179
moral development, 58–60
parenting, 46–47, **234**
perceptual speed, 120
personality, 131, 145
physical, 131–33, 157
play patterns of children, 68–70
politics and, 146
as positive thing, 124
psychological well-being, 131
questions surrounding, 129, 147
science ability, 113–18, 125, 128–29,
133–34
self-esteem, 85, **85**
senses, 132–33
sexism and, 114
sexuality, 145
social factors and, 123
socialization and, 142
spatial abilities, 120
stealing, **209**
Summers's comments on, 113–18, 125,
128–29, 133–34
telling lies, 207–8, **207, 208**
tender-mindedness, 145
trust, 145
verbal ability, 120
in word association tests, 145
Gender diversity, 210
Gender Equality Center (Norway), 186
Gender Equity Ombudsman (Norway), 186
Gender expectations, 77–79
Gender gap
in business, 150
Business Week article on, 202
in Norway, 186–87
ranking of nations based on, 184–86
in Sweden, 187–88
in U.S., 185, 188–90
Gender intensification, 77–78
Gender Portrayal guidelines (Canada), 25
Gender roles
changes in, 155–58
culture and, trends in, 155–58
shaping, 53–54, 62–64, 70–72
stereotyping, 22, 70, 220
Gender similarities, 138, 146
Genetics
advances in, 118, 146

gender differences and, 114, 129, 131,
133, 146
height and, 131
politics and, 146
separation-connection dichotomy and, 67
"Genius Studies (Terman), 181–82
Genome mapping, 118, 146
Gen-Xs, 219–20
Gen-Ys, 219–20
Georgia Bar Association, 3
Germany, women in government of, 195
Gifted women, research on, 181–84
Gilligan, Carol, 56, 59–60, 67, 77, 108–9
Gilligan dynamic, 108–10
Girls. *See* Alpha girls; Father-daughter
relationship; Mother-daughter
relationship; Non–alpha girls
Girl Scouts of America, 204–5
Globalization, 202
Goldstein, Daniel, 55
Gottesman, Erving, 99
Government
alpha girls in workforce of, 194–95
women in
in Chile, 194
expectations about, 189
in future, 189–90
in Germany, 195
in Liberia, 194–95
in Norway, 186
in U.S., 9, 10, **11, 12**, 189, 195
Green, Tony, 31, 38–39
Greenfield, Patricia, 21
Group, The (McCarthy), 92
Gur, Ruben C., 137–39

H

Hamm, Mia, 34
Harriss, Cynthia, 204
Harvard, 116–17
Harvard Model Congress, 29
Hasbians, 231
Hearing, 132
Heffernan, Margaret, 202
Height differences, male-female, 131
Helgesen, Sally, 205
Henning, Margaret, 50
Heredity. *See* Genetics
Heritage Foundation, 160
Hertz, Rosanna, 235–36
Hewlett, Sylvia Ann, 236
Homosexual relationships, 107, 228–32, 236
Hopkins, Nancy, 116, 125
Household chores, gender differences in,
221
How Schools Shortchange Girls (Bailey et al.),
93
Hyde, Janet Sibley, 131–32

Hypermasculinity, 166–67
Hysterical neurosis, 57

I

Identification with parents, 37, **51**, 53–55
Identity crisis, 72
Identity formation
  in adolescence, 72–73
  Freudian theory of, 62–64
  gender, 53–54, 62–64, 70–72
  gender expectations and, 77–79
  influences on, 71–73
  process of, 70–71
  separation-connection dichotomy and,
    63–64, 70–73
  "true self" and, 77
Illinois Valedictorian Project, 95, 184
Imitative behavior and ability, 20–21
In a Different Voice (Gilligan), 59
Income gap, 13, 154, **155**
Inevitable domesticity, myth of, 26–29
Inherent or intrinsic ability, 114, 123, 126,
  129, 141
Intelligence (IQ)
  gender differences in, 140–41
  performance, 140
  racial differences in, 125–26
  test design and, 133, 181
  verbal, 130–31, 140
Internalized discrimination, 143. *See also*
  Sexism

J

Janoff, Liza, 198–99
Jobs and alpha girls. *See* Workforce and
  alpha girls
Johnson-Sirleaf, Ellen, 194
Jolie, Angelina, 22
Jo March (fictional character), 26–28, 92
Judgeships, female, 198–201
JUMP (charter school), 158
Jung, Carl, 97–98
Justice orientation, 59

K

Kerr, Barbara, 182–83
Kindlon, Dan, 33–36, 166, 179
Kohlberg, Lawrence, 57–59, 61

L

L.A. Law (television show), 232
Language development, 130
Law
  alpha girls in workforce of, 195–200, **196**
  women in, 9

Lawless, Lucy, 22
Leadership, 9, 202–6, 209–12
Learning, 76, 141–43. *See also* Education
Lechner, Johnny, 149
Lesbian relationships, 107, 228–32, 236
Lewis, Marlyn McGrath, 222–23
Liberia, women in government of, 194–95
Lies, telling, 207–8, **207**, **208**
Lin, Henry Huan, 43
Lin, Maya, 43
Liswood, Laura, 188–89
Little Hans (case), 62
Little Women (Alcott), 26–28, 92
Liu, Cynthia, 222
Lives of Promise (Arnold), 95
Love and alpha girls
  alternative ways to manage love and
    work, 225–26
  careers and, feelings about, 225–27
  delaying motherhood, 215–18
  lesbian relationships, 228–32, 236
  marriage, desire for good, 213–14, **214**
  oral sex, 232–34
  parenting, feelings about, 234–36
  single-parenting, 234–36, **235**
  stay-at-home mother and, 222–23
  virginity, 232–34
  working mother dilemma and, 214–16,
    216
LUG (lesbian until graduation)
  phenomenon, 231
L Word, The (television show), 232

M

Male-dominated society, 18–19, 73–79,
  104–5
"Male model" of competitive learning, 76
Managerial Woman, The (Henning), 50
Marr, Antonia, 194
Marriage
  alpha girls and, desire for good, 213–14,
    214
  descent of men and, 160–63
  gender differences about goals of, 225
  men and, benefit to, 160–63
  power in, 154–56
Masculinity, traditional, 165–67
Mask of Sanity, The (Cleckley), 208
Masters degree data, 9, **9**, 10
Maternity leave, 188, 193–94
Math ability, 120–25, 134–35, **134**, 137
Math SAT scores, 134–35, **134**
McCarthy, Mary, 92
McCarthy, Rosaline, 195
Mead, Margaret, 92
Media
  advertising, 23–25
  alpha girls and, 20–26

Parents (*cont.*)
  gender roles and, shaping, 71–72
  household chores and, **221**
  identification with, 37, **51**, 53–55
  principles to live by, instilling, 208–9, **209**
  self-evaluation, 101
  separation-connection dichotomy and,
    influences on, 62–64, 71–72
  single, 234–36, **235**
Patriarchy, 18–19, 73–79, 104–5
Pediatrics (journal), 31–32
Penis envy, 63
Perceptual speed, 120
Performance intelligence, 140
Personality, 65, 131, 145. *See also* specific
    traits
PET scans, 137–38
Phthalates, 174
Physical differences, male-female, 131–33,
    157
Piaget, Jean, 58
Planned Parenthood Federation of America,
    29
Plastic surgery, trend toward, 24–25
Play patterns of children, 68–70
Polgreen, Lydia, 194–95
Politically Incorrect Wife, The (book), 94–95
Politics
  conservative, 94–95, 126–27, 160
  drama of, 29
  gender differences and, 146
  genetics and, 146
  separation-connection dichotomy and,
    66–67
Pollutants, 172–74
Power in home and marriage, 154–56
Pregnancy
  alpha girls and, choice about, 29–30
  of married *vs.* unmarried women, 235,
    235
Prentice, Holly, 103–8
Principles to live by, 208–9, **209**
Profile of alpha girls, 6, 26, 30
Psychoanalytic movement, 57, 61–66
Psychological well-being, 131. *See also*
    Self-esteem
Psychology. *See also* Emancipation,
    psychology of
  of alpha girls, 80, 86, 110–12
  evolutionary, 67
  Freudian theory and, 57, 61–66, 98
  of non–alpha girls, traditional
    conceptions, 110, 110–12
  of separation-connection dichotomy,
    56–57
  women's movement and, view of, 8, 11–13
Puberty. *See* Adolescence
Purcell, Phillip, 206
Purkey, Betty, 157

Q

Queen Bees and Wannabees (Wiseman), 79

R

Racial differences, 125–26
Raising Cain (Thompson and Kindlon), 166
Reagan, Ronald, 201
Reproduction of Mothering, The (Chodorow),
    64
Resource display of men, 165
Revolution from Within (Steinem), 95
Rice, Condoleezza, 190, 195
Risk taking, 50
Roberts, Alfred, 44
Roe v. Wade, 8, 94, 183
Role expectations, 98
Role theory, 98–100
Roper poll of corporate corruption, 205
Rosenberg Self-Esteem Scale, 75, **75**, 84–85,
    85
Rother, Larry, 194–95
Rules of attractiveness, 165

S

St. Ann's Mock Trial teams, 4–7
St. Luke's Mock Trial team, 4–5
Samuelson, Robert, 146
Sanger, Margaret, 29–30
SAT scores in math, 134–35, **135**, 137
SchoolGirls (Orenstein), 73
Science
  ability, 113–18, 125, 128–29, 133–34
  women in, 113–14, **115**
Second Sex, The (de Beauvoir), 10–12
Self-esteem
  in adolescence, 73–76
  of alpha girls, 47–48, **47**
  Arnold and, 95–96
  of boys, 97, 108
  of college women, 95–96
  depression and, 100
  father-daughter relationship and, 47–48,
    47
  gender differences, 85, **85**
  index of, 75
  male-dominated society and, 73–74
  of non–alpha girls, 84–85, 85, 108
  popular culture and, 76
  risks for low, 100–108
  Rosenberg Self-Esteem Scale and, 75, **75**,
    84–85, **85**
  Steinem and, 95–96
Senses, gender differences in, 132–33
Separate and unequal doctrines, 127
Separateness. *See* Separation-connection
    dichotomy

U.S.
  gender gap in, 185, 188–90
  maternity leave in, 188
  women in government of, 9, 10, **11**, **12**,
    189, 195
U.S. Congress, 9, **11**, 94
U.S. Constitution, 8
U.S. Supreme Court, 8, 94, 183, 200–201

V

Values, societal, 13
Verbal ability, 120
Verbal intelligence, 130–31, 140
Vietnam Veterans Memorial design, 43
Virginity, 232–34
Vision, 133
Visual-spatial ability, 140

W

Wealth, interest in, 178–79
WEF, 184–86
West Point, challenges of, 7
"What Women Want" (Tierney), 211
Why the Best Man for the Job Is a Woman
    (book), 202
Will, George, 125
Wiseman, Rosalind, 79
Witelson, Sandra, 140
Women. *See also* Gender differences
  birth rates for married *vs.* unmarried,
    235, **235**
  brain of, 126, 140
  in business, 9, 150, 203–5, **203**, 210–11
  in courts, 198–201
  feminism and careers of, 15
  in government
    in Chile, 194
    expectations about, 189
    in future, 189–90
    in Germany, 195
    in Liberia, 194–95
    in Norway, 186
    in U.S., 9, 10, **11**, **12**, 189, 195
  in law, 9
  leadership and, 205–6
  in medicine, 9, 192–93
  powerlessness of American housewives
    and, 154

in science, 113–14, **115**
sex ratio and, 169–70, **170**
sexual intimacy among, 232
sexuality of, 145
in state legislatures, 10, **12**
Summers's comments about, 113–18, 125,
    128–29, 133–34
in U.S. Congress, 9, **11**
Women's movement. *See also* Feminism
  alpha girls and, 7–8, 13–14, 30–31, 90
  birth control and, 30
  emancipation psychology and, 90
  psychological view of, 8, **11**–13
  victories of, 8, 30, 183
Word association tests, 145
Work ethic of alpha girls, 177–78
Workforce and alpha girls
  Arnold's research and, 184
  in business, 202–6, 209–12
  choice of career fields and, 16, **16**, 37,
    41–46, 190, **191**, 225–27
  corporate corruption and, 205–6, 212
  in courts, 198–201
  expertise in field and, desire for, 180,
    180
  gender gaps and
    in Norway, 186–87
    ranking of nations based on, 184–86
    in Sweden, 187–88
    in U.S., 185, 188–90
  in government, 194–95
  Kerr's research and, 182–83
  in law, 195–200, **196**
  leadership and, 201–2, 206
  marketplace realities and, 179–80
  in medicine, 190, **191**, 192–94, **193**,
    199
  overview, 181
  Terman's research and, 181–82
  wealth and, interest in, 178–79
  work ethic, 177–78
World Economic Forum (WEF), 184–86

X

X chromosome, 168–69, 171

Y

Y chromosome, 168, 171